Helion & Company Limited
Unit 8 Amherst Business Centre
Budbrooke Road
Warwick
CV34 5WE
England
Tel. 01926 499 619
Email: info@helion.co.uk
Website: www.helion.co.uk
Twitter: @helionbooks
Visit our blog http://blog.helion.co.uk/

Text © Dagmawi Abebe 2019
Photographs © as individually credited
Colour profiles © Anderson Subtil 2019
Maps © Tom Cooper (unless stated
    otherwise) 2019

Designed & typeset by Farr out Publications,
    Wokingham, Berkshire
Cover design by Farr out Publications,
    Wokingham, Berkshire
Printed by Henry Ling Limited, Dorchester,
    Dorset

ISBN 978-1-912866-31-1

British Library Cataloguing-in-Publication
    Data
A catalogue record for this book is available
    from the British Library

We always welcome receiving book
proposals from prospective authors.

CONTENTS

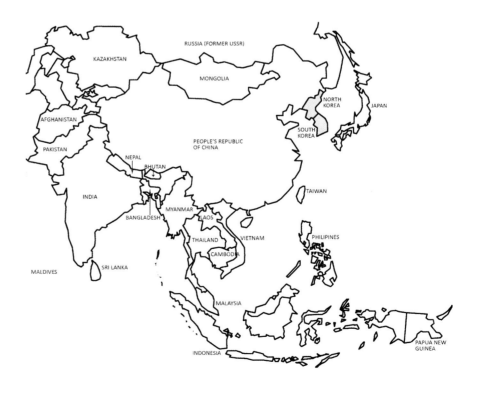

Note: In order to simplify the use of this book, all names, locations and geographic
designations are as provided in *The Times World Atlas*, or other traditionally accepted major
sources of reference, as of the time of described events.

PREFACE

Ethiopian names follow a different set of rules than English names. In Ethiopia just as in most other places, your first name is your given name. But there is no such thing as a last name or family name. The name that follows your first name is your father's first name, which is followed by his father's first name. Consider the name Kebbede Guebre. Kebbede is the man. And Guebre is Kebbede's father. So it would be inaccurate to refer to General Kebbede Guebre as General Guebre. Since Guebre is his father, we would be referring to a completely different person. We can correctly refer to our subject as General Kebbede. Furthermore, this book has resorted to sometimes referring to Ethiopians using just their first names and non-Ethiopians with their last names. This is contrary to Ethiopian culture, but was done for ease of reading and not meant to slight these highly distinguished individuals. Also, a person's rank during their service in Korea was used throughout the book until the Epilogue chapter.

Ethiopia has her own alphabet. So things get even more complicated when it comes to spelling because no standard has been developed for transliteration of words (including names) to English. Mulugeta Bulli, for example, could be spelled as, Moulougeta Buli or Bouli. Whenever possible, the spelling that was preferred by the subject or is in common usage was adopted here. Ethiopian names were transposed in many US official records. For instance, Kebbede Guebre's citation for his Legion of Merit read "Wolde Emanuel Kebbede Guebre." Best efforts were made to correct such mistakes. The names used in the narrative chapters reflect the correct names as shown in the Kagnew rosters (no roster was found for the Second Kagnew).

Readers might come across some discrepancies when comparing dates in this book to other publications. While researching the Kagnew's history, it was not uncommon to find conflicting dates between official unit records, award citations and other publications. In some instances, this book made a departure from the official unit records because these records were prepared by men engaged in warfare and as such were not immune to human error. A judgement call was made when two official records showed different information for the same event. Discrepancies were also noted in daily and monthly friendly casualty figures reported by Kagnew's parent units (the US 32d Infantry Regiment and US 7th Infantry Division). It was ultimately impossible to reconcile some of these differences.

All reasonable effort was made to present the reader with accurate information. This, unfortunately, was complicated by the lack of documentation which can be attributed to the propensity on the part of Ethiopians for oral history. Still it is amazing that complete and accurate biographies could not be found in English or Amharic for some of the most influential figures in that nation's history, including high-ranking officers, statesmen, and even a head of state. For instance, one English language source claimed Mengistu Neway served as "commander with the Kagnew Battalions during the Korean War." Another noted historian erroneously attributes the "Kagnew" name to Emperor Menelik's war charger.

Despite painstaking efforts, even this book is not warrantied against error. In the words of Dr. Daniel Crosswell, "the perfect is the enemy of the good".

GLOSSARY

1st Lt.	First Lieutenant	G-2	Brigade or higher level staff for Intelligence
2d Lt.	Second Lieutenant	G-3	Brigade or higher level staff for Operations
BAR	Browning Automatic Rifle	G-4	Brigade or higher level staff for Logistics
Bn	Battalion	Gen.	General
Brig. Gen.	Brigadier General	GHQ	General Headquarters
Capt.	Captain	GOPL	General Outpost Line
CCF	Communist Chinese Forces also referred to as People's Volunteer Army (PVA)	H&I	Harassment & Interdiction
		HIM	His Imperial Majesty
CG	Commanding General	HQ	Headquarters
CINC	Commander-in-Chief	I&R	Intelligence & Reconnaissance
C.O.	Commanding Officer	IBG	Imperial Bodyguard
Co	Company	ID	Infantry Division
Col.	Colonel	JCS	Joint Chiefs of Staff
CoS	Chief of Staff	KIA	Killed in Action
CP	Command Post	LCpl.	Lance Corporal
Cpl.	Corporal	LP	Listening Post
DMZ	Demilitarized Zone	Lt. Col.	Lieutenant Colonel
DOD	Department of Defense	Lt. Gen.	Lieutenant General
DPRK	Democratic People's Republic of Korea	KMAG	Military Advisory Group to the Republic of Korea
EEFK	Ethiopian Expeditionary Force to Korea	KPA	Korean People's Army
EUSAK	Eighth United States Army in Korea	MAAG	Military Assistance Advisory Group
FA	Field Artillery	Maj.	Major
FEC	Far East Command	Maj. Gen.	Major General
FO	Forward Observer	MASH	Mobile Army Surgical Hospital
G-1	Brigade or higher level staff for Personnel	MLR	Main Line of Resistance

MSR	Main Supply Route
MSTS	Military Sea Transportation Service
NCO	Non-Commissioned Officer
OCS	Officer Candidate School
OP	Observation Post
OPLR	Outpost Line of Resistance
PFC.	Private First Class
POW	Prisoner of War
PVR	People's Volunteer Army
Pvt.	Private
RCT	Regimental Combat Team
Rgt	Regiment
ROTC	Reserve Officer's Training Corps
ROK	Republic of Korea
S-1	Battalion or Regimental Staff for Personnel
S-2	Battalion or Regimental Staff for Intelligence
S-3	Battalion or Regimental Staff for Operations
S-4	Battalion or Regimental Staff for Logistics
Sgt.	Sergeant
Sgt. Maj.	Sergeant Major
UN	United Nations
UNC	United Nations Command
UNRC	United Nations Reception Center

USNS	United States Naval Ship
WIA	Wounded in Action
X.O.	Executive Officer

List of Ethiopian Titles

Abba	Father
Kegnazmatch	Commander of the right flank
Lij	Literally means "child", but also title given a young noble
Ras	Literally means "head", but also title given a general or field marshal

List of Ethiopian Administrative Divisions

Awraja	Sub-province
Kebele	Neighborhood or village
Teklay Gizat	Province or State
Wereda	District/subdivision of an awraja

US Army Unit Nicknames

7th Infantry Division	Bayonet Division, Hourglass Division
17th Infantry Regiment	Buffalos Regiment
31st Infantry Regiment	Polar Bears Regiment
32d Infantry Regiment	Buccaneers Regiment

INTRODUCTION

History of Korea

Korea is a peninsula in East Asia whose history has largely been shaped by its strategic position between China, Japan and to some extent Russia. It is approximately one-fifth the size of present-day Ethiopia or roughly the same size as the state of Utah. The climate and terrain are very extreme. The peninsula is dominated by mountain ranges which extend the entire length. The summers tend to be hot, humid and rainy. The winters, especially in the North, are bitterly cold as a result of arctic winds blowing from Siberia.[1]

At the close of WWII, as Soviet troops moved into northern Korea, an apprehensive US decided to enter the peninsula from the South. US Army officers were given 30-minutes to decide on a boundary to mark the zones of control for the two world powers. They chose the 38th parallel.[2] As explained by General Matthew Ridgway, the man who would later command all UN forces in Korea, "The 38th parallel is not a border in any true sense. It is not militarily defensible, nor does it wear any traditional significance."[3] There weren't any differences between Koreans who lived on either side in terms of language, food, clothing, customs or national identity.

After some futile attempts at reunification, the US brought the issue before the United Nations General Assembly which established a temporary commission to hold free elections in both zones. But the Soviets barred the commission from entering the North. In May 1948, general elections were held in the South and the Republic of Korea (ROK) was created under President Syngman Rhee. The Soviets created the Democratic People's Republic of Korea (DPRK) in the North under Kim Il-Sung. Both leaders were committed to reunification, but only under their own government.[4]

By August 1949, the US military had left Korea with the exception of the 500-person Military Advisory Group to the Republic of Korea (KMAG) tasked with creating an ROK Army capable of repelling Communist aggression without being able to initiate an attack of its own. The poorly equipped and barely trained combat troops numbered 65,000, with another 33,000 support personnel. They had no heavy artillery, tanks, effective anti-tank weapons or combat air power.[5]

Unfortunately, the Communists did not share America's view when it came to training and arming their allies. Kim Il-Sung had a total of 135,000 men, of which 89,000 were combat troops. The departing Soviets had also bequeathed the KPA with small arms, mortars, howitzers, self-propelled guns, T-34 tanks and 180 new airplanes.[6]

On Sunday, June 25, 1950 at 0400, the KPA launched a well-coordinated attack spanning the width of the peninsula. After an artillery barrage, 90,000 troops supported by columns of T-34 tanks made multiple thrusts into South Korea with the main attack following the ancient invasion route down the Uijeongbu Corridor to the capital. The South Koreans and their US advisers were completely caught off guard.[7]

KPA divisions supported by T-34 tanks sliced through ill-equipped ROK division towards Seoul. Faced with the grim prospect of being cut off, ROK units often scattered or as it was termed at the time "bugged out."[8] On the night of June 26, the South Korean government decided to relocate to Taejon. The US Ambassador and his staff left for Suwon on the 27th. Seoul fell on the 28th.[9]

Word of the invasion quickly made it to the US President Harry S. Truman who was at his home in Independence, Missouri. He boarded a plane to Washington D.C. to meet with members of his cabinet and the Joint Chiefs of Staff (JCS).[10] During his three-hour flight, Truman thought, "In my generation, this was not the first occasion when the strong had attacked the weak. I recalled some earlier instances: Manchuria, Ethiopia, Austria. I remembered how each time that the democracies failed to act it had encouraged the aggressor to keep going ahead. Communism was acting in Korea just as Hitler, Mussolini, and the Japanese had acted, ten, fifteen, and twenty years earlier.... If this

North Korean Army troops with their original mounts – Japanese-made tanks. (via Doug Dildy)

This Soviet-made T-34/85 tank of the North Korean Army collapsed a bridge damaged by US air strikes during the advance south of Seoul in the summer of 1950. (US Army)

North Korean forces to the 38th parallel.[14]

On June 26, Gen. Douglas MacArthur, Commander-in-Chief, US Far East Command (CINC-FEC), headquartered in Tokyo, Japan, got authorization from Washington to intervene in Korea with air and naval forces.[15] The UN Security Council passed a second resolution asking "Members of the United Nations furnish such assistance to the Republic of Korea as may be necessary to repel the armed attack."[16]

On July 7th, the UN Security Council voted to establish a unified command in Korea and for the United States to name the first ever UN commander. President Truman in turn designated General MacArthur who was then also authorized to fly the United Nations flag at his headquarters. MacArthur ordered the US Eighth Army under the command of Lt. Gen. Walton "Johnnie" Walker to Korea. All ROK forces were soon after placed under US command at the request of President Rhee.[17]

UN member nations started fulfilling their commitment. The British dispatched a brigade, which was later re-designated as a Commonwealth Brigade with the addition of troops from Australia, Canada and New Zealand. The Netherlands, France, Belgium and Turkey were also contributing their own contingents to Korea.

In the meantime, elements of the US 24th Infantry Division fought a series of delaying actions. Although all these engagements ended in KPA victories, the US troops succeeded in slowing the enemy advance in order to create the Pusan Perimeter – a toehold around the southeastern port of Pusan, which was needed to

was allowed to go unchallenged it would mean a third world war."[11] Truman told Secretary of State Dean Acheson, "…we've got to stop the sons-of-bitches no matter what."[12]

An emergency meeting of the United Nation Security Council was held at 1400 on the 25th.[13] The members adopted a resolution calling for an immediate cessation of hostilities and the withdrawal of

handle the influx of men and material coming into the peninsula.

The UN assembled a formidable force around the Pusan Perimeter. Four US Army divisions, one Marine brigade, one British Commonwealth brigade and five ROK divisions were dug-into defensive positions. Overwhelming air and naval assets were also allocated to provide support. The KPA had 10 infantry divisions, one armored division, one motorized regiment and one independent infantry regiment. The UN combat forces outnumbered the KPA approximately 92,000 to 70,000.

Repeated North Korean attacks were repulsed by Gen. Walker's skillful employment of his small reserve. By this point the KPA supply lines were dangerously over-stretched. Their troops were fighting with little food and ammunition. Mounting casualties had forced them to replace combat veterans with untrained and unenthusiastic conscripts. The UN, on the other hand, enjoyed complete air superiority, naval dominance off the coast and had received about 500 tanks, as well as effective anti-tank weapons. But the UN still needed something drastic to turn the tide.[18]

General MacArthur proposed a daring amphibious assault at the northwestern port of Inchon. The intent was for UN forces around Pusan to push the KPA back and smash it against the amphibious units pouring out of Inchon.[19] MacArthur's amphibious force landed at Inchon on September 15 and drove towards Seoul, liberating the city on September 25 – exactly three months after the start of the invasion. At the same time, UN forces around Pusan broke out of the perimeter and pushed the enemy north. Even with UN forces chasing what

US Marines concentrating at Chosin before their evacuation. (US Army)

US Army troops inspecting a knocked-out, Soviet-made T-34/85 tank of the North Korean Army. (US Army)

remained of the KPA troops north, the US policy concerning possible operations past the 38th parallel was unclear.

On October 15, President Truman arrived at Wake Island to have his first face-to-face meeting with Gen. MacArthur. Truman was impressed by MacArthur who assured him the window for a decisive intervention by the Chinese had passed, nonetheless, if the Chinese moved south, he predicted for them "the greatest slaughter." He hoped to have US troops "home by Christmas."[20]

MacArthur's forces attacked into North Korea and by the 19th the ROK I Corps entered Pyongyang, forcing Kim Il-Sung to relocate his government further north. UN forces continued their race to the Yalu River which separated North Korea from the Manchuria region of China.[21]

Meanwhile the Chinese had been holding emergency meeting to determine their response to the "imperialist" invasion of their neighbor. By late October, an estimated 300,000 members of the Chinese Communist Forces (CCF) crossed the Yalu undetected by

marching only at night and observing strict camouflage discipline during the day.[22] UN forces soon began discovering Chinese troops among their prisoners. But MacArthur was still unconvinced of a possible Chinese intervention. Around the same time, the ROK 6th Division was attacked by the CCF and eliminated as an effective fighting force. The rest of the ROK II Corps routed as a result. The Communists then attacked and shattered the 8th Cavalry Regiment, part of the US 1st Cavalry Division.[23] But, on November 6, the CCF abruptly broke contact and disappeared. The Chinese had achieved their first objective by disrupting the UNC momentum and were able to assess the enemy's strengths and weaknesses. They also hoped to lure the UN further north into the Chinese trap. MacArthur obliged by ordering Walker to push to the Yalu.[24] On November 24, several Eighth Army units and ROK divisions were ambushed and shattered. The mission quickly changed from the destruction of the KPA to the perseveration of UN forces and soon "bug-out fever" took over. [25]

To make matters worse, the harsh Korean winter was setting-in.

Ethiopian troops taking leave at parade in front of the Emperor before leaving for Korea, 1951

Ridgway. The energetic Ridgway had commanded an airborne division and corps in WWII. MacArthur, who knew Ridgway from their time as instructors at West Point, told him, "The Eighth Army is yours, Matt. Do what you think best," and gave him a free hand in Korea. Ridgway immediately set out assessing the Eighth Army. What he found was a demoralized force which lacked aggressiveness and clung to luxuries. Staff officers and field commanders who didn't meet his high standards were replaced. He ordered all units to patrol aggressively and to make contact with the enemy.[32]

The New Year kicked off a new Chinese offensive. UN forces withdrew from the 38th parallel, and Seoul was retaken by the Communists, switching hands for the third time in six months. The enemy stopped after crossing the Han River because its supply lines were again stretched. Ridgway in turn ordered a series of operations codenamed Operation *Roundup*, Operation *Killer* and Operation *Ripper*. The last of which enabled the allies to retake Soul on March 14. In similar successive operations, UN forces advanced to an area slightly north of the 38th parallel dubbed Line Kansas.[33]

Among other things, MacArthur's belligerence towards Communist China, his desire to use Chinese Nationalist troops, and his desire to use radioactive fallout to seal off the Sino-Korean border were in direct conflict with the moderate position Washington and the UN wanted to adopt.[34] But the *coup de grace* came when a letter he had written criticizing the president's policies was read to Congress by one of the general's allies. His perceived insubordination was creating a constitutional crisis. The president had no choice but to fire him.[35] In Tokyo, half a million Japanese lined the streets to bid him farewell. Just as many people greeted him when he returned to American soil for the first time in many years. Before a Joint Meeting of Congress, America's most senior and popular general concluded 52-years of military service with the words, "…old soldiers never die; they just fade away."[36]

In the Far East, Ridgway was elevated to four-star general and appointed CINC-UNC. Lt. Gen. James Van Fleet took over Eighth Army.

On April 13, 1951, two days after MacArthur was fired, Kagnew Battalion left Addis Ababa for French-Somaliland (present-day Djibouti), and eventually, Korea.

The cold caused weapons to jam; tanks and trucks were rendered inoperable. It was necessary to mix alcohol with gasoline in order to keep gas lines and carburetors from freezing. Water-soluble medication, morphine and plasma had to be kept against the body or specially heated before use. The troops suffered frostbite from lack of proper winter clothing.[26]

In the east, US Marines and the 31st Regimental Combat Team (RCT) positioned on either side of the Chosin Reservoir were also encountering fierce resistance. In fact, the 5th and 7th Marine Regiments were surrounded and hit by enemy forces which severely outnumbered them.[27] The unyielding Marines managed to fight their way out to the relative safety of Hagaru-ri, engaging the CCF in a running gun battle which lasted five days.[28] After days of fierce combat, the 31-RCT had taken almost 600 casualties and its commanding officer had been captured by the enemy. Now under the leadership of Lt. Col. Donald C. Faith, 31-RCT had to run a gauntlet in order to reach the Marines at Hagaru-ri. It suffered friendly fire from aircraft, a continuous enemy barrage, as well as various obstacles and physical roadblocks. When the column finally reached a second blown bridge just miles from safety, it became every man for himself as able-bodied soldiers ran across the frozen river abandoning the wounded. The Marines at Hagaru-ri raced forward over the treacherous ice and rescued a total of 319 souls. But 1,000 of the 2,500 members of what has come to be known as "Task Force Faith" were killed, wounded or captured.[29]

The Marines and the survivors of Task Force Faith withdrew from Hagaru-ri towards the port of Hungnam.[30] Under air cover as well as offshore naval gun support, 105,000 troops, 91,000 refugees, 350,000 tons of cargo and 17,500 vehicles were evacuated out of Hungnam by December 24 in one of the greatest logistical feats in modern military history. Above all else, events at the Chosin forced MacArthur to admit that, "We face an entirely new war."[31]

On December 23, Eighth Army suffered another blow when its commander, Lt. Gen. "Johnnie" Walker, was killed in a jeep accident during one of his frequent visits to the front. But this tragedy brought with it an opportunity to infuse fresh blood into the broken UN forces. The man tapped to replace Walker was Lt. Gen. Matthew B.

History of Ethiopia

Ethiopia, which in the past was also referred to as Abyssinia, is an ancient empire located in East Africa. The terrain is dominated by mountain ranges but also includes lowland and semi-desert areas. Consequently, the country has diverse climate zones ranging from near freezing at high altitudes to temperate and hot. The oldest humanoid remains, dating back 3.5-million years, were found in the Afar desert, making Ethiopia the birthplace of mankind. Unlike Korea, which is ethnically homogeneous, Ethiopia is home to various ethnic groups as

Construction of the Ethiopian railway at Dire Dawa. (Mark Lepko Collection)

well as many languages and dialects.

Around the first century AD, a Christian kingdom emerged around the northern city of Axum and expanded to include parts of present-day Sudan, Somalia and even Yemen across the Red Sea. But the rise of Islam in Arabia during the seventh century, and its expansion into Africa, diminished their influence.[37]

The Zagwe Dynasty, most notably known for the rock hewn churches of Lalibala, came to power in Ethiopia around the 10th century. In 1260, the Zagwe was replaced by the Solomonic Dynasty which emphasized its direct lineage from Emperor Menelik I, the purported son of the Queen of Sheba and King Solomon. In 1527, a Muslim by the name of Ahmed Gragn (Ahmed the left-handed) swept the kingdom until he was defeated in 1543 with the help of Portuguese troops who had rallied to aid their fellow Christians in Ethiopia.[38]

Zemene Mesafint (Era of the Princes) lasted from the mid-1700s until 1855 when *Ras* Kassa, a bandit of noble blood, defeated his rivals and was crowned Emperor Tewedros II.[39][40] The ambitious Tewedros unified Ethiopia and enacted much needed reforms, often by force. This lack of diplomacy, which alienated him from the church, the nobility, the people, and ultimately foreign empires, proved to be his undoing. He took his own life rather than surrender after suffering his first ever military defeat at the hands of a British expedition.[41]

In 1889, Emperor Menelik II ascended to the throne. Around the same time, territory on the bay of Assab, in present-day Eritrea, which was purchased from the local Sultan by an Italian company was taken over by the Italian government and used to expand deeper into Eritrea. The Italians then used their foothold in Eritrea to encroach into the Ethiopian highlands.[42] Also in 1889, Ethiopia and Italy tried to define their boundaries as well as their overall relationship with the Treaty of Uccialli. The Italian copy of the treaty differed from the Ethiopian version in that it contained an article declaring Ethiopia an Italian protectorate. Emperor Menelik ended the treaty upon discovering this treachery. Not willing to take no for an answer, the Italians invaded Ethiopia.[43]

Emperor Menelik achieved an unprecedented feat by rallying the whole nation under one banner, that of freedom. The Ethiopian vanguard consisting of the armies of *Ras* Makonnen and two other nobles defeated Italian forces occupying the natural fortress of Amba Alagi. *Ras* Makonnen's war mount was named *Abba Kagnew* and per tradition that was the general's *nom de guerre*.[44]

Menelik's army then proceeded north to siege the Italian fort at Makale. The Italians there soon ran out of supplies but were allowed

Tigrayan tribal warriors of Ethiopia in the 1930s. (Mark Lepko Collection)

to leave by Menelik who offered honors of war and safe passage under escort. Unfortunately, the fleeing Italian troops, along with reinforcements from their homeland, took up a fortified position farther north and resumed hostilities. Menelik managed to lure the Italians out of their forts by employing a network of double-agents to feed the enemy false information. The three-pronged Italian advance to Adwa was beset with tactical blunders and resulted in them being routed after a bloody battle. With his supply lines over-stretched, Menelik returned home without fully exploiting his victory.[45]

Adwa marked the first ever defeat of Europeans at the hands of colored people. A triumphant Menelik turned his attention to the expansion, unification and modernization of his country. Emperor Menelik's victory over the Italians and Emperor Tewedros' suicide before the British would define Ethiopian chivalry for centuries to come, including during the Korean War.

Menelik was succeeded by his grandson *Lij* Iyasu whose reign only lasted three-years as a group of nobles led by *Ras* Tafari Makonnen had him excommunicated, deposed and imprisoned. *Ras* Tafari, who was *Ras* Makonnen's son and Menelik's nephew, then seized power, first as regent and later as emperor, under the name Haile Selassie, and became a pioneer of modernization and reform.[46] The early days of Haile Selassie's rule saw the completion of the Franco-Abyssinian railway between Ethiopia and French-Somaliland (present-day Djibouti), the establishment of a constitution, the development of governmental ministries, banks, newspapers and schools.[47]

Realizing that Ethiopia, as the only free African nation, offered a tempting target for colonization, Haile Selassie prepared to defend her sovereignty both militarily and diplomatically. His crowning achievement, or what was thought so at the time, was Ethiopia's acceptance into the League of Nations, which offered its members the promise of collective security. Haile Selassie also began to modernize the military. The professionalization of the military began in 1917 when Haile Selassie, as regent, formed a regular standing force.[48] In 1919, he appointed a small group of Russian officers and some Ethiopian veterans of the King's African Rifles to train his troops.[49] A year later, some Ethiopian officers were sent to study at the French military academy at Saint-Cyr. Upon their return some of those officers were also assigned as trainers.[50]

A Belgian military mission was secured in 1929 for the purpose of training a modern Imperial Bodyguard.[51] Later, an Imperial Bodyguard academy was opened at *Genet* (the Emperor's summer estate in Holeta) to develop a modern officer corps under the tutelage of Swedish officers. The chief instructor, Capt. Viking Tamm, along with the principals of the schools in Addis Ababa, selected 148 of the nation's brightest youths, some as young as fifteen, to become the first cadets. Some came from very prominent families and many would go on to play significant roles in their nation's history. In fact, two of the cadets, Mulugeta Bulli and Mengistu Neway would later command the Imperial Bodyguard.[52 53]

In the meantime, an Italian veteran of the Great War named Benito Mussolini was stoking nationalistic fervor as one of the leaders of the Fascist movement. In 1922, he led thousands of paramilitaries known as Blackshirts on the "March on Rome" and secured for himself the prime ministership.[54]

In late 1934, a joint Anglo-Ethiopian Pasturage Commission studying grazing and watering rights in Wal-Wal, deep inside Ethiopian territory, came under attacked by Italian airplanes and colonial troops based in neighboring Italian-Somaliland (present-day Somalia). While the Ethiopians took the heaviest casualties, it was the Italians who demanded an apology and indemnity. Using the incident as a pretext, the Fascist government ramped up a military buildup in their adjoining colonies: Eritrea in the north and Italian-Somaliland in the southeast. Mussolini was hoping to usher in the rebirth of the Roman Empire and avenge his nation's humiliating defeat at Adwa.[55]

Emperor Haile Selassie brought the matter before the League of Nations for arbitration. But the League dithered as it had done four-years earlier in the wake of the Japanese invasion of Manchuria. France and Britain slapped both sides with an arms embargo which in reality only affected Ethiopia. For Haile Selassie, the promise of collective security was turning out to be an illusion.

On October 3, 1935, Italian forces in East Africa invaded Ethiopia from Eritrea and Italian-Somaliland. Haunted by the ghosts of Adwa, the Italians fielded a large, modern army, supported by hundreds of airplanes and tanks. By contrast the defenders were mostly feudal levies armed with antiquated weapons and only a handful of planes and armored vehicles. The Italians captured the Northern cities of Adigrat, Adwa, Axum and Mekele over the next few weeks with little opposition as Ethiopian forces had withdrawn to more defensible positions further south.[56] The forces of *Ras* Imru, *Ras* Seyum, *Ras* Kassa and *Ras* Mulugeta reached the north and created a defensive line.[57]

The League of Nations condemned Italy's aggression but failed to impose oil sanction, which was the only measure capable of crippling the Fascist war machine.[58] Later, the press uncovered secret negotiations between France and Britain to appease the Italians by granting them considerable territories and influence over Ethiopia. Public outrage caused the two governments to abandon the plan and to sack the masterminds. Unfortunately for Ethiopia, the concurrent oil sanctions debate ended without

Italian motorcycle troops in Somalia. (Mark Lepko Collection)

Armoured trucks and tankettes of the Italian Army fording a river in central Ethiopia. (Mark Lepko Collection)

a firm decision.[59]

On the Western flank of the northern front, *Ras* Imru's army of 25,000 was almost halved after its first encounter with the Italian Air Force and the desertion of one of his subordinate commanders, but the dutiful general pushed forward.[60] *Ras* Imru began adapting his tactics to counter Italian air supremacy by employing camouflage and night marches (as the Chinese would later do in the Korean War). His troops scored a string of early victories, at times resorting to mounting tanks and beheading the Italians crews with swords. Following these victories, *Ras* Imru decided to leave the larger part of his army behind and took a small force to make a bold thrust into the enemy's rear to destroy the supply base and disrupt his line of communication. Aware of his precarious position, Badoglio unleashed the Regia Aeronautica. When the Italian planes finally appeared over *Ras* Imru's army, they did not bring the usual fiery destruction but instead dropped canisters of mustard gas.[61] To the Italians, the advantages they enjoyed in numbers, training and material were not enough. The Battle of Dembeguina was too close a call. Therefore, Badoglio requested and Mussolini authorized the use of poison gas in violation of the Geneva Convention. The Fascists also bombed Red Cross field hospitals and destroyed an Ethiopian aircraft being used to evacuate casualties. That plane which was part of Haile Selassie's tiny fleet was named *Abba Kagnew.*

The subsequent battles in the northern front played out in a similar fashion. The armies of *Ras* Seyum, *Ras* Kassa and *Ras* Mulugeta were holding their own until Italian planes armed with poison gas tipped the scale. With the entire front collapsing, what remained of these armies retreated south and consolidated with the Emperor and additional troops advancing north.

On March 31, the last major battle of the northern front and the most emblematic of the whole war was fought when the two marshals faced-off at Maychew. Haile Selassie hurled his outnumbered and outgunned troops, including his Imperial Bodyguard at the Fascists. Although they fought valiantly, they were no match for the Italian Air Force and artillery. With his forces disintegrating, the Emperor made his way back to the capital.

The Ethiopians in the southern front did not fare much better. General Rodolfo Graziani, who would later earn the nickname "The Butcher of Ethiopia," also used airplanes armed with poison gas to

Emperor Haile Selassie. (Author's collection)

soften up the defenders before breaking through with his mechanized infantry.

With their training interrupted by the outbreak of war, the Imperial Bodyguard cadets at Genet Military Academy took volunteers and organized themselves into a brigade. They didn't have enough rifles for all their men and their few cannons had no shells. Kifle Nesibu became brigade commander with the rank of lieutenant colonel. Lieutenant Colonels Belay Haile-Ab and Ketema Beshah commanded the two regiments. Major Kebbede Guebre was on the brigade staff, possibly as the operations officer. Major Mulugeta Bulli was assigned as one of the battalion commanders, Major Matias Gemeda was a company commander, and Lieutenants Mengistu Neway and Woldeyhanis Shitta were platoon leaders.[62] The young officers, along with their Swedish advisers, planned to confront the Fascist invasion force at the mountain pass of Termaber. The brigade commander and his chief of staff took a small group to reconnoiter the proposed ambush site, but after experiencing countless setbacks, they realized the untenability of the position and aborted the mission. They lived to fight another day.[63]

Haile Selassie also took a similar course of action. Unlike past emperors who chose to fight to the death, he opted for exile. This controversial decision would cast a shadow on his legacy even to this day. The loyal *Ras* Imru was named regent with orders to carry out a guerilla campaign.

On May 5, 1936, Badoglio entered the capital and merged Ethiopia, Eritrea and Italian-Somaliland to form Africa Orientale Italiana (Italian East Africa). On June 30, Emperor Haile Selassie pleaded his country's case before the League of Nations amidst jeers from Italian journalists. It is said as he stepped from the podium at the end of his speech, the Emperor uttered those most prophetic words, "It is us today. It will be you tomorrow." But the League did not heed his warning and in the end self-interest trumped collective security.

With the Italians only maintaining nominal control of the country, the conflict made the natural progression from conventional to guerilla warfare. Thirty-five of the young cadets-turned-officers from the Genet Academy, along with their troops, headed west with hopes of forming the nucleus of a larger guerilla force. After a grueling march, they set up camp around the city of Lekemte. They established a leadership council, a gendarmerie for the city, a pay scale for the soldiers, and a constitution. The first article of their constitution recognized the group as "*Tikur Anbessa*" – meaning Black Lion, while another article barred the mistreatment of civilians and prisoners of war.[64] *Tikur Anbessa* was comprised of both officers and young educated Ethiopian civilians. Among the former cadets were Lt. Cols. Kifle Nesibu, Belay Haile-Ab, Ketema Beshah and Maj. Matias Gemeda.[65]

In June 1936, *Tikur Anbessa* dealt the enemy a devastating blow. They ambushed an Italian military mission at a remote airfield, destroying three airplanes and killing twelve of the thirteen Italians, including the second highest ranking Italian in East Africa, Deputy Viceroy/Brig. Gen. Vincenzo Magliocco. The young officers demonstrated not only great tactical proficiency but unimpeachable warrior ethos. When the last of the enemy soldiers succumbed to his wounds days later, these Patriots buried him with full military honors. In this daring attack, *Tikur Anbessa* suffered three killed and four wounded. Among the wounded was Maj. Matias Gemeda.[66]

Tikur Anbessa then joined up with *Ras* Imru and what remained of his guerilla force. They searched for a new base of operations while engaging the Italians in running gun battles which were punctuated by aerial bombardments and poison gas attacks. With their mobility and fighting ability diminished by a swelling civilian refugee population, the weary patriots were finally confronted by a numerically superior, fresh, well-supplied enemy force. After negotiating safe passage for the civilians, *Tikur Anbessa* laid down its arms and surrendered.[67]

On February 19, 1937, two young patriots attempted to assassinate the Italian viceroy, General Rodolfo Graziani, using hand grenades. The general received hundreds of shrapnel wounds but survived. In the end it was the natives who got the worst of it.[68] Italian security forces, the Blackshirts and laborers retaliated with an orgy of violence. They killed, burned, raped and looted with impunity for several days. The US representative in Addis called it, "unbridled brutality and cowardice." The young educated class, including many of the *Tikur Anbessa* who had been paroled after their capture, were targeted for execution but they remained defiant to the end. Lt. Col. Belay Haile-Ab refused to be escorted to his execution by anyone of a lesser rank and was subsequently thrown out of a plane mid-flight. Facing a firing squad, Lt. Col. Ketema Beshah asked for a cigarette and five-minutes to smoke it. Lt. Col. Kifle Nesibu and Maj. Matias Gemeda were also among those executed. When the dust settled an estimated 30,000 Ethiopians lay dead.[69]

The brutal retaliation, however, had the opposite effect on the populace than what the Fascists intended. Patriots flocked to join the resistance. The Italians had to raise additional colonial troops

A scene from the outskirts of Addis Ababa in the late 1940s, showing a jeep of the Ethiopian Army passing by a camel caravan. (Albert Grandolini Collection)

and send 40 more Blackshirt battalions from Italy to suppress the rebellion.[70] But Ethiopia's salvation would not come until the outbreak of World War II when the Nazi blitzkrieg swept across Europe in 1939. Mussolini declared war against Britain and France, and soon Italian forces started attacking British outposts in East Africa. An integral part of British Prime Minister Winston Churchill's war plan was the use of Ethiopian irregular/patriot forces. To this end, Emperor Haile Selassie was flown to Khartoum in June 1940 from England where he had sought exile. The British also established a military training camp at Soba, twelve miles from Khartoum, for Ethiopian ex-pats. Many who had been in exile, including former Genet Military Academy cadets, found their way to the camp.

On January 18, 1941, the Emperor crossed into his country at the head of a small force and rallied his war weary people to re-take Addis Ababa on May 5, 1941, five-years to the day from when the Fascists had captured it. As the rest of the world became ever more embroiled in another great war, the nation that had been one of the first casualties had come out on the other side and the Patriots who fought for five long years to liberate her were now trying to find their place in society. Most returned to their farms, while others pursued careers in the police and military.

Haile Selassie still believed a modern military consisting of an Imperial Army under a Ministry of War and an independent Imperial Bodyguard was essential for repulsing foreign invaders as well as maintaining internal stability. On May 8, 1945, Ethiopia joined the rest of the world in celebrating Victory in Europe (VE) Day. The Emperor addressed a large crowd of diplomats, nobles, school children, ordinary citizens and thousands more listening on the radio to reaffirm his commitment to collective security. He said,

There is no need for renewal of Our offer to send troops to fight against the common enemy side by side in the battle with the forces of Our Allies. Though Our country, Ethiopia is now far from the scene of battle, Our thoughts are there. All help which may be asked of Us, even the Lives of Our People, will be given willingly. We do not believe that distance need prevent Our land from giving assistance in the common cause.[71]

Training of an Ethiopian Army mortar team by a US instructor. (Albert Grandolini Collection)

A month later, representatives from 50 countries met in San Francisco, California, to put together a charter for the "United Nations," a term coined by US President Franklin D. Roosevelt in 1942. The Emperor sent representatives of his government and made his country one of the signatories on June 26, 1945, and subsequently ratified the charter on November 13, 1945.[72][73]

The late 40s were a time of rampant change for most nations around the world. And Ethiopia was no exception. In 1948, Ethiopia

Czechoslovak-manufactured CKD-IV tankettes were the first armour operated by the Ethiopian Army after the liberation from Italian occupation. These two are seen together with one of the US-supplied M8 reconnaissance cars. (Albert Grandolini Collection)

US Army troops on withdrawal 'north of Seoul', on 14 January 1951. (US Army)

US Army Prisoners of War paraded through the streets of Pyongyang. (Korean Central News Agency)

and ammunition to sufficiently equip two or three divisions, in addition to a limited number of military aircraft.[74]

The task of re-establishing the Imperial Bodyguard fell to an Ethiopian officer. Mulugeta Bulli was born in Sidamo Province and attended primary school in that area in Amharic and French before going to Addis Ababa for his secondary education. The studious Mulugeta was selected to be a cadet at the Genet Academy. Following the Italian invasion, he received a captain's commission and commanded one of the battalions when the young officers stood up a brigade to march to the mountain pass of Termaber.[75] He spent the occupation years in French-Somaliland (Djibouti) and later traveled to the Sudan to join Haile Selassie. He attended the Soba military academy, marched with the Emperor throughout the liberation campaign and with a small party preceded him into the capital.[76] At the rank of major, Mulugeta was appointed commander of the Imperial Bodyguard after it was reconstituted with 300 of the old-breed Guardsmen.[77] He spent the decade after the war shaping the Imperial Bodyguard into a modern military unit and in 1951, he was promoted to brigadier general. He was intelligent, disciplined, cautious and loyal, especially to the Crown.

Mulugeta's academy classmate Mengistu Neway was his right-hand man and the second most influential officer in the Guard. Mengistu was born around 1915 or 1917 in Addis Ababa. He attended Tafari Makonnen School before being selected for the Imperial Bodyguard academy at Genet. At the outbreak of war, he was commissioned as a first lieutenant. He joined the patriotic resistance during the Italian invasion and like so many of his peers eventually sought exile in Djibouti and then Kenya. Later he trained at the Soba academy and re-entered the capital with the Emperor. He helped Mulugeta with re-establishing the Imperial Bodyguard as his special assistant. For a time (as late as 1947) he commanded the 3d Battalion of the Imperial Bodyguard.[78] He also served as staff officer (hybrid of present-day G1 and G3) overseeing the training and personnel needs as well as the hospital, engineers, athletics, the band and the press for the IBG.[79]

reoccupied Ogaden after reaching an agreement with the British. The Italians reoccupied Somaliland, renewed their military buildup and started making a show of force close to the Ethiopian border. Haile Selassie's armed forces were still small in number, barely trained and ill-equipped. Determined not to get caught flat footed again, he sought help from wherever he could get it. He signed a contract with Czechoslovakia for a small arms factory and technicians. He obtained 10,000 rifles and 1,000,000 rounds of ammunition from the British. Similar attempts were made with the governments of Belgium, Canada and Sweden. After both Ethiopia and the US raised their respective missions from Legation to Embassy in 1949, the imperial government made repeated inquires to the US regarding the purchase of arms

General Viking Tamm, who had been the chief instructor at the Imperial Bodyguard Academy in Genet as a captain a decade earlier, arrived in Ethiopia in 1945 to resume his work of training a new corps of cadets for the Guard. When he returned to Sweden in 1946, he left twelve Swedish instructors in his place.[80]

Once again school administrators and the military advisers handpicked capable youngsters for military training regardless of their wishes. Viveca Halldin Norberg highlights that each cadet upon enrollment was asked by Tage Olihn, the chief Swedish instructor at that time, why he wanted to become an officer. Norberg wrote, "Not one of the cadets sought enrollment because he wanted to be an officer. The reason why they did not want to become officers was, according to Olihn, that they thought that they could get better and more well-paid jobs after completing civil education."[81] While the Swedes managed the curriculum, the academy was administered by an Ethiopian officer – Capt. Asfaw Habtemariam – who would later command troops in Korea. The first course with approximately 150 cadets, ages 16-19, started in April 1946, in Addis Ababa, because the original Genet Military Academy in Holeta was being used to train officers for the Imperial Army. The Imperial Bodyguard Academy graduated the first of three successive post-liberation cadet courses on September 9, 1948.[82]

The Post-WWII US Military

At the close of WWII, Communism had replaced Nazism, Fascism and Japanese Nationalism as the biggest threat to global peace. The Soviet Union had gone from an ally of necessity to bitter adversary. To make matters worse, their successful testing of an atom bomb in 1949 marked the beginning of the nuclear race. In Asia, the Communists emerged as the victors of the Chinese Civil War. In 1950, China and the Soviets signed a treaty of mutual assistance. The US government in return adopted a policy of containment against Communist expansion.[83]

At the same time, US policymakers started to rapidly demobilize the armed forces. Overall spending on national defense was slashed by 83% from 1945 to 1950.[84] The US Army with a peak of 5.9-million ground troops in 1945, was down to 591,000 by June 1950.[85][86] Of those, 231,000 were deployed overseas, with approximately 108,500 in the Far East. The Army Air Forces were cut from 243 combat groups and reorganized as the US Air Force with 48 groups at the beginning of hostilities in Korea. The Navy was similarly demobilized.[87]

The Far East Command, which had responsibility in Asia including Korea, had four divisions. Each division had the requisite three regiments, but most regiments were short a battalion and were stripped of their organic armor. These changes would haunt the US in the early days of the Korean War because US Army doctrine called for three maneuver elements.[88] A month into the conflict, a frontline officer would bitterly comment, "What can you do with a damn two-battalion infantry regiment? You have no base to deploy around, no reserve—and no tactics, because all our tactics are founded on the assumption that you have three full battalions to maneuver with."[89] Even artillery battalions had two instead of the normal three batteries.[90]

The US military, especially the Army, was suffering from a critical lack of supplies, training and overall direction, as boots on the ground were thought to be obsolete in the atomic age. Units did not have the weapons and equipment they were required to have per the Table of Organization and Equipment (TO&E). And what they had was mostly left-over from the last war.

On the policy front, Washington had tunnel-vision on Europe because that was where the decisive showdown with Communists was expected to take place. Asia was only a sideshow. When MacArthur was awakened and informed of the North Korean invasion on that fateful Sunday morning so reminiscent of Pearl Harbor, he thought to himself, "…in the short space of five years [America's] power had been fritted away in a bankruptcy of positive and courageous leadership toward any long-range objectives. Again, I asked myself, 'What is United States policy in Asia?' And the appalling thought came, 'The United States has no policy in Asia.' "[91] Or as Gen. Matthew Ridgway put it so succinctly, the US was "in a state of shameful unreadiness."[92]

1

FIRST KAGNEW BATTALION

On June 27, 1950, Ethiopian Ambassador *Ras* Imru met with State Department officials in Washington. In response to the US President's statement from earlier that day, *Ras* Imru expressed his hopes for peace and added, "the Korean incident is a matter which could not be considered of a local nature but on the contrary is a matter of concern for the entire world." He regretted the outbreak of armed conflict but commended the US for implementing the Security Council resolution.

On July 3, 1950, the Ethiopian Vice-Minister of Foreign Affairs responded to the June 27 Security Council Resolution reaffirming the Imperial government's "unswerving loyalty to principle of collective security and its prompt application to limit and control aggression and to secure and maintain international conditions that will permit the self determination of all peoples."[1]

After the UN Secretary-General subsequently sent an urgent request for assistance, in particular for ground forces, General MacArthur outlined the basic requirements for troop contributions. Ground units were to number approximately 1,000, with enough English-speakers and if possible armed with US weapons and equipment for attachment to existing US command structure at the regimental or division levels. These units were to be supplied on a reimbursable basis. Pledges poured in, but some offers, such as the ones from Iran, Lebanon and Pakistan never materialized.[2]

Ethiopia's position on geo-political issues brought before the United Nations at that time was complex. She was aligned with India, the Soviet Union and Middle East countries on anti-colonialism and independence, but she voted with the West on matters of human rights and territorial integrity. *Ras* Imru, Haddis Alemayehou and several other prominent Ethiopians were openly Communist sympathizers. Haile Selassie, however, favored the US and remained committed to collective security, and when the UN plea for troops came in, he offered to send a battalion to Korea without consulting his legal adviser John Spencer, or Minister of Foreign Affairs Aklilou Abte Wolde, who according to Spencer, did not view this as "a wise move."[3]

On August 5, 1950, Aklilou reported to the UN, the Imperial Ethiopian government was prepared to provide military assistance and was examining the logistics of such an undertaking. His Imperial

Majesty was also pledging 100,000 Ethiopian Dollars for the purchase of medical supplies.[4] On November 2, Aklilou clarified the Imperial Ethiopian Government would provide a contingent of 1,069 officers and men.[5] On November 16, 1950, the Department of the Army advised UNC that Ethiopia had offered one infantry battalion for service in Korea and that the unit would need to be trained and equipped. A week later, the UNC replied that the offer was acceptable.

In February 1951, the American military attaché in Addis Ababa provided a preliminary report on the Ethiopian contingent preparing to join the war in Korea. The unit was to be led by a colonel and organized as an expeditionary force, consisting of an infantry battalion and base section, including a stores and a replacements subsection. The infantry battalion under the command of a lieutenant colonel, rifle companies, a heavy weapons company and a headquarters company with signal, quartermaster, and military-police platoons as well as a medical platoon with European personnel. A Coptic priest would also accompany the unit as chaplain.

The attaché reported that all officers and very few of the enlisted men spoke English. He judged their proficiency with their own weapons to be good but added that they would need a two-month familiarization if they were to use US weapons and equipment. Apparently, the Emperor was anxious for the unit to depart immediately for political reasons and preferred that any further training be given in theater. Another battalion of 81 officers and 1,069 men including primary replacements were reportedly on standby.

While each soldier would have his individual equipment and arms, supplies, including rations, crew-served weapons and transportation from Djibouti to Korea and back were to be furnished by the US or others. The imperial government expressed its willingness to let UNC make any changes in organization deemed necessary and granted complete operational authority to the CINC with no stipulation made as to use of troops, except that unit integrity be maintained.

Colonel Kebbede Guebre was being floated as the probable commander of the unit. General Dothée and Colonel Nilsson, personal military adviser to the Emperor and chief of the Swedish training mission respectively, recommended a US officer initially command the battalion until the Ethiopian commander became familiar. They both allegedly expressed doubts in the quality of the senior officers and pinned their hopes to US leadership.

Colonel Kebbede Guebre was born in Addis Ababa in 1916 to *Kegnazmatch* Molaw. He received his early education at Tafari Makonnen and Menelik II schools before entering the Genet Military Academy in 1935. After the Italian invasion, he was commissioned as lieutenant and then promoted to captain and major in rapid succession. During the occupation, he fought as a patriot before eventually seeking exile in Djibouti. Kebbede later traveled to Sudan to join the liberation campaign. He attended the British training camp at Soba and was chosen as bodyguard to the Emperor. He then served as Intelligence Chief in the re-established Ministry of War. From 1942 to 1944, he was the commanding officer of the 9th Regiment in Harar at the rank of lieutenant colonel, before being appointed Secretary General of the Ministry of War. In 1949 he was promoted to colonel and made acting C.O. of the 1st Division and later, governor of Bale Awraja. He was 5-foot-6 and spoke English, French and some Italian.

Col. Kebbede Guebre greeting Ethiopian troops on arrival in Korea, May 6, 1951. (US Army)

Ethiopian troops disembarking USNS *General McRae*, May 6, 1951. (US Army)

ADMINISTRATIVE DIVISIONS
OF
ETHIOPIA

Map of Ethiopian administrative divisions (federal states) as of 1952, when Eritrea was federated into the country. (Guidebook of Ethiopia, The Chamber of Commerce, 1954, via author)

While Kebbede would command the overall expedition, Lieutenant Colonel Aman Mikael Andom would lead the fighting element (the infantry battalion). Aman was of Eritrean origin. After some schooling there, he attended a missionary school in Sudan before returning to Eritrea to continue his education. Aman first entered military service at the military training camp in Soba, Sudan, and fought in the liberation campaign. After the war, he attended the prestigious British military academy at Sandhurst. One source claims he was a platoon leader in the Imperial Bodyguard and later a platoon leader and company commander with the Imperial Army's 1st Battalion in Gonder. He subsequently served in staff assignments in the Ministry of War before returning to Eritrea as a battalion commander where he participated in the campaign against local separatists.[6] He spoke Arabic, English and French.[7] When he left for Korea, Aman Andom was 28 years old. The US military attaché said Aman was "reputedly Ethiopia's best officer." He was considered a soldier's soldier. In Korea he was quoted by Stars and Stripes as saying, "My men like hand-to-hand fighting… That's real combat."[8] Later in his life Aman would be characterized by the US as "brash, aggressive, intelligent, racially sensitive and at times emotionally unstable."[9]

A request from the Ethiopians for Col. Nilsson, Chief of the Swedish training mission, and two other officers to accompany the unit and assist with training was debated by Sweden's General Staff and Foreign Office. While the former supported the idea, the latter objected over the risk of having Swedes associated with any failure on the part of the Ethiopians in combat.

Aware of the realities of mid-century America, General Mulugeta Bulli bluntly expressed "his sincerest hope that his men would not encounter any racial discrimination as they want to fight enemy and not allies." He was assured they would not be segregated but treated as comrades.

On April 11, the Emperor inspected the Imperial Bodyguard academy, paying close attention to the officers destined to Korea. On April 12, the battalion assembled in *Janhoy Meda* (also referred to as *Jan Meda* – a large field/horse track in Addis Ababa also used as parade field by the Guard) in front of their Swedish instructors, other military officers, the diplomatic corps and tens of thousands of spectators. They received from the Emperor the unit colors and the designation "Kagnew Battalion".[10]

The Emperor addressed the departing troops:

Soldiers… These flags you will carry in valour throughout the campaign. You will, We are sure, bring them back to Your Emperor and Commander-in-Chief, to whom you have sworn allegiance, as cherished battle standards, glorified by your exploits and heroism.

…

Soldiers: The spirits of your ancestors, heroes of the thousand-year long struggle

Ethiopian troops arrive in Korea, May 6, 1951. (US Army)

Ethiopian troops in formation at UNRC, May 6, 1951. (US Army)

for the defense of Our freedom will follow you, and will strengthen your hand and hearts in the heat of battle.

Remember that you are about to pay a debt of honour for your Homeland which was liberated thanks not only to the blood of her patriots, but also that of faithful allies, likewise members of the United Nations. Remember also that, in paying this debt, you are laying the basis for a universal system of collective security in behalf of your own Homeland as well as of nations of the world, be they great or small, powerful or weak.

May God protect you, give you courage to acquit yourselves as heroes and bring you back safely to your beloved Homeland.

After the parade, the entire battalion along with the VIPs were invited to the Imperial Palace for a feast.

First Lt. Desta Gemeda commanded 1st Platoon, 1st Company, Kagnew Battalion. Desta was born in Lekemte Awraja in Wolega Province. He attended a missionary school in his hometown until his education was interrupted by the Italian invasion at the age of seven

Lts. Bekele Mengheshia and Lemma Gebresadick being interviewed, May 6, 1951. (US Army)

Ethiopian troops awaiting billeting at UNRC, May 6, 1951. (US Army)

Matias and his fellow patriots marched to Wolega to join *Ras* Imru before Maj. Matias was captured and later executed.[12] Desta was enrolled into the first post-liberation Imperial Bodyguard cadet course and was commissioned in 1948, after three years of grueling training. He and the other graduates received their assignments within the Guard and began their military careers. Their primary responsibility was the training and care of their troops, but they also tried to become well-rounded by rotating to different assignments and taking evening classes .[13]

Twenty-year-old Corporal Bulcha Olika also from Wolega Province was assigned to a signal unit in the Guard when he received a transmission that Ethiopia would be joining the war in Korea. He prepared a written report and submitted it to his commanding officer. After reading the report, the officer immediately asked who took the message. Bulcha was summoned for questioning. The officer asked where he got the message and called him a liar. Everyone was hearing about the Korean War on the news radio… about how many planes were destroyed and how many people were killed, so it was unfathomable to this officer that his small country would be joining such a remote conflict. The two went to the radio room and listened to the transmission with dual headsets. The message was as Bulcha had transcribed word-for-word. The officer apologized.[14]

The accuracy of the message should not have come as a surprise to the officer as Bulcha

or eight. After the liberation, he attended the Haile Selassie School in Lekemte and was sent to the Tegbareid School in Addis Ababa. After finishing the 6th grade, he was studying for the entrance exam to the Kotebe Secondary School when he was hand-picked for the Imperial Bodyguard academy. Following a directive from the Ministry of Education, the school's director had chosen him because of his good grades.[11]

Desta had never really considered a career in the military until that time, even though he thought he possessed the qualities of a good soldier. His older brother was Maj. Matias Gemeda of *Tikur Anbessa*. A young Desta had spent some time with his brother as

was one of his best radio men. Bulcha had left home at the age of 11 for schooling. He enrolled in an Italian missionary school on some type of work-study program where he labored his way through for a year and a half. When the other students played outside, he had to tend the grounds, split firewood, and wash dishes for 600 students under the watchful eye of the school's tyrannical cook.[15] Bulcha was then recruited into the budding Imperial Ethiopian Air Force where he endured close order drills from his instructors in addition to daily beatings from the other recruits. After his countless complaints went unanswered, he forged a letter stating his mother had passed away and secured a discharge from the force. He returned to school until he

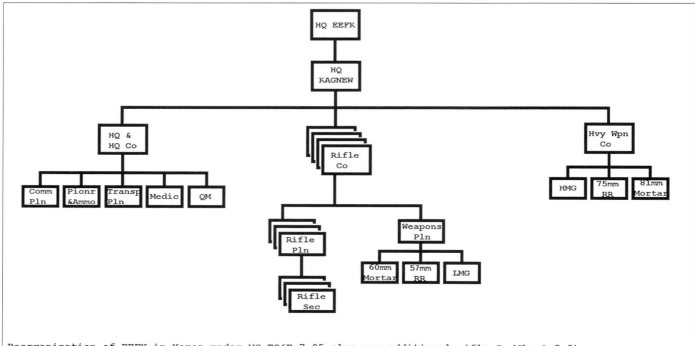

Reorganization of EEFK in Korea under US TO&E 7-95 plus one additional rifle Co (Chart 3-2)

Source: Fox, William J. History of the Korean War: Inter-Allied Co-operation During Combat
         Operations. Fort Leavenworth: US Army Command & General Staff College, 15 Aug.
         1952, p. 3.

Ethiopian troops getting chow, May 8, 1951. (US Army)

Ethiopian troops examining a carbine, May 8, 1951. (US Army)

was recruited six months later to the Imperial Bodyguard by an officer named Woldeyohanis Shitta.[16]

He underwent four-years of training with the Guard and attended night classes at the British Consulate. Bulcha's superiors recognized his aptitude and offered him assignments in the band and later in the engineers. He turned them down. He later accepted an assignment with the signal corps where he continued to excel until he eventually ended up in the press unit. This is how he got to be in that fortuitous position on the eve of Ethiopia's involvement in Korea. It also did not hurt that the signalmen got paid more and were the envy of other soldiers.[17]

Desta Gemeda said, as the only force trained in modern military science at that time, the Imperial Bodyguard was the obvious choice

Ethiopian troops cleaning mess kits with water and sand, May 9, 1951. (US Army)

Ethiopian officers asking questions, May 9, 1951. (US Army)

Ethiopian troops drilling, May 9, 1951. (US Army)

Ethiopian troops relaxing after a day of training, May 9, 1951. (US Army)

the Korean geography and read about the culture. Units were organized, officers were assigned commands, and men were recruited among the new recruits and veterans.[18]

The train station in Addis Ababa was filled with weeping friends and relatives, Desta recalled, "But we wanted to go. As professional soldiers we wanted to go to the front and use our training."[19] On April 13 at 0900, the battalion departed from Addis Ababa to French-Somaliland (Djibouti) on the country's sole railway for the 487-mile trip. The battalion was leaving during the Lent fasting season when Orthodox Christians abstained from consuming meat, dairy and eggs and so a traditional feast was out of the question. The Emperor did his best with vegetarian fare.

At each stop, local officials gave the troops a similar reception. When the troops arrived in Dire-Dawa however, Prince Makonnen (Duke of Harar), the Emperor's second son, who had flow ahead, greeted them with a carnivore's delight. Those more devout and unwilling to break their fast, respectfully accepted the food but threw it away later. The reception was followed by a one-hour furlough in the city. The troops were then collected by officers and military-police to resume their journey.[20]

By then the King of Sweden had intervened and a compromise had been reached on the issue of Swedish advisors accompanying the unit to Korea. While Col. Nilsson, chief of the training mission, would not be permitted to go, two other officers would be allowed to provisionally resign from the Swedish Army and accept commissions in the Ethiopian Army with the added stipulation that they not remain in Korea beyond June 15, 1951. They were further prohibited from joining the battalion in combat.[13] The advisers were to provide training to the battalion *en route* to Korea.

Captains Sten-Eggert Naucler and Orvar Nilsson were the two officers chosen for the task. Capt. Naucler was a decorated war hero. He had volunteered to fight for the Finns in the Russo-Finnish Wars, first as a platoon leader and later as a company commander. After the war, he served in a series of command and instructor billets before joining the Swedish training mission to Ethiopia in 1948. He was fluent in Swedish, English, German, and spoke some French, Finnish and Amharic.

Captain Nilsson, on the other hand, was just a 20-year-old cadet at the outbreak of the Russo-Finnish Wars. But that did not deter the young patriot. He dropped out of training in order to serve in the Volunteer Corps. After the first campaign (the Winter War), he resumed his training and graduated in 1941. He then returned to Finland to fight in the Continuation War. He came to Ethiopia as a member of the training mission in 1950.

The battalion arrived in Djibouti at 1100 on the 15th. Since some nations contributing troops did not possess the capability to transport their forces to the theater of war, the task fell to the US Military Sea Transportation Service (MSTS). The troop transport ship *General J.*

for the mission once the decision was made to get involved and so the young officers took the initiative and started preparing. They studied

Philippine, Dutch, Ethiopian and Thai soldiers taking a break, May 18, 1951. (US Army)

1st Lt. Mulugheta Natnael inspecting the equipment of one of his men, June 9, 1951. (US Army)

Members of Ethiopian Ammunition & Pioneer Platoon bridging a river, June 6, 1951. (US Army)

H. McRae would pick up Dutch, Belgian, Greek, Ethiopian and other UN troops on the way to her new final destination – Pusan.[21] The *McRae* weighed anchor and sailed into history on April 16.

The men spent the first week attending safety briefs, learning the hygiene rules and getting acclimated to life aboard a crowded troopship. The officers bunked two or four to a room, while the enlisted men were packed with as many as 250 in the largest berth. They all suffered from seasickness. The weather was so hot, they sometimes had to strip down to their skivvies.[22]

Naucler and Nilsson studied the small number of US weapons

Medic Hahene Reta and US Army sergeant at the firing range, June 8, 1951. (US Army)

US Army Sergeant explaining the operations of US M-1 Rifle to Capt. Tadesse Shibel, June 5, 1951. (US Army)

Ethiopian officers being briefed on air-ground coordination, June 10, 1951. (US Army)

aboard the ship and prepared written instruction for their use and care.[23] The Swedes provided instruction to the Ethiopian officers who in turn taught their men in their native tongue. As Desta Gemeda put it, "[they] discussed the situation and learned theory."[24]

On May 1, Private Zenabu Gebrehywot of the signal platoon, who had a pre-existing respiratory condition, complained of chest pains and was taken to the infirmary. He passed away during the voyage off the coast of Vietnam.

An advance party consisting of Colonel Kebbede, Captains Yohannes Meseker and Yohannes Paulos had left Addis Ababa on April 25 on a British airliner. Upon their arrival in Tokyo on May 4, they visited the commanding general and his chief of staff. They also met with the G-4 section to figure out the supply situation. The

Americans were surprised to find the Ethiopians would be arriving with practically just the clothes on their backs which included: one British-style battle dress suit, shoes with leggings, one haversack, one blanket, one sun helmet (not steel helmet), suspenders (not belts), and one mess kit with canteen, but no canteen cup. Their British .303 rifles were inspected and left behind because they were unserviceable for field use.

Ethiopian officers inspecting a captured Russian-made tank, June 10, 1951. (US Army)

battalion for combat. Maj Tadesse Wendemaghegnehu was put in charge of the Depot Company. Individuals were issued weapons, uniforms, helmets, blankets and packs. Clothing the troops was somewhat challenging because the Ethiopians "were taller than US Army standards and their feet were longer and more narrow."[25] The unit was issued tents, kitchens and vehicles. A major stir arose over the issue of footwear. The Ethiopians had arrived with only one pair of shoes – the ones on their feet. An inspection by the quartermaster showed 65% of these shoes to be badly worn. So the UNRC issued replacements. Both Kebbede and Aman, however, insisted on combat boots (which were in critical supply). Eighth Army eventually relented and combat boots were issued prior to the unit's departure from the UNRC.

The first week of real training commenced on May 14. US Army personnel with at least six months of frontline experience instructed the Ethiopian officers. The Ethiopian officers in turn instructed their soldiers. The Americans judged the unit to be highly disciplined with a well-established relationship between officers and men. Efficiency of the force was satisfactory and expected to improve as training progressed. However, the troops were having difficulty in signal training since they had little prior experience with modern communication equipment, but they worked diligently at it and ultimately surprised the Americans by becoming highly proficient. There were also deficiencies noted in proper handling of rations and field sanitation, with the latter being an issue with other UN contingents as well. The 57mm team was having trouble with the technical aspect of the training. The situation improved when the battalion C.O. replaced the platoon leader and gunners with personnel that had some artillery experience. All other training was progressing rapidly and was in most cases judged to be excellent or above. The American trainers were impressed by the Ethiopians. They all "[claimed] they never had better or more eager pupils." One US liaison officer commented, "They wanted to learn, as much as possible as fast as possible 'Probably so they could get their hands on the Reds as soon as possible.'"[26]

Another American concluded,

The Ethiopians had little or no training with modern equipment when they arrived, but, if anything, they learned faster and tried harder than any other unit processed through the Center. If they ran into a point of information which they didn't understand, they would ask for more details until they felt they fully understood it.[27]

Sergeant Asseba Badada was profiled in Stars and Stripes as the typical Kagnew soldier. "He was tall, sinewy, agile, dark brown skin, clear friendly eyes… curly but soft, black hair." The married 28-year-old was a nine-year veteran of the Imperial Guard. "He's a professional soldier… never worked at any other occupation." He had two years of high school education before joining the military. According to the

The eager troops crowded the deck as the *McRae* pulled into Pusan at 0800 on May 6. President Rhee, the US Ambassador, other high ranking officers and Col. Kebbede were also present. On the same day, GHQ issued General Order 18 attaching the Imperial Ethiopian Expeditionary Force to Korea (EEFK) to the US Eighth Army. The EEFK then boarded trucks and moved to the United Nations Reception Center (UNRC) in Pusan for processing for an eight-week training program.

The initial organization of the EEFK was a bit nebulous, but it resembled a reinforced infantry battalion under the British system of four rifle companies, instead of the US three, and included other attachments such as a depot company. When the Americans suggested reorganizing the unit according to the US Army's TO&E, the two Ethiopian senior officers objected among other things to the size of the rifle squads and the utilization of automatic weapons in the platoons. They organized the squads into 10-man squads instead of nine and chose to employ the automatic weapons separately from the rifle platoons. Consequently each company contained three rifle platoons and one weapons platoon. Each rifle platoon had three squads. The weapons platoon consisted of 60mm mortars, a 57mm recoilless rifle section plus a light machinegun section formed from the weapons squad of the rifle platoons – again in contradiction to the US system. Later the unit would be reorganized under US TO&E 7-95 as an infantry battalion headquarters with headquarters company, heavy weapons company and four (instead of the normal three) rifle companies.

US officers reported the training of the battalion was unnecessarily delayed due to Aman's decision not to commence training prior to the issuance of American uniforms, arms and equipment. After considerable discussion, limited training was conducted for all officers, drivers and maintenance personnel. All troops did, however, participate in physical training.

The staff at the UNRC got on with the business of equipping the article, he thought "rifle, bayonet, and hand grenade are the soldier's best friends—coupled with confidence in those weapons and in himself." He is disciplined and demands as much of his subordinates as his superiors ask of him. The reporter noticed that he and the other Ethiopians were at ease on the mountainous Korean terrain. Asseba explained, "that the terrain is directly similar to that of his country. 'So similar that the men actually get a bit homesick at times.'"[28]

Kagnew's training culminated in a battalion field exercise held from June 24 through July 1 in the vicinity of Hopo-Ri. Unfortunately Kagnew suffered a series of tragedies. One soldier drowned in the Naktong River during training on the 29th. On July 2, as infantrymen were engaged in a simulated attack, the supporting 75mm recoilless rifle fired a round which hit a tree immediately above the advancing troops. One soldier was killed and nine others wounded. Later that day one of the injured succumbed to his wounds.

Despite these setbacks, the troops showed aggressiveness and "Unexpected inherent tactical ability." "Difficult terrain was traversed quickly; indicating a high degree of physical fitness." However,

Ethiopian troops learning how to operate a switchboard, June 12, 1951. (US Army)

the battalion staff (S-1, S-2, and S-3) was not put to maximum use and communications, especially wire communication was underutilized. "It appeared the staff members… were just along. The battalion commander accomplished all of the minor details normally done by the staff."[29]

Each foreign contingent was authorized a liaison group at United Nations Command Headquarters in Tokyo for the purpose of providing liaison between its troops in the field, the General Headquarters and the home government. On June 17, Maj. Naucler and Capt. Tamrat Tessema arrived in Tokyo for liaison duty. In their new capacity they would work with Col. Edward Farnsworth Jr., the Chief Liaison Officer for the UNC.

In June, the other Swedish adviser, Maj. Nilsson, left Tokyo and arrived in Addis. Upon his arrival, Nilsson reported "the training program… was good but that morale was low due to the abusive attitude of the two senior Ethiopian officers who are also non-cooperative with American personnel." He added, "Certain Ethiopian troops and officers were agreed to dispose violently of Kebbede and Aman at the first battle opportunity." After receiving the report, it seems General Mulugeta Bulli had contemplated replacing both officers with Lt. Col. Teshome Irgetu. On June 30, 1951, Col. Nilsson, chief of the training mission, presented the same report to the Emperor along with a petition the two officers be relieved in hopes of "preserving the reputation of the Swedes and ensuring decent leadership of otherwise good contingent."

This friction between Ethiopian junior officers and the two senior commanders in Korea reported by Nilsson and later repeated by

Naucler could be difficult to understand since Kebbede and Aman were two of their nation's ablest field grade officers. It is even more puzzling when considering the legendary status they have since attained in Ethiopian society. Nonetheless, Kebbede and Aman came from the Imperial Army and not the Imperial Bodyguard. And as it turned out, the insular Guard officers were unhappy with the decision to have Army officers lead them in combat, since they had expected to flight under their own officers. There were three Imperial Army officers in the battalion. The third was Capt. Mehretab Tedla.

A report by the British military attaché in Addis to his home government seems to corroborate this. He wrote, "…there was not one Bodyguard officer considered fit to command the Korea battalion and the C.O. was brought in from the Army." He added, "It is said the Emperor was so annoyed that he ordered all field officers to attend a special tactical course at the cadet school." On the other hand, the attaché identified the junior officers sent to Korea as "the pick" of the litter.[30]

In the end, this episode turned out to be one big misunderstanding. After serving under Kebbede and Aman, members of Kagnew Battalion grew to respect, if not love, both men. These two were fiercely protective of their troops, looked out for their interest and made sure they suffered no slight, at times to the chagrin of the Americans. This conflict was in no way caused by a desire on the part of the Swedes to command Kagnew Battalion as has been suggested in recent years by some authors. It was made abundantly clear by the Swedish government that Naucler and Nilsson would only travel to Korea to provide training and not to participate in combat operations.

Lt. Col. Aman Andom, Lt. Col. John Hightower, and his X.O. watch the Kagnew parade, July 23, 1951. (US Army)

Ethiopian Battalion Medical Section celebrating the Emperor's birthday, July 23, 1951. (US Army)

to Kaesong and met with their Communist counterparts. And with that, peace negotiations commenced.

By the end of June, the 7th Division was in IX Corps reserve at Kapyong tasked with preparing a defensive position at Line Kansas (one in a series of defensive lines used to denote the Main Line of Resistance) in addition to conducting maintenance and training. This was the first time the division was placed in reserve since entering the war in September 1950.

The Ethiopian troops departed Pusan aboard trains on July 9 and arrived at the 7th Division area July 11. They were now scattered in four locations. EEFK HQ with Col. Kebbede was in Teague (attached to 2d Logistical Command). There was a depot in Pusan, operational forces at the front and a liaison group in Tokyo.

On the morning of July 11, EEFK with an assigned strength of 84 officers, 8 warrant officers and 1,037 enlisted men was officially attached to the US 7th Infantry Division. It was further attached to the 32d Infantry Regiment for operational control and training. The combat battalion consisted of 56 officers and 796 other ranks.

The US 7th Infantry Division was first activated on December 6, 1917, as part of the American Expeditionary Force during World War I. After seeing action in the Western Front, it was disbanded in 1923. The division was reactivated in 1940, absorbed the 32d Infantry Regiment and deployed to the Pacific Theater where it fought in some of the bloodiest battles of World War II. It was then dispatched to Korea with the

On June 23, during a radio address, Yakov Malik, the Soviet Representative to the UN, advocated an armistice in Korea. On June 30, General Ridgway proposed meeting on a Danish Hospital Ship to discuss it. The Communists replied they were ready to meet at the 38th parallel in Kaesong between July 10 and 15. Ridgway said his representatives were ready to meet their representatives on July 10 or sooner, but that liaison officers should meet first to work out the details. On July 8, a liaison group of three officers flew by helicopter

mission of patrolling the 38th parallel until it was transferred to Japan in 1948 for occupation duty.[31] It is nicknamed the "Bayonet Division," but is also referred to as the "Hourglass Division" because of the shape the two reversed 7s make on the division insignia. The US 32d Infantry Regiment was designated as the "Queen's Own Regiment" after receiving its regimental flag from the last queen of Hawaii, where it was first activated in 1916. It is also referred to as the "Buccaneers".

On July 12, 1951, at 1000, Lt. Col. John Hightower who had

assumed command of the 32d Regiment only a week prior, welcomed the Ethiopians to the "Queen's Own" Infantry.[32] Hightower, a 6-foot-4 Texan, came from humble beginnings. He grew up during the Great Depression and worked in the Civilian Conservation Corps as a laborer before attending college on a football scholarship. He was commissioned into the Army in 1940 and served in WWII until he was wounded.[33] As any good officer, Hightower lobbied hard for a combat command and became the youngest regimental commander in Korea at the age of 34.[34] While he was very successful in the Army, those who knew him best said he was never comfortable with violence. His family called him a "warrior for peace."[35] Following Hightower's speech, Lt. Col. Aman addressed the regiment. He spoke of collective security and said he and his men were honored to "take [their] place amongst the allied nation's[sic] of the free world, and to be a part of the 32d Infantry."

Lieutenant Colonel Hightower and his wife had met and entertained Col. Kebbede in Tokyo before both men proceeded to Korea. According to the Hightower family, "keeping in mind the times were the 1950s, there was a bit of a flap when the Ethiopians arrived. The only place to put the new [commander] was in the tent with [John]. His men were stewing around [so John] asked them what was up. They haltingly explained their dilemma and [he] said there was no problem, commanders shared tents, so billet [us] together. A lifelong friendship ensued" between Hightower and Kebbede.[36]

Maj. Terefe Teklemariam and the Ethiopian Color Guard present arms, July 23, 1951. (US Army)

Maj. Gen. Claude Ferenbaugh performing a ceremonial dance on the Emperor's birthday, July 23, 1951. (US Army)

The 7th Division had been training since going into IX Corps reserve on June 23. Colonel Hightower and his staff observed a series of small unit demonstrations by Kagnew Battalion in order to determine their combat proficiency. The officers and men were found to be of high caliber but still uncomfortable with some US weapons and so the battalion was put through another round of intensive training.

On July 23, the Ethiopian Expedition celebrated their Emperor's birthday. The division commander, Maj. Gen. Claude Ferenbaugh, Lt.

Col. Hightower and others were in attendance. There were parades, feasts and traditional dancing which even the general participated in. Kagnew resumed its training on July 25 and from July 26 through July 29, the battalion participated in a division-wide field exercise.

On July 30, an Ethiopian ambush patrol departed at 2000, reached its objective at 2130 and returned to base at 0815 the next morning without any enemy contacts. Another patrol from 2d Co departed at 0800 reached and remained in observation at its objective and at

Maj. Gen. Lemnitzer awards Silver Star Medal to Capt. Tefera Woldetensai, April 4, 1952. (US Army)

formation for a memorial service honoring their comrades who gave their lives in Korea. The day also marked the 35th anniversary of the regiment's activation. The next day, with morale high, the regiment started toward the frontline held by the US 24th Infantry Division. On August 8, the 7th Division relieved the 24th Division on Line Wyoming. The 17th Regiment was on the right, the 31st on the left and 32d in reserve. By this point, Line Wyoming had been fortified into a defensive line organized in depth with security for the Main Line of Resistance (MLR) provided by a GOPL of reinforced platoon strong-points 800-2,000 yards forward of the MLR. The 3d Battalion with 2d Company of the EEFK attached, relieved elements of the 24th Division on Patrol Base X also forward of the MLR. The division was now in contact with the 27th CCF Army.

1355 received small arms and mortar from unknown enemy forces. The patrol called artillery on the suspected enemy site at 1445 and withdrew.

August 1951

August is normally the hottest month of the year in Korea with temperatures in the 80s during the day and 70s at night. However relative humidity ranging from 70% to 90% made the heat oppressive. At the beginning of August, the 32d Infantry was still in corps reserve tasked with fortifying Line Kansas. Training was focused on night patrolling, ambushing, and marksmanship in preparation for relief of the 24th Infantry Division on Line Wyoming.

The month also brought a major change to the battalion as Lt. Col. Aman Andom was relieved of command and ordered to return home, apparently at the request of the US government. The British attaché wrote, Lt. Col. Aman "proved so impossible in his relations with Europeans and Americans that he was finally recalled."[37] Although Lt. Col. Teshome Irgetu had arrived in Korea on August 16, it appears Maj. Tadesse Wendemaghegnehu was in charge of the battalion from the beginning of August until Teshome officially took command on October 1.

Lieutenant Colonel Teshome was born in 1921 in Addis Ababa. After attending the Tafari Makonnen School, he was employed by the French legation as an interpreter during the Italian occupation. He joined the military in 1943. And after completing his training the same year, he was promoted to 1st Lt. He made captain in 1945, major in 1948, and lieutenant colonel in 1951. He spoke French, English and some Arabic. It is worth noting Teshome is not listed in the rolls for the 1935 Genet Military Academy, Soba academy, post-liberation Imperial Army or IBG cadet courses. Skordiles nevertheless claims Teshome was born in 1914 and was a graduate of the Genet Academy in 1936.[38]

On August 7, the entire 32d Regiment turned out in parade

On August 14, at 1600, 2d Platoon, 2d Company, led by 2d Lt. Guebreyesus Mikael, left for a night patrol around the high ground forward of Hill 1073. At around 0150 on August 15, the patrol was attacked by a reinforced company which was supported by 82mm mortars, 120mm mortars and 57mm recoilless rifles. The patrol quickly rallied and set up defensive positions "to prevent the enemy from gaining the hill they were defending." Under the cover of heavy mortar barrage, the enemy attempted to encircle the patrol. But Lt. Gebreyesus went from position to position exposing himself to enemy fire in order to call fire missions. He silenced the 82mm mortars by successfully directing friendly artillery onto their position. The patrol repulsed three successive attempts by the enemy to encircle their positions but took some casualties in the process. When a soldier operating a Browning Automatic Rifle (BAR) was killed, Pvt. Gifar Fitala dashed a distance of 50 yards, picked up the BAR and "sprayed the area to his direct front, killing the enemy who attempted to take advantage of" the momentary lack of defense in that sector. "Due to his courage in that position the move of the numerically superior enemy was prevented." The enemy attempted to encircle the patrol a total of three times but withdrew at daybreak after being repulsed each time. The patrol suffered two friendly KIA and one WIA. The attack cost the enemy a confirmed 14 KIA, another estimated 35 KIA, and an estimated 50 WIA. Despite having paid for the outcome with their own blood, Kagnew was still being doubted by their American comrades. In reference to the enemy casualty figures reported, the staff of the 3d Bn, to whom the 2d Co was attached to, notated "not probable" in the battalion diary.

On August 17, 2d Bn with 3d Co EEFK attached was to replace 3d Bn with 2d Co EEFK attached. But before the relief, at 2130 on August 16, a two-squad patrol led by 2d Lt. Abebe Kassahun left for the river junction at the base of Hill 1073. The patrol was forced to take cover after coming under heavy mortar fire. Once the barrage lifted, "2d

Lt. Abebe moved from position to position checking on his men" and gathering intelligence on enemy disposition. By 2300 the patrol reported being cut off by an enemy company which mounted grenade attacks from the northwest and southwest supported by a heavy machinegun firing down the trail and two light machineguns at another position. The patrol "engaged the enemy for 3.5-hours suffering one casualty." Later 2nd Lt. Abebe called in fire missions on enemy units blocking his egress route. The 3d Bn opened a path back to Company K lines for Abebe and his men using 60mm and 81mm mortars and artillery fire. Carrying their wounded comrade, the men followed the artillery concentration. At this point, Sgt. Molla elected to act as the rear guard and covered the patrol as it withdrew uphill. "After assaulting the enemy position… he engaged the enemy in a hand-to-hand struggle" and incapacitated four of them. "This gave the men in the platoon who carried the wounded comrade, and the remainder of the men in the platoon, ample time to climb the hill to a place of comparative safety. The patrol withdrew through two enemy platoons and arrived at friendly positions at 0335. The enemy suffered four KIA counted and an estimated 20 KIA. Another patrol that was dispatched to that area almost four hours later counted four killed.

Hanging the Presidential Unit Citation streamer on the Kagnew flag. (US Army)

The Ethiopians were showing their comfort with hand-to-hand fighting early on. Lt. Abbeba Dawit was observed by a reporter thoughtfully "[running] his finger along the sharp edge of a steel blade. 'The Turks say the bayonet is the key to the Chinese kingdom,' he mused smiling. 'I think perhaps they are right.'"[39]

By August 19, the unit had been in combat for 105 days and suffered a cumulative four killed in action, two wounded and 40 non-battle casualties. On August 19, General Ferenbaugh came to the front and awarded US Bronze Star Medals for Valor to 2d Lts. Guebreyesus Mikael, Abebe Kassahun, Sgt. Molla Filate and Pvt. Gifar Fitala for distinguishing themselves in battle.[40]

The 1st Company had been attached to the 17th Regiment after relieving the 4th Co EEFK on August 20. 1st Lt. Desta Gemeda remembers taking his platoon to their new position on a dark and rainy night. His platoon was attached to Item Company. The

American company commander called him to the tent and explained that friendly units had not captured any POWs in a while. Since fresh intelligence was needed, Desta was ordered on a prisoner snatch and bunker destroying mission. A machinegun squad of US soldiers would be attached to the patrol, so Desta thought it was a big deal that the C.O. trusted him with American lives.[41]

Early the next morning, Desta took out his map and showed his men where they would go. As the patrol departed friendly lines, the fog was so thick visibility was restricted to ten meters. Desta was advised to wait an hour until the fog lifted. When the patrol started moving again, Desta was able to see their objective through binoculars. As they advanced, they came under automatic weapon and mortar attack. Desta silenced it by exposing himself to hostile fire to call accurate friendly indirect fire. He then positioned his men and

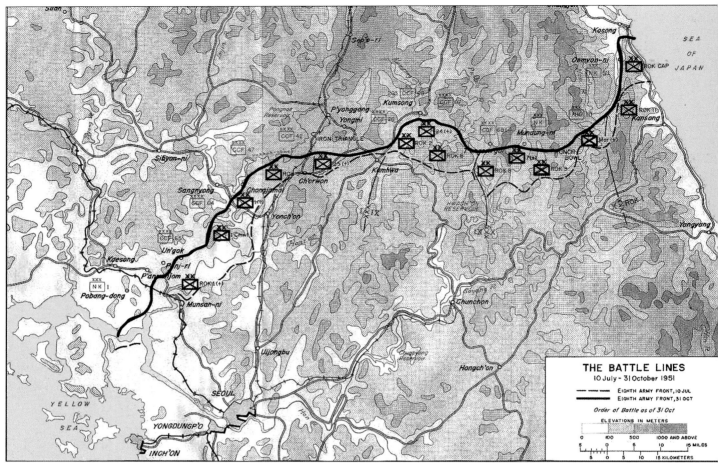

Battle lines of July-October 1951. At the time, the 7th Division was deployed, along with the Kagnew Battalion, in the centre of the eastern flank of the front lines held by UN forces, opposite to Mundung-In. (Hermes, Walter G. *Truce Tent and Fighting Front*. Washington D.C.: Center of Military History, United States Army, 1992, p. 98.)

began waiting for movement. He eventually saw one North Korean soldier leave his bunker with a water jug on his shoulder heading to a small stream. He called over one of the squad leaders and pointed out the soldier. The patrol was prepared – they had even brought towels to gag the prisoner's mouth. As the enemy soldier was fetching water, they pounced. The North Korean was strong and put up a fight. They tried to drag him back but he continued to struggle so they resorted to wounding him in the thigh with a bayonet to gain compliance. When Desta radioed to report their status, he was ordered to send the POW to friendly lines immediately. The C.O. asked him what he saw. Desta reported the enemy was digging foxholes, but that the bunkers were too far to hit with weapons the patrol had on hand – even their 57mm. Desta was ordered to provide the coordinates of the bunker. He was told that artillery would be incoming and to provide adjustments. The first shot missed – it was too long – so he called an adjustment. The second shot also missed. It was too short. Using the two points, the gunners were able to bracket the target. The C.O. radioed, "Battery three, rounds on the way." The patrol heard the shells flying overhead and the bunker was completely destroyed. They reported estimated enemy casualties. The C.O. asked for the whereabouts of the POW. Desta replied, "On the way." The C.O. then ordered them to recon the enemy position. As the weary patrol prepared to recon, the company C.O.'s voice came over the radio again and told them to just return to base as time was running out. Before they could leave, they observed another enemy position with a lot of activity – people going in and out. They destroyed it with their 57mm before returning.[42]

At one point during 1st Lt. Desta's patrol, the communications between the Command Post and the leading patrol failed. That was

when Capt. Tefera Waldetensye who was liaising between the patrol and Item Company "voluntarily exposed himself to the enemy fire and moved forward, carrying instructions to the platoon. He personally directed and supervised the repair of communications facilities and then returned, enabling the [commander] of Company I to plan for the future operations of the platoon…."

Captain Tefera Waldetensye was Lieutenant Desta's company commander and academy classmate. Tefera started his career in the Imperial Army and was at the signal school when he was picked to attend the first Imperial Bodyguard cadet course. After graduation he served as platoon leader before being promoted to company commander.[43]

On August 22, 3d Company led by Capt. Wendemu Negatu left at 0530 to patrol Hill 752. The patrol split into two with two platoons proceeding down the hill on the left flank, while the third platoon moved independently on the right flank. The bigger force reached the objective at 0845 and split off in to two groups. At 1000, one platoon remained on position as reserve while the other platoon assaulted the objective. Ten minutes later an enemy squad opened up on the assault force with small arms and automatic fire. Capt. Wendemu "exercising sound judgment and great tactical ingenuity led [his men] in an attack against the hostile forces." The enemy routed after suffering two killed and one wounded. Since part of their mission was to capture enemy prisoners of war, the patrol attempted to capture the wounded soldier and in the process they wounded another enemy soldier. To prevent their capture by the Ethiopians, the Communists machinegunned their two wounded comrades. Sporadic exchange of gunfire continued until 1120. After observing a company sized enemy force preparing for a counterattack, Capt. Wendemu immediately "deployed his men in positions of advantage" and once the enemy attack started, he moved from position to position exposing himself to hostile fire to direct the artillery support. "So effective was the coordinated fire of friendly troops that the onrushing masses of the enemy were repulsed with extremely heavy casualties." The fearless Negatu started pulling back his men at 1155 after the patrol suffered five wounded and one dead (four from mortars and two from booby traps). Enemy losses were significantly higher with 13 killed and four wounded with an additional estimated 19 killed and 23 wounded.

On August 29, 7th Recon Co relieved Kagnew Battalion on Patrol Base Able. Kagnew in turn replaced 2d Bn on Patrol Base X and began aggressive patrol activities. That same

Sgt. Maj. Mamoushet Goshime visiting the UN General Assembly in Paris, December 1951. (UN photo)

day, a reinforced platoon patrol, codenamed Patrol Fissiha, from 2d Co departed at 0800. When the patrol reached their objective at 1145, they found no enemy. But at 0105 the patrol was attacked by an estimated enemy platoon. The patrol called in artillery and killed 15 Communists. The patrol continued the assault inflicting seven more KIA. The patrol observed another enemy platoon preparing for a counterattack and again brought down an artillery barrage which caused the enemy to withdraw with ten KIA. As the friendly patrol withdrew, the enemy answered with its own mortar fire, killing one of the Ethiopians.

The next day, a 2d Co patrol which was sent out to establish physical contact with Company G on Hill 658 received one company sized and another platoon sized attack at 0100 and 0430. They suffered one friendly KIA and one WIA. On August 31, the CCF threw grenades into the 2d Co area killing one and wounding two.

During the month of August, the bulk of Kagnew Bn HQ remained in reserve while individual companies were attached to frontline US battalions to receive their baptism by fire. In addition to the actions mentioned above, they repulsed many attacks on friendly positions and sent out numerous patrols ranging in size from squad to several platoons, both in day and night. Desta attributed the growing trust between the Americans and Ethiopians to the time spent attached to US companies. He said, "After seeing how well we were doing through these types of missions, eventually they had enough faith in our fighting abilities to deploy us to the front as a battalion. We soon started attacking in company strength and moving as a battalion."

At some point during their time in the Far East most soldiers went on R&R, which was usually five days spent in Tokyo. The Japanese called it I&I (Intercourse and Intoxication). Capt. Tefera, 1st Lts. Mamo and Desta went on R&R together. They had a great reception at the officers' area where they got to shower, shave, and receive a fresh set of uniforms. Unfortunately, that meant spending some of their precious free time sewing on unit patches. They dined on T-bone steak, which was a welcomed change from dry rations. They also toured the city

and went to the cinema.[44] Dressed in civvies, they stopped at a saloon where they were greeted by a curious owner who wanted to know all about these black men. Of course, they were happy to explain. The man complimented them on their great voices and asked them to perform on stage. They did not think they had any musical talents and they only knew schoolboy songs, but they decided to be good sports. The owner introduced them by saying they came from Africa for the Korean War, they are in town on R&R and that they are our friends. The trio put on quite a show and were a hit with the crowd.[45]

September 1951

The 7th Division began the month of September in bitter fighting for the high ground approximately 5,000 meters in front of Line Wyoming. The objective was secured on September 4 and the following four days were spent consolidating it as a GOPL. The 32d Regiment was positioned in the vicinity of Sanyang-Ni and took advantage of its semi-reserve status at the beginning of the month to put two battalions through intense training; 1st Bn occupied a blocking position on the right flank of the division's sector while the EEFK maintained Patrol Base X on the left flank of Hill 1073.

On September 10, a combat patrol from 1st Company departed friendly lines at 0530. At 0900 the patrol received small arms fire from its right flank. Unfazed, the patrol continued, but again came under further small arms attack at 0935 suffering one friendly wounded. The patrol placed artillery on the suspected enemy position and pushed forward. At 1052 the patrol observed six to ten enemy troops and again placed artillery causing an estimated three KIA. At 1120 the patrol observed 200 CCF troops. The patrol called in artillery killing at least 35 enemy. The patrol then advanced forward and assaulted the crest of Hill 602 which was garrisoned with 350 Communists. After a literal uphill battle, the Ethiopians secured the objective by 1400. They remained on the hill for another hour under a barrage of enemy machinegun and mortar fire. Lt. Col. Hightower was flying over the action at this point and observed his men were "in a hell of a fire fight."

The patrol which had suffered three killed and eight wounded (three from friendly booby traps) evacuated its casualties and withdrew under the cover of a smoke screen provided by friendly artillery units. It returned to base at 2015.

It was estimated the artillery scored 100 enemy KIA, while the patrol accounted for another 70 with small arms. They destroyed one mortar and silenced another mortar and an artillery piece. A US artillery liaison officer attached to the unit reported the patrol ran into an estimated 400 enemy. He said the enemy was routed with an estimated 150 casualties from artillery, and 100 more from Ethiopian small arms and hand-to-hand fighting. He also added two mortars, two machineguns, and one artillery piece were knocked-out. Three more EEFK patrols were sent out that same day.

On September 11, during a night reconnaissance, as a patrol reached its objective, it encountered "devastating automatic fire" from enemy soldiers whose fire was so intense the patrol was unable to advance. The patrol leader, First Lieutenant Tesfaye Wolde Sadik, "[ordered] his men to take cover and [directed] a rifleman to harass the enemy by firing on the position." He then maneuvered to the enemy's right flank and "fearlessly running through the fire-swept impact area to within a few yards of the emplacement, he silenced the defenders with a grenade. 1Lt. Tesfaye Wolde Sadik almost singlehandedly broke the enemy's defense and secured the position. He was awarded the Bronze Star Medal for Valor.

From September 12 through September 15, the battalion made daily raids on Hill 700 and withdrew back to the MLR.

On September 12, Communist reinforcements were attempting to link up with one of their units being heavily assaulted by Ethiopian forces on the reverse side of a key terrain feature. As the reinforcements approached, 1st Lt. Berhanu Tariku "deployed his platoon in hastily prepared positions on the slope of the hill in anticipation of the attack. Constantly vulnerable to intense hostile fire, Lieutenant [Berhanu] plotted mortar concentrations upon the enemy and his route of approach when the assault occurred and moved fearlessly about the perimeter to coordinate and direct the defense." Over the next three and a half hours of bitter fighting, his platoon repulsed repeated attacks allowing the friendly main effort to seize the objective. For his actions, 1st Lt. Berhanu earned a Bronze Star Medals with "V" device for valor. He would later earn a second such medal during his second tour of duty in Korea in 1953.

On September 12, 4th Company initiated a patrol at 0530. The company encountered an enemy company at 0950 and engaged it with small arms and automatic weapons. The patrol seized the hill inflicting two KIA for their one friendly wounded. By 1100, the enemy completely surrendered Hill 700 to the patrol after suffering an estimated 20 killed. 4th Company remained on the hill and placed artillery on another group of 20 Communists with good effect as all 20 were thought to be wounded. Several bunkers and one machinegun were destroyed. An enemy artillery was neutralized. After the battle, the American liaison officer who accompanied the patrol provided his own account, adjusted enemy casualty figures up and concluded the enemy company that was defending the hill was determined to hold the ground more than any previous battle. He reported 20 enemy soldiers were killed on Hill 700, with an added 70 soldiers caught in the open by artillery fire as they withdrew from the hill, resulting in an estimated 35 wounded. Additional artillery rounds fired to silence a Communist mortar which was targeting the patrol inflicted another 20 enemy wounded. The 4th Company suffered one more casualty from small arms and another from artillery.

On September 14, the 2d Co launched a company sized patrol and departed friendly lines at 0530. It moved through the 31st Regiment

position to the Hill 602 complex. By 0855 the patrol was on Hill 700 receiving heavy fire from an estimated enemy company on Hill 602. The artillery liaison officer reported they were receiving fire from three to four 150mm artillery. The patrol called for counter-battery fire but continued to receive intense shelling. They kept pushing forward until intense machinegun fire from Hill 602 halted their progress around 1315. Undeterred, the patrol remained in position on Hill 700 calling in fire missions and weathering the enemy barrage for almost nine hours against an enemy who was fighting from fortified positions using heavy machineguns. They were close enough to observe the Communists evacuating some of their casualties. The patrol even managed to kill one enemy with small arms and recovered the soldier's weapon, ammunition, grenade, newspaper, photograph, and notebook. Having bloodied the enemy, they closed on friendly lines at 1830. For their one WIA, the Ethiopians inflicted five or six casualties and one machinegun destroyed on Hill 700, an additional 45 casualties on Hill 602, and another 45 casualties in the surrounding area.

The 32d Regiment was subsequently ordered to relieve both the 17th and 31st Regiments on the GOPL, so the two regiments could take up positions on Line Wyoming. On September 16, Kagnew Battalion relieved elements of the 31st Regiment north of Chupa Ri and west of the MSR and continued with the aggressive patrol designed to disrupt the enemy's offensive capabilities and protect the MLR on Wyoming from enemy concentrations on Hill 602 facing Kagnew Battalion, and Hill 569 facing 1st and 3d Battalions.

On September 17, 1951, Sgt. Maj. Aneley Teghegn's unit was "heavily engaged against a well-entrenched hostile force on commanding terrain and the assault platoon, coming under devastating small arms fire near the summit of the hill, was forced to seek cover." Exposing himself to mortal danger, the sergeant major moved through the enemy's field of fire to evacuate the wounded. He then rallied the remaining men forward "in a daring charge up the hill, routed the fanatical defenders, and seized the objective." Despite being wounded, he refused medical aid for himself but organized their defense and repulsed two enemy counterattacks before finally agreeing to be evacuated. Sgt. Maj. Aneley Teghegn was awarded the Bronze Star Medal for Valor.

By this time IX Corps was finalizing plans for Operation *Cleaver* a tank-infantry raid on enemy emplacements in the Iron Triangle approximately 5,000 yards beyond the GOPL along a two-division front for the purpose of disrupting and destroying enemy concentrations. The Ethiopians were tasked with capturing and holding Hills 602 and 700, and the high ground in this area. D-Day was set for September 21.

On September 19, a patrol of two reinforced squads from 4th Co advanced on Hill 700 and began receiving small arms fire from Hill 602. The patrol suffered two friendly wounded and in response they directed an air strike on the hill resulting in an estimated 75 casualties and 13 bunkers destroyed. That same day, other patrols from 2d and 3th Companies engaged the enemy around 1900. These patrols suffered three friendly killed and 13 wounded from small arms and mortar fire.

In one of these battles, Captain Assefa Meshesha's patrol "forged up a rugged mountain defile, hampered by rain and heavy underbrush. He positioned most of his men to provide flanking fire, and "ordered the leading platoon forward." After observing his assault platoon get repulsed by enemy automatic and small arms fire, he had the support element to provide covering fire while he personally led the bogged down platoon "in a daring frontal assault against the [well-fortified] hostile positions." After summiting the hill, he engaged the enemy in hand-to-hand combat routing the stubborn foe from the strongpoint." He was awarded a Bronze Star Medal for Valor.

On September 20, Pvt. Abitte Abitew's unit came under attack while conducting an operation on an enemy held terrain. His unit was forced to pull back and take cover on the slope of the hill. After regrouping, they discovered two soldiers were missing. Pvt. Abitte voluntarily left his position of cover, "crept 100 yards through intense enemy fire, only to discover that both his comrades had been killed. Fearlessly, he maintained a singlehanded stand until his company renewed the assault and then, joining the leading elements, fought courageously until the enemy was driven from the commanding ground and the objective secured." Pvt. Abitte was awarded the Bronze Star Medal with "V" device for heroic achievement in battle.

On September 20, the CG

Ethiopian troops celebrating the 21st anniversary of the Emperor's coronation, November 3, 1951. (US Army)

met with Colonel Hightower who advised he foresaw danger awaited his Ethiopian troops on Hill 602. That morning, a reinforced platoon from 3d Co departed at 0700 and headed for Hill 700. At 0830 it was engaged by an enemy platoon on Hill 700. The fighting grew fierce and by 1000 the sides were locked in hand-to-hand combat. Enemy small arms and grenades resulted in two friendly wounded. The close nature of the fighting precluded the artillery from lending a hand, but by 1035 the Communists unleashed their 60mm mortars. Five rounds fell on the patrol wounding the patrol leader and his radio operator, leaving the patrol without comms until a replacement radioman could arrive. The enemy, which had grown to a reinforced company, was stronger than before and for some reason holding onto ground for longer than usual. By 1225 the situation became critical. The patrol had suffered three KIA and 14 WIA and a relief platoon was dispatched to help. To make matters worse, one of their enemy prisoners succumbed to his wounds.

At 1315, the relief patrol from 3d Co arrived on Hill 700 and assisted in pushing back the enemy and securing the area. As the enemy fled north to Hill 602, it was taken under friendly artillery. The patrol remained in position and directed artillery fire until 1350. An enemy counterattack on the left flank was quickly stopped. The Ethiopians then left a small force to watch the left flank while the main body of the patrol went right to surround the enemy. They advanced forward to reach the ridge on Hill 602. The patrol then pulled back to the foot of the hill and bombarded the enemy with air strikes. At 1505, they observed the enemy on Hill 602 preparing to mount another counterattack. They placed artillery on the massed troops and closed on friendly lines at 1810. The patrol suffered relatively heavy casualties while trying to take a POW and recover the body of one of their own. They suffered three KIA and 15 WIA. As for the enemy, they counted a total of 67 KIA and estimated an additional 40 KIA.

On the morning of September 21, the main effort of Operation *Cleaver* in the regiment's sector was conducted by the 2d Bn and 32d Tank Co with other elements including, Kagnew Bn patrols providing supporting and diversionary attacks on the flanks. While infantry from Companies E and F moved forward against light opposition, the armored column became bogged down by extensive mine fields and small arms fire directed at mine clearing personnel. The column inched forward over the next hours, delivering devastating fire at enemy positions despite the loss of four vehicles along the way. At 1730 the column was ordered to withdraw without reaching its objective. A patrol from 1st Bn moved towards Hill 569 fighting for more than four hours against stiff resistance but was unable to overcome it.

Meanwhile two companies of the EEFK departed at 0845 towards Hill 602. They were tasked with inflicting as many casualties as possible. Following artillery prep, the lead element, 2d Co, came up against stiff resistance on the first objective, Hill 700. "Realizing that his men were threatened with annihilation in their present, untenable positions," the C.O. of 2d Co, Capt. Merid Gizaw "left his position of cover" and began to move among the troops shouting words of encouragement. He then charged towards the enemy exposing himself to intense hostile fire. Inspired by his courageousness, the men followed their leader up the hill and drove the enemy off the crest. Capt. Merid "quickly [deployed] his men into positions of vantage" that enabled them to rain fire onto additional enemy forces which were holding up the advance of 1st Co which had passed through the 2d Co position and was advancing towards Hill 602 on the adjacent slope. The Bronze Star Medal for Valor cited his "heroism and intrepid leadership."

The 1st Co advanced along the ridgeline through heavy small arms and automatic fire from an estimated enemy company in well-fortified bunkers on Hill 602. After calling in two air strikes on the objective, 1st Co continued to fire and maneuver towards its target under the shield of friendly artillery. The patrol closed with the enemy at 1450 and engaged him in fierce hand-to-hand fighting. Having spearheaded the attack personally, Capt. Tefera Waldetensye was wounded by an enemy bullet and was "bleeding profusely and in great pain."[46] Despite being unable to use his right arm, Capt. Tefera, refused to be evacuated and "relentlessly pressed the assault throughout more than eight hours of bitter conflict. Inspired by his courageous action, his troops inflicted numerous enemy casualties" until the patrol occupied Hill 602 at 1615.

When the 1st Co and 2d Co patrols were ordered to withdraw, Captain Tefera again refused medical aid until his entire company had withdrawn to its original position. Both Kagnew elements departed from the objective at 1700 and returned to base around 1800. Their success came at a high cost. They suffered eight KIA and 14 WIA, but they counted 29 enemy KIA, another estimated 29 KIA, 21 WIA from small arms, 100 KIA from artillery and 50 KIA from air strikes. They also captured or destroyed a 60mm mortar, 12 rifles, five burp guns, 50 ammo pouches, two heavy machineguns, an ammo dump, and 150 enemy rations. Capt. Tefera was awarded the Silver Star Medal for his valor. An official history of the 7th Division also credits Capt. Tefera with being awarded a Bronze Star Medal.[47]

Operation *Cleaver* cost the Communists 1,098 dead, 823 wounded and 79 taken as prisoner.

On September 22, an Ethiopian patrol was sent back to Hill 700. A reinforced platoon from 4th Co departed at 0700 and by 0845 reported assaulting the objective against heavy resistance from an enemy platoon employing small arms, machineguns and grenades. Upon reaching the crest of the hill at 0920, the patrol was again engaged in hand-to-hand combat with the enemy. An Ethiopian soldier wanted to capitalize on the enemy's proximity by chasing down a Communist soldier in hopes of taking him prisoner. Unfortunately, the Ethiopian found himself surrounded by the enemy. Like a cornered beast he fought ferociously and kept the enemy at bay until four volunteers from the patrol came to his aid. While these soldiers were withdrawing, one was wounded and two were killed. They laid down their lives as a testament to their credo that no one got left behind. Still, the patrol was not done. They feigned a withdrawal and returned to Hill 700 at 1315 and fired on the fleeing enemy. An hour later, the patrol observed an enemy platoon (later accounts placed the enemy force at company

strength) moving up around Hill 602 and again placed artillery. The patrol finally withdrew at 1545 having inflicted a confirmed 11 KIA and an additional estimated 25 KIA.

The Stars and Stripes described the gallantry of "Haile Selassie's Kamikaze troops" during their first big battle in which they beat back the Communists nearly a mile as well as the men's frustration at not being able to take prisoners. Capt. Ayalew Haile Selassie was quoted as saying, "We do everything we can to capture the Chinamen, but they have been told we eat prisoners, and won't surrender. We are all hunters. We like to take the enemy alive, but it is becoming very difficult in battle." He explained that it was easier on patrol. "We crawl in the brush a leetle, we look a leetle, we wait a leetle, then we crawl a leetle more and pretty soon we have a prisoner." One American officer who was with an Ethiopian group when it was being counterattacked noticed their fire slackening. When he asked the patrol leader if the troops were running low on ammo, the officer answered they had stopped firing to encourage the Chinese to attempt a banzai charge "so [his] children can go to work on them with the bayonet."[48]

On September 25, Kagnew Battalion was relieved from its position on GOL and attached to the 31st Regiment on the MLR. The CO thought it would be a good idea to put the battalion on the line two to three days before the relief was to be effected.

During the month of September, the battalion suffered 17 killed and 58 wounded in action. At the end of the month, Old Man Winter was rearing his head. The UNC started issuing cold-weather clothing underwear, mufflers, sweaters and gloves. In September, two officers and 113 enlisted men from the replacement company joined the battalion.

In the 7th Division sector, Hill 602 was judged to be the most difficult objective. At least four separate multiple platoon-to-company sized patrols were sent out. In some instances they were able to dislodge the enemy from his positions, but other times they just managed to bloody him. The division assessed the "disadvantage to such actions is that since line is static, friendly units cannot consolidate on gains. Captured real estate [had] to be abandoned for the enemy to recapture by night." While the presupposed reversal was disappointing, the attack nevertheless kept the enemy off-balance and unable to consolidate.

The Kagnew Battalion received a US Presidential Unit Citation "for outstanding performance of duty and extraordinary heroism in action against the enemy in the vicinity of Sam-hyon, Korea during the period of September 16 to September 22, 1951."

Early in September, Kagnew soldiers had put their daring on display "when attempts to capture a prisoner were failing miserably." Sgt. Maj. Ayele Kassa and Cpl. Kebe Defair volunteered to capture a prisoner. They crawled from their position, across no man's land, down to a river with known enemy activity. At their objective, they saw a Chinese soldier washing himself in the river. When they moved to capture him, they were

Weary Ethiopian troops departing from the frontline after many days of fighting, December 2, 1951. (US Army)

suddenly met with enemy fire, but they still managed to wrestle him into submission and bring him back as a POW.[49]

Ever proud of their heritage, the Ethiopians formally requested that UNC medical records refer to their soldiers as 'Ethiopian' rather than "Negro."

October 1951

At the beginning of October, 7ID was at Line Wyoming. The 31st and 32d Regiments minus EEFK were positioned on the GOPLR 5,000 meters to the north. The EEFK was still temporarily attached to the 31st Regiment. The battalion was now officially under the command of Lt. Col. Teshome Irgetu.

On October 1, General Ferenbaugh met with Colonel Hightower at the regimental CP. He brought up the fact that 31st Regiment had not reported any probes since relieving Kagnew. He once again cast doubt on the abilities of the battalion by concluding that enemy probes reported by the Ethiopians were "probably imaginary." This was

Lt. Amare Checkol, Chaplain conducting church service, December 10, 1951. (US Army)

an incorrect assessment of the situation since the CCF was known to direct concentrated attacks at an area and then completely ignore that same area after a while. One reason for this was that the Communists sometimes used probes to maintain contact with the opposition, while at other times they sat back and relied on UN forces to initiate contact. The division's own intelligence section would publish reports stating the same. For example, from February 15, 1952 through February 18, 1952, the Communists launched concentrated attacks on 7ID positions. The attacks ceased when the 25ID relieved 7ID on February 18. "The enemy again lapsed into a defensive role and initiated no contacts" for the whole time the 25ID was on the line. The enemy would also attack a section of the front or a certain unit to test for weaknesses.

By the October 7, Kagnew returned to the 32d Regiment and moved into reserve with the rest of the 7th Division in Kapyong. The regiment started intensive training which progressed from individual to small unit and ultimately to regiment problems over the coming weeks. The training and recuperation which was to last four to six weeks was cut short and the regiment was ordered to move to Worun-ni to become part of X Corps. On October 20, the 7th Division relieved the 2d Division on Line Minnesota above Yanggu, between Mundung-ni and Satae-ri valleys. The 31st and 32d Regiments formed abreast on the MLR. Kagnew Battalion was ordered to relieve the French Battalion, which had just concluded a month long savage battle against the Communists. They were assigned an area known as "Heartbreak Ridge," which was a narrow ridgeline consisting of three peaks: Hill 894, Hill 931 and Hill 851. A month-long intense aerial and artillery bombardment by UN forces had turned the steep hillsides into barren moonscape. Hand-to-hand fighting had caused considerable human

loss on both sides. The US 2d Division (with Dutch, French and Thai battalions attached) had suffered 3,700 casualties while inflicting 25,000-40,000 casualties on the enemy.

The 7th Division's mission was to occupy and defend Line Minnesota by employing aggressive patrols to determine enemy positions, prevent him from building up supplies and repel attacks on friendly positions. Additional patrols in the regiment's rear area were also initiated to screen for enemy infiltrators. Patrols in the Kagnew and 3d Battalion sectors were severely restricted due to the terrain and proximity to enemy strongpoints.

On October 22, forty-eight veterans representing the 19 nations in the Korean War arrived in Washington D.C. to attend in the UN Day observance and for a thirty-day tour of US cities where they would participate in local civic programs, bond rallies and Red Cross blood drives. They were greeted by government officials and later taken on a tour of the capital.[50] On October 24, they met President Truman at the White House where he congratulated them on their service and sent them off by saying, "Have a good time now, and if there's anybody around the country that doesn't treat you right, why you tell me!"[51] After New York City, they split into two groups with one group taking a northern route across the US while the other went through the south. The black soldiers, including the two Ethiopians, Sgt. Maj. Mamoushet Goshime and Sgt. Molla Kebede, were placed on the northern route for obvious reasons.

US Army Capt. Harold Myers was also selected for the tour. Myers, who was part Cherokee, grew up poor in Shoshone, Idaho. As the oldest of many siblings, he went out on his own during the Great Depression and like Col. Hightower was a laborer in the Civilian Conservation Corps. He was disallowed from enlisting in the Army

Ethiopian 75mm recoilless rifle team blasting enemy-held position, December 9, 1951. (US Army)

Korea, he said, "the less hope h[...] has." Gaining ground "means little in Korea... and that's what removes hope and a goal. A patrol gains ground during the day and then pulls back at night and relinquishes that same ground." These statements were printed in the local paper and later picked up by newspapers in the D.C. area. His superiors were not happy. The only reason he was not severely reprimanded was because the Ethiopian government allegedly intervened on his behalf.[55]

Back in Korea, Colonel Teshome placed 3d and 4th Companies on the line and placed 1st and 2d Companies in the battalion reserve, and got on with the business of thrashing the enemy. On the 23rd, they called in air strikes on Hill 871 destroying ten bunkers and four mortars, with an estimated 50-100 enemy casualties. The Communists replied with

at first for failing the urine test (for health conditions and not drug use). Since the process was not centralized in those days, he went to a recruitment office in a different city and paid someone five dollars to take the test for him. He passed and was a corporal at the time of Pearl Harbor.[52]

During WWII, he served in the 3d Division from North Africa through southern France all the way to the German border. He deployed to Korea as an officer in the 7th Division and was a member of the ill-fated Task Force Faith. Capt. Myers was in the back of a truck, suffering a relapse of malaria when he was left behind with the other wounded after the enemy hit the column on the last night. A determined Myers crawled on the ice until some US Marines found him. He was embittered by his experience with Task Force Faith and wrote to his wife, "...this never would have happened in the 3d Division... If our son ever goes to war, I hope that he goes into the Marines... they take care of their own..."[53] After leaving the hospital, he was assigned as artillery liaison officer between Kagnew and the 48th Field Artillery Battalion. He judged a new home with the Ethiopians. He found them to be professional soldiers with an impeccable record for night fighting. He was convinced the Ethiopians were some of the best troops on the planet, and shortly before his return to the US, he was awarded the "Ethiopian Star" medal by Lt. Col. Teshome.[54]

When the tour group arrived in Myer's home state of Idaho, they were given a hero's welcome with the press and even the Governor in attendance. Later on, they took Capt. Myers out for drinks. With everyone buying him drinks, the captain who hadn't imbibed in a long time, let his guard down. Assuming things were off the record, he began to speak candidly about the war. He declared, "MacArthur was right– you can't win a war with one arm tied behind your back." He continued to criticize the strategy, "the average fighting man in Korea with all respect to General Ridgway, believes that MacArthur was right in his call for all out war." He advocated the use of the atomic bomb. He also spoke about morale; the longer a man stays in

mortar fire of their own over the next few days, wounding a few Ethiopians. Battalion members also suffered battlefield accidents, including a bullet that was cooked-off by burning refuse.

A recon patrol was dispatched on the 28th. This time it was a platoon from 3d Co which departed at 0500 and made contact with an enemy platoon at 0635. The platoon leader called in artillery support and advanced towards the objective, reaching it at 0800. The patrol was confronted by a larger enemy force, estimated at company strength. "The brunt of this assault centered on the avenue of approach to two positions occupied by" Pvts. Bayessa Kenate, Ishete W Mariam, Negga Tessema and LCpl. Tesfaye Beyene. This foursome "fighting with great courage and skill... repulsed the initial thrust and, maintaining their valiant stand throughout two hours of bitter fighting, contained three subsequent onslaughts and contributed significantly to thwarting the enemy's attempt to breach the friendly perimeter." The patrol employed automatic weapons, 60mm mortar, 57mm and 75mm recoilless rifles in a firefight which lasted until 1000. They suffered two killed from enemy mortar fire and four wounded. They recovered their casualties and withdrew at 1130, after counting ten enemy killed. They estimated an additional 40 KIA from artillery. The four men who not only prevented a breach, but also inflicted heavy casualties on a numerically superior enemy force, were awarded Bronze Star Medals for Valor.

October saw a significant increase in the number of mortar attacks with as many as 500 in one day, compared to a previous average of 600 a month.

Psychological warfare was extensively employed in Korea. 7th Division light aircraft and artillery showered enemy positions with tens of thousands of "anti-morale, good treatment and safe conduct" leaflets. The Eighth Army loudspeaker team was also assigned to further exploit the Communist soldiers' frailties. However, the UNC did not have a monopoly on psychological warfare. The Communists were responding with their own leaflets. One advised UN troops

'Rotation isn't going to get you out of this war. Rotation is only a new trick. You have to risk your lives for a nine-month period in Korea before it comes to your turn." Another leaflet asked, "Why freeze when you can be home with your loved ones?"

In October Kagnew had four killed and fifteen wounded. They had suffered a cumulative 31 KIA to date.

November 1951

The UN troops continued the cold weather preparation. By now every man had been issued complete winter gear, in addition, bunkers, tents, vehicles and weapons were winterized. No major offensive action to the north was being planned due to the armistice negotiations taking place at Panmunjom, but the division continued to launch aggressive patrols a short distance north of the MLR. Even the Communists had scaled back, conducting fewer night patrols at squad or smaller strengths compared to previous platoon to company strength patrols.

Lieutenant Colonel Hightower wrote to his friend "Eddy" Farnsworth, Chief of the UNC Liaison Group, extoling the Ethiopian Battalion. But he also related that the officers had reported ill-treatment while on R&R at Camp Drake, including being processed last and being assigned less-desirable billets. He asked his friend to look into the matter informally and to ensure the Ethiopians receive equitable treatment.[56] Farnsworth wrote back assuring Hightower that no discrimination was taking place that he was aware of, but he promised to investigate the allegations.[57]

The 7ID was dug in on the new MLR, Line Minnesota, with 32d Regiment on the right and 31st Regiment on the left. The 7ID area of responsibility was extended to include the northern rim of the area known as the Punchbowl. In the 32d's sector, the EEFK Bn was in the center on Hill 851. The regiment would spend the entire month on the line, initially with three battalions on the line and one battalion in reserve every week on a rotating basis per the C.O.'s desire to distribute the burden equally among his men.

In early November, Kagnew Battalion sent out patrols with mixed results. The enemy put up a stiff resistance when patrols approached his MLR. The enemy in turn probed EEFK positions, usually at squad strength, but the effort was halfhearted resulting in quick withdrawals when facing opposition. The CG paid a visit to Kagnew Battalion and was displeased that enemy patrols were getting within hand grenade range of their position. The general wanted the matter straightened out. He also found out that the enemy was playing a cruel trick on the troops by firing artillery at night – just enough to disrupt their sleep.

The general returned the next day to the battalion rear area to attend the 21st anniversary of the Ethiopian Emperor's coronation. When he visited their CP on November 5, he saw for himself the reason the enemy was able to get within grenade range was due to low visibility. Apparently, there was still some vegetation on the ravine in the battalion's sector.

After personally inspecting the Ethiopian positions on the 7th, the Regimental C.O. found the men were looking pretty shabby. Hightower, who was regarded as a judicious officer, did not want his men to suffer needlessly. He had made plans for the men to get at least one hot shower a week, as many hot meals as possible, and for each battalion to spend the same amount of time on the line. He ordered Kagnew pulled out next for some rest, and the battalion went into reserve on October 10 and initiated a training program.

Unfortunately, Col. Hightower had to abandon his plan to rotate his battalions as the entire division was needed to cover their extended front. Consequently, all four battalions in the 32d Regiment were ordered to occupy positions on the MLR. Kagnew relieved elements of the 31st Regiment on November 19 and took up a position on the

Lt. Zegheye Yemeru, Asst. S-3, interrogates enemy soldier, December 9, 1951. (US Army)

left flank of the 32d sector. It was now in contact with 610th Regiment, 204th Division, 68th CCF Army Corps.

At 0730 on November 21, a platoon from 1st Co on patrol was engaged by an estimated 40 enemy troops. The patrol advanced under fire for 15 minutes, driving the enemy from the objective, capturing two prisoners, killing four and wounding an estimated ten. They stayed in the area calling artillery on several clusters of enemy troops and withdrew at 1130. Later that day, Gen. Ferenbaugh went to the 32d CP to get the scoop on the 1st Co patrol from that morning. Ethiopian guards brought the two POWs for interrogation. The prisoners were from the 9th Co, 3d Bn, 610th Reg, 204th Div. The general decided to not only sit in, but also conduct part of the interview.

The prisoners told him they had only received two weeks of training. They were fed 900-grams twice a day, at dawn and dusk and were weak from starvation and dysentery. They were allowed to sleep a couple of hours during daytime. They claimed to have been at the front for eleven days with orders to defend. The first prisoner was 20-year-old Pvt. Chun Wi Chai. He was POW Number 1454. Before his capture, he had been a rifleman in the CCF for seven and a half months. He was judged to be in good health and of average intelligence. Although hesitant at times, he provided information on the disposition of enemy forces. He spoke of how his fellow soldiers were too frightened to leave their foxholes at night because of UN airstrikes and artillery. He went on about how the enlisted men were overworked and treated badly by officers. Therefore, he said, many men, encouraged by the UN propaganda leaflets, wanted to desert the CCF, but could not find the opportunity.

A more comprehensive report compiled by 3d Division's Interrogation Prisoner of War (IPW) Section discussed the overall morale problem in the CCF. The eleven POWs who were surveyed painted a portrait of a divided class system. According to the prisoners, Communist party members had priority to medical treatment when sick or wounded. When supplies became scarce, as they often were, again party members and CCF veterans had priority, over recruits and ex-Chinese Nationalist Army members. Raw recruits, often teenagers as young as 14, were being treated with increasing brutality by officers and NCOs when their young bodies were unable to stand the strains of combat. While in the rear areas the troops were bombarded with Communist propaganda, until they arrived at the front and the unrelenting UN firepower saps their morale. They had to be driven into combat at gunpoint. This was no idle threat as those who showed

Ethiopian troops constructing new bunkers on the line at Heartbreak Ridge, December 2, 1951. (US Army)

signs of cowardice were executed. Of course, the survey participants were mostly new recruits and ex-Chinese Nationalists, so the findings may have been skewed.

Although the winter remained relatively mild to this point, the area had received some snow. On the morning of November 22, 2d Lt. Dejene Tekle was leading a patrol from 2d Co. The Ethiopians were fish out of water as they had never experienced snowfall in their homeland. They moved cautiously through no-man's land trying to get their bearings. But the enemy was in his element. Only a week prior the Communists had been issued white camouflage uniforms and were lying in wait for the patrol.

When the Ethiopians got within throwing distance, they sprang the trap. Thirty enemy soldiers opened up with small arms and grenades. The stunned patrol initially recoiled, then placed artillery and sprang forward to counterattack. 2d Lt. Dejene started getting his casualties evacuated and assigned his men fields of fire to suppress the enemy's machineguns. As the patrol engaged the enemy in hand-to-hand combat, Dejene was mortally wounded. But his men fought like lions and forced the enemy to withdraw. When the patrol started receiving machinegun and mortar fire from another group of enemy troops, they had supporting US tanks open up and silence the enemy. The patrol returned to base having counted 15 enemy KIA and four WIA, and an estimated eight KIA and nine WIA. Kagnew suffered seven wounded and one killed. 2d Lt. Dejene Tekle earned the distinction of being the first Ethiopian officer killed in action during the Korean War.[58]

November 23 saw the first major snowfall of winter. The area received several inches of snow from early morning to noon that hampered patrol activities. That morning at 0720, an estimated enemy platoon engaged a platoon size patrol from 1st Co. The patrol immediately killed six CCF soldiers and forced them to withdraw. Friendly forces pursued the enemy until an enemy platoon counterattacked using small arms, automatic weapons and mortars. "They untangled themselves from the enemy" under covering fire by the regiment's tanks and withdrew to base with four killed and six wounded. They had killed sixteen, wounded seven and captured two prisoners. The tanks damaged ten bunkers with an estimated 25 KIA.

The Ethiopians suffered 33 wounded and five killed in November.

In October, the first group of battlefield casualties were transported by ship to Aden and then flown in two planes to Addis Ababa. Five out of the 27 required stretchers; the rest were walking wounded. They were greeted at the airport by a large crowd as well as the Duke of Harar and the American Ambassador. However, families were not present.[59] The British attaché reported there was a shroud of secrecy regarding their return until "late the day before they arrived."[60]

The Duke addressed the troops:

We have been eagerly following your heroic actions against a modern and ruthless enemy in a new environment, far from your homeland… The world has just witnessed the bravery and skill the Ethiopian warrior is renowned for. The blood that was spilled from each of you on the battlefield is a testament to your deeds. The scars you carry on your bodies are badges of honor as good as any medal. We wish the wounded a speedy recovery, and challenged those still on the battlefield to bring equal glory to their country.

That afternoon, the troops were visited by the Emperor and the Empress at the Imperial Bodyguard Hospital and presented with medals.[61]

December 1951

At the start of December, the division remained on Line Minnesota and continued to strengthen its position after adopting a defensive posture in accordance with the deal reached by mediators. The UN was trying to show goodwill by not attempting to take real estate it had not taken by November 28. The Communists were also on the defensive for the sixth month in a row.

Since infiltrators had been a problem from the very start of the war, on December 12, the 32d Regiment was assigned Operation *Hideout*, which called for a minimum of one battalion to screen the area 5,000 meters behind the MLR and to apprehend all persons without proper identification.

On December 7, Kagnew Battalion started a training program. That day the regiment got word from Department of the Army, that 230 Ethiopian replacements were expected to arrive around December

2. A cadre of Ethiopian officers and NCOs as well as one US officer trained the new arrivals for five weeks at the UNRC in Pusan. They were there the same time as an Italian Hospital Unit, and despite Col. Kebbede's initial concern about his men harboring a grudge, there was no bad blood. The magnanimous Ethiopians even helped the Italians set up their tents.[62]

On the 15th, the battalion began patrolling the rear area in support of Operation *Hideout* in addition to maintaining its training schedule. It conducted six screening patrols with nine huts and 23 bunkers destroyed. The patrols also found 5,500-rounds of M1 ammunition and 300-rounds of 60mm mortar ammunition. Over the coming days, the EEFK conducted additional screening patrols destroying 82 bunkers and capturing four Koreans, including two who were armed with rifles.

The battalion continued these patrols but with less success until December 24 when it was relieved by 2d Bn and went under the operational control of 31st Regiment. That morning, one soldier was wounded by a sniper. Kagnew conducted additional patrols but again with minimal contact with the enemy. Night patrols by the Communists were of a harassing nature and as the weather got colder and snow heavier, enemy activity became less frequent.

Major Naucler was ordered to return to Ethiopia on December 28. He visited the Kagnew troops in Korea before leaving the Far East, and upon his arrival in Addis, submitted a "Report of the Work at the Imperial Expeditionary Force of Korea" to General Mulugeta Bulli. The report was a scathing critique of the two senior commanders (Kebbede and Aman), but it also gave a glowing review of the junior officers and enlisted men. Capt. Tamerat succeeded Naucler as the Ethiopian Chief Liaison Officer at the UNC in Tokyo.

On the last day of the year, Kagnew was relieved by 3d Battalion and returned to the operation control of 32d Regiment. Since coming to Korea, the battalion had suffered 37 KIA and 139 WIA.

January 1952

Average temperatures in December were between 25 and 40 degrees Fahrenheit. In January they would average 12 to 30 degrees. 7ID was still on Line Minnesota with the 32d Regiment in reserve. The division was facing 7,600 enemy troops, as well as, a reserve force of 9,100. The prior agreement reached by mediators to restrict patrols for one month was now rescinded. All units were ordered to increase the number and aggressiveness of their patrols. Plans were drawn to increase artillery fire by five to seven times the normal intensity of the past three months. In turn, the Communists were defending their MLR with such tenacity, it was nearly impossible to drive them out of their positions. Friendly patrols had to kill every defender.

The division started settling in. Comfortable camps were established for the reserve regiment complete with squad tents for sleeping and prefabricated wooden buildings for mess halls.

On January 3, forty-eight members of Kagnew Battalion were awarded Ethiopian medals for combat in Korea. Four US medals were also awarded by Gen. Lemnitzer. On January 7, 32d Regiment relieved 17th Regiment on the MLR. Its first priority was improving the position. 1st Co was attached to 1st Bn, and 4th Co was attached to 2d Bn. And what remained of Kagnew Battalion moved to regimental reserve around Hill 1181.

On the 12th, a 4th Co patrol was engaged by a large enemy force fighting from fortified positions. The Ethiopians "sought cover but, because of the open nature of the terrain, they faced annihilation unless immediate, aggressive action was taken." As the saying goes, the best defense it a good offense. Sgt. Mamo W. Mikael, Pvts. Hailu Meshesha and Kassaye Hunde with sheer disregard for their own safety, left their positions

and charged directly into the intense enemy fire… [they] raced across the fire-swept terrain toward the hostile positions and, upon reaching the first of the interlocking trenches… unhesitatingly leaped inside and engaged the foe. [Their] fearless actions forced the hostile troops to slacken the fire which they poured against the remainder of the friendly force and caused them to concentrate on defending their positions. As the heavy enemy fire abated, the friendly units charged up the slopes and drove the hostile troops from their positions with heavy casualties.

Meanwhile, platoon leader 2d Lt. Bekele Mengheshia also braved hostile fire in order to evaluate the terrain and the situation. "Following his reconnaissance, he dauntlessly remained in the open to direct the fire of his men against the hostile positions." He then positioned himself on an exposed knoll "and directed the fire of friendly mortar and artillery batteries in the area." The fighting lasted 20 minutes with the patrol inflicting eight KIA and ten WIA.

On January 21, 3d Company relieved 1st Company and was attached to 1st Bn. While 2d Company relieved 4th Company and was attached 2d Bn. The 1st, 4th and Heavy Weapons Companies moved into blocking positions. For the rest of the month, elements of Kagnew Battalion continued to dispatch patrols. On January 20, a reinforced platoon from 4th Co raided an enemy position killing six with small arms and two more with grenades. They inflicted an additional ten wounded in the trenches. After recovering from the shock, the enemy opened up on them from defensive positions wounding four Kagnew men. The patrol still managed to destroy two bunkers with 57mm recoilless rifles before withdrawing. On the 25th, a reinforced squad from 3d Co went on a daytime combat-recon patrol and destroyed two more bunkers with the 57mm. Two days later, a daytime patrol from 2d Co again used the 57mm to destroy a bunker with an estimated three killed.

Colonel Kebbede informed the UNC that his government was planning to relieve the current battalion in Korea after one year in country. He added that the new unit may arrive all at once or divided into more than one expedition, but organized and supplied the same as the original unit. The new troops were said to be "volunteer" soldiers with many years of military service.

General Mulugeta Bulli requested the troops rotating home from Korea be permitted to retain their rifles and sidearms, citing an ancient custom that a soldier must return with his weapons or otherwise be disgraced and considered an unworthy warrior. His government of course offered to pay for the weapons as reimbursable aid.

At the close of the month, Kagnew went into regimental reserve while the three other battalions manned the line. The Ethiopians had suffered six WIA.

February 1952

On the first day of February, two enemy platoons were observed moving south. A 3d Company patrol which was outside the wire believed it was being encircled and withdrew back to base. Right at midnight enemy forces engaged the right flank of 3d Company and left flank of Baker Company, 1st Bn, with small arms and grenades. Friendly troops responded with small arms, automatic weapons, 60mm and 81mm mortar fire resulting in seven dead Communists. Unfortunately, 3rd Co suffered one killed, three wounded and one of their bunkers was burned by an illumination grenade that set-off 57mm ammunition. After about an hour the enemy withdrew north. The casualties had to hang in there until they could be evacuated in the morning.

Operation *Clam-Up* went into effect across the Eighth Army front and lasted from February 10 through February 15. As the name suggests all friendly patrol activity, daylight vehicular traffic, noise and firing was halted. Since the enemy had relied on UN patrols to initiate contact so as to conserve his own resources, *Clam-Up* was a ruse designed to force the Communists to initiate contact by making them believe UN forces had withdrawn. The enemy responded to the operation by fortifying his positions, moving heavy caliber weapons forward and building bunkers. He also reconned in-force from February 11 through 14 in groups of approximately 400 men in 14 night-probes which caused him high casualties.

Two incidents during the operation exemplified the discipline of the Ethiopian battalion. On February 11, at 0100, an enemy soldier snuck past the wire and closed on 1st Co positions. He then threw a grenade at a bunker. 1st Co fired a single shot in response and killed the infiltrator. On February 14, at 2110, 1st Co started hearing an enemy squad moving inside the wire. By 2130 the squad of five had grown to 40 enemy soldiers inside the wire. 1st Co did not panic even with the enemy almost on top of them. They continued to listen in silence. At 2145, the infiltrators setup three machineguns in front of 1st Co. Still, friendly troops waited motionless like a coiled viper. The enemy then started crawling forward under cover of long bursts from their machineguns. All the company's weapons in the vicinity, as well as a .50-Cal from a supporting tank were trained on the enemy but remained quiet. Baker Company also observed several groups of enemy to their front. All across the front friendly units started hearing bugles, singing, blasting, chopping and the ominous shouts of "Banzai!" In past instances, such signals had been used to launch massive human wave attacks. At 2240 the bulk of the enemy had gotten within 75-100 yards to the Ethiopian positions, but 1st Co kept silent and listened to the enemy continue to infiltrate. Then the enemy went silent until midnight and inexplicably started to withdraw. The withdrawal happened in trickles until 0500 the next morning. The defenders maintained noise discipline by not returning fire throughout the ordeal.

One should not get the impression the Korean War was a one-sided war just because the exploits of the CCF are not chronicled here. The Communist soldiers often fought fanatically and with great tactical proficiency, despite the advantages United Nations units enjoyed in almost all aspects of warfare. The enemy gave just as good as it got. During the month of February, an average of 179 rounds of mortar and artillery were fired on 7ID positions each day. Between February 16 and 21, Kagnew positions were hit with artillery and mortar fire with seven bunkers destroyed, but fortunately no lives lost.

On February 14, Col. Hightower completed his tour and rotated home. He was replaced by Lt. Col. William A. Dodds.[63] On February 23, elements of Kagnew Battalion which had been attached to other battalions were returned to their parent organization. Then the division (along with the 32d Regiment) was relieved by the 25th Infantry Division, after having spent the four coldest months of the year on Line Minnesota. It then moved to the reserve area sixty-five miles away at Kapyong for rehab and training.

During the month, the Kagnew Battalion averaged 1,206 men with 80 officers, 11 warrant officers and 1,115 enlisted men. They suffered one killed, six wounded and 43 non-battle casualties. Figures at the division level, however, show seven wounded and none killed.

March 1952

Word was out that the commanding officer of the replacement Ethiopian battalion would be Lt. Col. Asfaw Andargue. Asfaw was born on July 22, 1916 or 1917 in Addis Ababa. He completed his primary education at Tafari Makonnen School and joined the Imperial Bodyguard in 1934. It is at this point that his biography becomes murky. One source states that he was an Imperial Bodyguard band leader before the invasion and a merchant during the occupation. Another source claims he was an interpreter in the Guard and later a guerilla fighter who returned to the capital and joined the patriot underground until the Fascists imprisoned him for espionage. Yet another source states he entered Haile Selassie I Academy in 1934 as member of the Guard and had his education interrupted by the Italian invasion in 1935. During the occupation he operated as part of the underground resistance forces and was captured and sentenced to death. After a year and a half of imprisonment, he was released by the Italians "to regain favor with the Ethiopians." It is also written that he was released only after the cessation of hostilities.

After the Italians were ejected, he attended the Haile Selassie Military Academy and rejoined the Imperial Bodyguard in 1941. He attained the rank of Major in 1948 and Lieutenant Colonel in 1950. He previously served as platoon leader, company executive officer and battalion commander as well as an instructor for the Imperial Army's seventh cadet course. Asfaw who was regarded as an excellent soldier spoke no English and poor French.

The American military attaché in Addis, Col. Leo J. Query, reported that Asfaw had been the commanding officer of an "alert battalion." A report by the British attaché confirmed the existence of the "Ready Battalion" which would relieve the unit in Korea. While none of the Kagnew veterans interviewed were able to shed light on this, it seems the Ethiopian high command had plans for the rapid deployment of a reserve battalion should the unit then in Korea suffer heavy casualties and need urgent replacements or reinforcement.[64]

Captain Workneh Gebyeou was the new battalion's S-3. Colonel Query, who knew Workneh personally, described him as "very intelligent and alert." Workneh was born in Gonder. After completing traditional church schooling, he attended the Menelik II School and was one of the young men handpicked for the first post-liberation Imperial Bodyguard cadet course. The brilliant Workneh graduated at the top of his class and was retained at the academy as an instructor for the second course, while many of his classmates went to Korea.[65] After seeing that course through, he was put on the staff for the Second Kagnew Battalion.

The Swedish instructors reported to the US military attaché that all the officers were graduates of the cadet academy with at least three-years of experience. All NCOs had attended a four-month squad-leader course. Furthermore, all personnel were put through a special six-week individual training plus three weeks of organization and operational training based on US military doctrine. The Swedes gave the officers and men an overall high rating and added that the soldiers had good basic skills, but needed more training with US weapons and in the recognition of enemy equipment, signals, medical, and coordination with artillery and armor.

Yilma Belachew of Addis Ababa was a 20-year-old officer with the Second Kagnew Battalion. He tried to enroll in the first Imperial Bodyguard cadet course along with his friends but was turned away due to his young age. He continued his education and had completed six months at the School of Commerce when he was finally accepted to the academy. Yilma completed three years of military training under the tough Swedish instructors. The cadets were punished severely for any mistakes and were told, "You are not going to a party; you are going to war. You will get yourselves and others killed, and lose your country."[66] After graduation, Lieutenant Yilma was on his way to Korea before even drawing his first paycheck as an officer. He

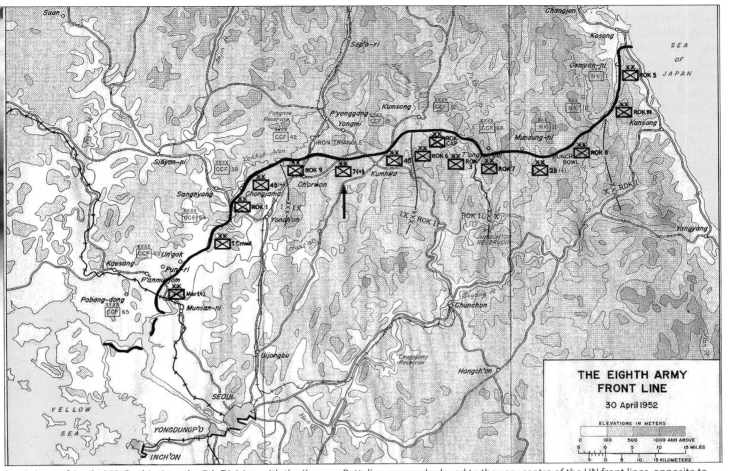

Battle lines of April 1952. By this time, the 7th Division with the Kagnew Battalion was re-deployed to the very centre of the UN front lines, opposite to the so-called 'Iron Triangle'. (Hermes, Walter G. *Truce Tent and Fighting Front*. Washington D.C.: Center of Military History, United States Army, 1992, p. 283)

had heard news stories about the Korean War and received some briefings. Soon the battalion was organized. The officers were selected and trained. They, in turn, with the help of the non-commissioned officers, trained the men.[67]

Private Vassilios Simatos was also headed to Korea. Vassilios was born in 1933 in Jimma to an Ethiopian mother and a Greek father. The young Vassilios was quite the loveable rascal. He spent his childhood working the crank on the record player at his father's saloon. His merchant father, who was on the road a lot, entrusted the care of his son to a Greek family in Addis Ababa. A few weeks after his father left, Vassilios found himself turned into that family's servant. They worked him mercilessly and barred him from attending school. They treated him worse than Arabi – the family dog, who even got to eat before Vassilios.[68] Some time later, a guest who was staying with the family discovered he was missing $500. Naturally, Vassilios was blamed. His father was called and proceeded to beat him. The boy falsely confessed to flushing it down the toilet. Later another man was arrested for stealing that money. Vassilios'

A field gun battery of the 75th Artillery Battalion, US Army, in action in the Kumwha area, on 4 April 1952. (US Army Historic Division)

father beat him again – this time for lying.[69]

After three years in that household, Vassilios told his father he would not go back to that family, so he was put up with an Ethio-Greek family. They enrolled him in school and all was going well until he had to move to another home and a new school. There, he became a bit of a hooligan, but he also worked, first as a shoeshine and later washing cars. He then managed to get lodging. The rent was $2 a month and there were 120 people living there. [70] Some time later, a Greek man found Vassilios on the street begging for money and asked why he did not work. The man got him a job as a baker in a hotel. This allowed Vassilios to prepare the dough at night and to go to school in the morning. Four years later he was hired by the Imperial Highway Authority. After getting laid off from there, he looked everywhere for another job to no avail. His frustration led him to start contemplating suicide. Then he heard about Ethiopian troops going to Korea. He told himself that he would rather die for his country than take his own life and flipped a coin to seal his fate. [71]

He made his way to the Imperial Bodyguard recruiting area. When they asked his name, he replied, "Vassilios Simatos." They told him, "Get out of here. We don't want Arabs or half-breeds." Vassilios was so angry he punched a wooden board causing his hand to bleed. [72] He left and started thinking of how to get around this obstacle. He decided to change his name from Vassilios to "Fasil" – the name of a 17th century Ethiopian emperor. He changed his father's name to "Gragn," meaning "left-handed" because that was the hand he hurt when he punched the wooden board. Fasil Gragn waited a while, went back to the recruiter and enlisted in the Imperial Bodyguard. [73] Fasil's training lasted around six months and included forced marches, weapons training and maneuvers. It was rigorous he said. At the end of the training the ones joining the Korean battalion were selected. [74]

The 7th Division started the month of March in IX Corps reserve. This time was used to train in offensive tactics as there had been a high turnover since the division conducted its last large coordinated attack last September. The training would last five weeks, with a third of the training occurring at night time.

On March 11, 600 soldiers from the Second Kagnew Battalion bade farewell to their Emperor and their families and started their journey to the Far East. [75] The Second Kagnew Battalion would be transported to the theater of war in two increments; this was the first increment. Modern sea travel was a new experience to most if not all of the Ethiopians. Yilma Belachew saw the colossal ship at the port in Djibouti but still could not believe all these people could fit on it. He said it was like a city; everything you could ever want was on there: stores, entertainment, athletic facilities, dining areas and so on. [76] They boarded the troop transport which already had Greeks, Dutch and Americans onboard. One day, Capt. Workneh saw Vassilios chatting with the foreign troops and called him over. He asked where he was assigned. Vassilios said he was a chauffeur. The captain said, "No, you speak English" and reassigned him to his S-3 section. [77]

Of course some Ethiopians felt Americans did not really speak English. Capt. Mehretab Tedla of the First Kagnew described to a reporter the one difficulty he and his men had in conversing with American troops. "Americans don't speak English," he stated with a smile. "They speak 'skoshi,' 'taksan,' and 'samey same.' This," he said "makes it very difficult for us." [78] Mehretab was the third member of Kagnew Battalion who came from the Imperial Army and not the Imperial Bodyguard. He was a graduate of the Army's Sixth Cadet Course. [79]

Vassilios joined the battalion staff which included Pvt. Assefa Demissie who was radio operator for both the S-2 and S-3 sections under Capts. Solomon Kadir and Workneh Gebyeou respectively. Assefa Demissie tried to enlist in the military at the age of 14 following in the footsteps of his father who was a patriot and whose heroics he had heard of as a child. When he was told he was too old, he argued saying it was brains that counted and not age. Mengistu Neway assigned him to the radio section. At the time of First Kagnew's departure he was stationed in Harar. After returning to the capital he was picked in place of another soldier and sent to Korea at the age of 17. He said he was "number one Morse Code" and even received an award from Mulugeta Bulli. [80]

Just like the First Kagnew Battalion, the men of the Second Kagnew underwent familiarization training with US weapons aboard the ship. To build morale and break up the routine, everything was turned into a competition, including chores. There was even a cleaning competition among the various contingents. That was where the battalion started earning a winning reputation. [81] The men were experiencing seasickness. Additionally, the food did not agree with them and so they mixed the traditional Ethiopian chili powder with water and started drinking it to strengthen their bodies. Yilma Belachew said the voyage which was supposed to take 18 days took 21. Their bodies were weakened from the trip. [82]

There were no Ethiopian combat casualties in Korea during March.

April 1952

At the start of April, the division was still in reserve. The 32d Regiment had the primary mission of training and the auxiliary mission of counterattack. With the arrival of warmer weather, the troops started turning in their winter clothing and gear. On April 1, a request was received from the Ethiopian government that half the men of the First Kagnew Battalion be rotated home immediately. The Eighth Army took issue with the request on tactical grounds since the Ethiopian government had restricted the first group of replacements from being committed until the arrival of the second group scheduled to land on July 4. This would leave the current battalion on the frontline at half strength. Eighth Army suggested the earliest the rotatees could be moved was April 7.

The next day the Ethiopian government lifted its prior restriction on the first group of replacements. And on April 3, the CG held a conference with his staff, Dodds, Teshome, and Kebbede regarding the imminent departure of approximately 40 officers and 625 enlisted men back to Ethiopia. Teshome concurred with the plan to move the 600 new arrivals from Pusan and to have them complete their training with the remainder of the First Kagnew Battalion in the 7th Division area. By this point, they had only completed one week of a scheduled six-week training in Pusan. Meanwhile, the holdovers from First Kagnew continued their training.

2

SECOND KAGNEW BATTALION

The Second Kagnew Battalion arrived dressed in shorts and was greeted by US and Korean officials as well as crowds of locals. Despite the First Kagnew Battalion having proved itself in battle, their successors were still viewed with suspicion. Yilma Belachew said the Americans weren't too enthused about us because our men who grew up eating *Injera* (Ethiopia's staple food) were skinny. He thought maybe they expected the Ethiopians to have a bigger build like [West] Africans. One US officer was overheard commenting, "How can they send us kids and how can they fight for us?"[1]

On April 5, General Lemnitzer gave a farewell speech to the rotatees of the First Kagnew. He told them, "It has been an honor and a privilege to have had you in the 7th Division. Your unit, the Ethiopian Kagnew Battalion of your Emperor Haile Selassie's own bodyguard, is one of the finest in the Eighth Army in Korea."[2] The CG then awarded one Silver Star and one Bronze Star to two members of battalion. The rotatees left for their homeland aboard the USNS *General McRae* on April 7.

The 32d Regiment completed five weeks of training at noon on April 12 and relieved the 2ID at the front on Line Missouri under the cover of darkness. The Ethiopian replacements

Gen. Ridgway greets wounded Pvt. Abdi Gurara on Hospital Ship Jutlandia, April 21, 1952. (US Army)

who were expected to arrive at the front on April 10, would not arrive until April 13 due to issues with transportation. Kagnew Battalion was placed into division reserve in the left sector with blocking and counterattack missions. It dedicated the remainder of the month to indoctrinating these new arrivals in US Army weapons and tactics.

Regimental records show 758 Kagnew soldiers were rotated home while 674 replacements were received in their place. On April 5, Kagnew Battalion's strength was at 349. By the 9th, it had increased to 446 and 1,058 by the 13th. The battalion was at 1,115 by the end of the month. It did not suffer any combat casualties for the second month in a row.

On April 18, 1952, the commander of the Military Sea Transportation Service sent a message to the captain of the *McRae* advising him to contact the US Naval Attaché upon the ship's arrival in Colombo with regards to individual weapons being flown in for issuance to the Ethiopian troops aboard. After much maneuvering by the Ethiopian government, US officials had relented and granted an exception.

Some of the wounded from the previous months of fighting were now stable enough for the long trip back home. They were to be transported aboard the Danish Hospital Ship *Jutlandia*. On April 21, Gen. Ridgway visited the ship to thank the hospital staff and award UN Service ribbons to the troops aboard. Later that day, the ship sailed from Yokohama with 194 patients, including 73 Ethiopian. When it arrived in Djibouti, the Danish expedition chief, the chief surgeon and a journalist were invited to Addis Ababa by the Emperor who received them three times in as many days and thanked them for the treatment given the Ethiopian patients.

The Duke welcomed the Ethiopian wounded in place of his father, their commander-in-chief. After he acknowledged the delay in sending the replacement battalion, he praised them for fighting well and carrying a heavy burden in the name of their country, despite being in a strange land under challenging conditions. He added,

My father had long since decided to support Collective Security so that peace and freedom are not extinguished by aggressors. The heroism you and your comrades from other nations displayed in supporting this stance and restoring South Korea's freedom will take up a chapter in the history books. You proved to your king, countrymen and even to the world, what an Ethiopian soldier armed with modern weapons could do. You have set a great example for the troops that follow you… Your sacrifices will be remembered not just by Ethiopia but by the entire civilized world… Welcome back to you country.[3]

The remaining First Kagnew men including Lt. Desta and Cpl. Bulcha would ensure continuity of operations and help train the new troops over the next couple of months. The lessons went beyond the tactical and technical to include the cultural. Desta said troops had to go to the bathroom and do their business in latrine stalls with others possibly nearby. This was taboo for Ethiopians and new troops who were not accustomed to using the field latrines would wait all day to answer nature's call in solitude, but Desta and the other veterans were used to it. He said, a few "of us would be on the toilets talking and the Americans would let one loose, shouting "On the way!" It was the same way with the showers. They had to teach the new arrivals the American and Korean cultures.[4]

May 1952

During the month of May, the 7th Division mission was manning Line Missouri. However, the relatively flat terrain in the Kumhwa sector created a unique set of challenges. It required defense in depth with an extensive outpost line. Patrols had to advance further, sometimes as far as 4,000 meters, before contacting the enemy. Rear area installations

A self-propelled artillery piece of the 92nd Field Armoured Artillery Battalion of the US Army, in action in the Kumwha area, on 8 June 1952. (US Army Historic Division)

had to be concealed because the flat terrain was suitable for long range observation by the enemy. Furthermore, the 2d Division had left the area in a shambles requiring the 7th Division to perform additional renovation and policing of trash.

During this period each regiment had two battalions on the line tasked with conducting aggressive patrols. The units on the line also dispatched listening posts, while the units in reserve dispatched screening patrols. The 32d Regiment sent out deep reconnaissance patrols which penetrated 2,000 meters past the enemy's outposts at night. The patrols sometimes had to stay camouflaged in these positions for up to 48 hours. The EEFK continued to conduct training as the division tried to get a true assessment of the unit's capabilities.

On May 5, the Ethiopians celebrated the 12th anniversary of their victory against the Italians. Maj. Terrefe Teklemariam, the battalion's executive officer, told the Stars and Stripes, "Each time we observe this day we realize more fully what a wonderful blessing liberty is to a nation… We all realize how dark were those days when our liberty was denied us."[5] And the next day, they commemorated their first year in Korea. On May 9, Lt. Col. Asfaw, who had been in Korea for about 10 days, took over the battalion.

During May, Kagnew did not suffer any combat casualties.

June 1952

In June, the division continued its active defense of Line Missouri at the base of the "Iron Triangle" and was stretched out over 26,000 meters. The 7th Division G-4 section supported 19,000 divisional troops, 12,000 US troops from attached units, 11,900 ROK Army and indigenous personnel, and 2,100 UN troops, for a total of 45,000 soldiers. Frontline troops were fed two hot meals a day (breakfast and dinner) instead of the usual three and ate combat rations for lunch. The food and mess gear were transported using tramways and the

Korean Service Corps who carry the loads up the hill and back down

The 32d Regiment occupied the left flank in the west central part of IX Corps' sector. The 1st and 2d Bns were on the line with 3d Bn and EEFK making up regimental and division reserves respectively. Recon patrols were dispatched to determine the disposition and strength of enemy forces. Snipers were employed to inflict casualties. Nightly ambush patrols and listening posts were used to protect friendly positions. The rear was secured with screening patrols and checkpoints.

Between June 2 and June 4, elements of Kagnew Battalion relieved the 2d Battalion on the MLR. On the 4th, right before midnight, as a larger group of enemy forces attacked George Company positions, five to six enemy soldiers broke off from that attack and fired on elements of 1st Co and 3d Co EEFK as they were trying to relieve George and Easy Companies on the MLR. The friendly units returned fire and hunkered down. These friendly units spent the night anxiously listening to cries of pain coming from no-man's land. At dawn, 1st Co dispatched a patrol to investigate. The patrol recovered three enemy dead and two wounded.

The two prisoners were moved up the chain for interrogation. Luang Chin, age 28, was a squad leader for 1st Sqd, 1st Plat, 44th Div Recon Co, 15th CCF Army Corps. He had three years education and had joined the CCF around June 1948. His statements were determined to be doubtful because he was still "shocked and confused" from being wounded. Nevertheless, he provided intelligence on locations, troop strengths and the supply situation. He said he and another soldier were sent out to recon a mountain when they got hit with machinegun fire. They were later captured while searching for a Communist regiment for medical aid. He admitted seeing UN propaganda leaflets and liking the one with Chinese revolutionary Sun Yat-Sen but he was afraid because he was told deserters would be shot and that the leaflets

Prince Makonnen Haile Selassie greeting Abebe Bikilia (future marathon runner) at the latter's homecoming with First Kagnew's wounded. (Author's collection)

Vassilios Simatos in Korea.

contained germs and poison.

The other prisoner was captured by the same Ethiopian patrol three hours after Luang Chin. Twenty-year-old Pvt. Cho Jo Nen from 5th Sqd, 2d Plat, 44th Div Recon Co, with two years of grammar school had been in the CCF for eight months. He was "under severe pain… and answered questions halfheartedly with eyes mostly closed." He alleged that he and three other men went out on a recon patrol and if possible were to capture a prisoner. They were later joined by 12 men from 1st Platoon and 3 men from the bazooka squad. They walked southwest and were joined by 12 more from the 131st Regiment. After heading southeast they were attacked, resulting in his capture. Unlike his friend, he had kept one UN leaflet guaranteeing clothing, safety, food and care, but claimed it did not have any effect on him.

On June 6, a 1st Co patrol encountered an opposing patrol and engaged it in a firefight. The friendly patrol was soon in danger of being encircled but fought its way out inflicting five KIA. The patrol attempted to retrieve the enemy bodies for intelligence. However, intense fire from enemy troops made it impossible. The patrol was ordered to withdraw by the Battalion C.O. and returned to the MLR safely around midnight. The next day at dawn a screening patrol was dispatched to the area where the firefight had taken place in order to search for bodies. However, none could be located as the enemy had policed the battlefield.

On June 9, the Ethiopians relieved 2d Bn on the MLR.

Three Kagnew soldiers were awarded Bronze Star Medals for Valor for action which occurred on June 9, 1952. Pvt. Gemechu Tsege had set up a perimeter defense and was fighting ferociously after his ambush patrol was unexpectedly attacked. "When six of the enemy attempted to capture one of his comrades, [Pvt. Gemechu] led a counterattack, annihilated the six enemy soldiers and released his comrade." Similarly, Pvt. Fitaweke H. Guebrel shouted words of encouragement to his fellow soldiers and engaged the enemy in hand-to-hand fighting after the surprise attack, inspiring the rest of his patrol to inflict heavy casualties on the enemy. Cpl. Tefaye Gebresillasse was at a friendly outpost that was being subject to preparatory mortar fire. When the ground attack started, he was moving from position to position shouting words of encouragement and directing fire. He called for artillery fire, "some of which landed within twenty yards of his post." He the engaged the enemy in hand-to-hand combat until they were "repulsed with heavy casualties."

On the night of June 10, the battalion received 22 rounds of 76mm mortar, suffering six wounded.

Second Lt. Yilma Belachew and his 75mm recoilless rifle platoon took over a frontline position on June 10. Right away he started studying maps of the area and the disposition of the enemy facing him. One night, he was told a patrol composed of holdovers from the First Kagnew Battalion was set to depart for a patrol through his sector but their officer fell ill. The operations officer, Capt. Workneh Gebyeou, came to the front seeking a volunteer. Yilma raised his hand. His friends thought he was crazy, but he felt confident as the enemy was right in front of him and he had studied his movements. Yilma and 14 men were sent to the rear for two days to rehearse for the mission – an ambush patrol tasked with taking prisoners.[6]

On June 18, 1952, the patrol moved three kilometers north of the MLR to its objective. Yilma and his men surprised an enemy platoon with small arms and grenades. Despite the brief confusion, the enemy regained its composure and counterattacked. The two sides locked in hand-to-hand fighting. Yilma and his men managed to rout the

Chinese at the tip of their bayonet.[7]

The Ethiopians instinctively gave chase but found themselves under an artillery barrage and encircled by enemy reinforcements. After unsuccessful attempts at a breakthrough, Yilma radioed for artillery support. The American guns roared to life to break the enemy's stranglehold.[8]

When the patrol returned to friendly lines the next morning, 2d Lt. Yilma was dispatched to the Regimental Command Post for a debrief since the regiment was starving for fresh intelligence on the enemy. After the debrief, Col. Kebbede, who was in attendance along with Lt. Col. Asfaw and Capt. Workneh, recommended Yilma be transferred to the S-3 section as Workneh's assistant.[8]

Despite their greenness, the Ethiopians had performed flawlessly. Yilma remarked, "God was with me. I had great soldiers. The leadership was mine, but the valor was theirs." The same US officer who was disappointed at their slight physical appearance when the Second Kagnew first arrived in Korea, paid them a visit after hearing about the patrol. He concluded, "You can't judge a person by his size, but by his heart."[9]

Before assuming his duties on the battalion staff, Yilma was sent back to the front for about eight days. On the morning of June 21, it was all quiet in the 1st Company sector. A soldier was on watch at every bunker while the others rested inside. Korean Service Corps (KSC) laborers – Korean civilian units composed of workers used for manual labor such as laying wire and carrying supplies and ammunition up steep, rugged hills – were out front laying wire to strengthen the company's defenses.[10] Incoming enemy mortar fire shattered the silence catching one of the Koreans in the open. He was critically wounded and began to cry in pain. Private Melese Berihun, heard the man's cries and emerged from the bunker to investigate. Even though Melese did not understand exactly what the man was saying, the cries of pain moved him to action. While enemy mortars were still exploding all around, he left the safety of his position and dashed forward. As Melese picked up the wounded man to evacuate him back to the bunker, a mortar shell exploded nearby. They died together. Yilma said they were found and buried together at the Pusan Cemetery in that embrace.[11]

On June 21, seven rounds of 60mm mortar hit Kagnew positions resulting in one KIA and two WIA. There was another notable mortar attack on June 25. This time Capt. Workneh reported the mortar shells landed near two platoons in the 4th Co area. Apparently, some of the soldiers started vomiting and fainting and one can only imagine their anxiety. Most of these men had heard of, if not personally witnessed, the effects of poison gas during the Italo-Ethiopian War. Workneh requested experts from division medical and chemical sections. The illness was later determined to be food poisoning.

Private Fasil Gragn, the Ethio-Greek soldier formerly known as Vassilios Simatos, was working on patrol and fire support plans in Workneh's S-3 section. One day, an American patrol was going out through the Ethiopian position, so they requested a translator. Captain Workneh assigned Fasil.[12] It was a two-day recon mission with strict orders not to fire at the enemy unless fired upon. The patrol left the wire, got into position, set up the machineguns and the Americans went to sleep. An astonished Fasil raised Capt. Wokneh on the radio. He reported that his American friends had fallen asleep and asked what he should do. Workneh replied, "Listen, you're the only mixed race we brought here, so you better not be the first to be taken prisoner. We haven't had a prisoner taken to date. Don't sully our name or I will court-martial you!"[13]

Fasil pulled out his pistol, woke up one of the Americans and warned him, "Sir, I'll be keeping an eye on you while you keep an eye

on the enemy." The American was beside himself and told him that he would have him court-martialed and sent to jail." Upon hearing this threat for the second time that day, an unfazed Fasil replied that he was already headed to jail. While the two were arguing, the area was rocked by a grenade explosion. Enemy artillery quickly followed. The next thing Fasil remembers was his American friend on top of him slapping him back into consciousness. Fortunately, he did not suffer any serious injuries. After that patrol Fasil was promoted to corporal.[14]

On June 26, Kagnew was relieved by 2d Bn and went into division reserve to start training again.

In June, Kagnew's lucky streak was broken – it lost two soldiers during the month. Twenty-nine men comprising the EEFK HQ at Taegue joined the battalion at the front. As of June 30, 1952, Kagnew's total strength was at 1,142 and the unit had been in combat 421 days, receiving a cumulative 41 killed and 153 wounded.

It would be an understatement to say life at the front was extremely difficult. The troops faced danger from all angles. Weather in the form of extreme heat or cold was a big factor. They had to take measures against vermin and the diseases they carried and when they were deloused, DDT was used extensively. In April, broken equipment caused the regiment to go two weeks without showers. When the shower units started operating normally the next month, the troops could once again start showing once every five days. They lived under the threat of enemy raids, snipers, mortar and artillery fire, as well as booby traps, landmines and natural hazards. They had to watch for infiltrators in the rear area. Physical exhaustion and mental fatigue were a constant companion. The fear of falling into enemy hands was an ever-present danger.

June was an active month for the division. Patrols of all kind (including ambush, recon, sniper, combat, screening and raids) went from 444 in May to 942 in June. Contacts with the enemy totaled 59%, representing a 44% increase over the previous month. The driving force behind this trend was a IX Corps directive for enemy identifications through prisoners and captured documents. The 26th Infantry Scout Dog Platoon was also attached to the division and the four-legged troops greatly assisted in detecting the enemy on ambush patrols.

July 1952

At the beginning of July, 2d and 3d Battalions were on Line Missouri, while 1st and Kagnew Battalions served as regimental and division reserve respectively. Infantrymen with the line units kept up with the aggressive patrols, while the tank units were bunker busting. The primary focus was capturing prisoners. The operational tempo continued to pick up and there was almost a 100% jump in reconnaissance patrols month over month, a 73% increase in combat patrols and 30% more listening posts were sent out.

On the first day of July, Gen. Lemitzer, who himself would be rotating out in a couple of days, visited the Ethiopian Battalion to say farewell to the departing troops. The next day Lt. Col. Asfaw Andargue officially replaced Col. Kebbede as commanding officer of the Ethiopian Expedition. On July 3, Brig.Gen. Wayne C. Smith relieved Lemitzer.

Around July 4, the second increment of Second Kagnew Battalion troops arrived in Pusan aboard the USNS General LeRoy Eltinge. The next day, the remaining Ethiopian rotatees embarked on the same ship for the return trip home. The battalion lost 29 officers and 266 men in the rotation but gained 50 officers and 504 enlisted men.

Second Lieutenant Melesse Tessema was Yilma Belachew's classmate from the second course. Melesse was born on January 8, 1931 in Sidamo Province, Aleta Worno Wereda, Dande Kebele (village). He moved from Sidamo to Arussi and eventually to the capital by the age of 10 where he entered the Tafari Makonnen School. He was older and consequently bigger than the other students when he started the second grade. He progressed through that grade, third grade and fourth grade the same year. The next year, he skipped the fifth grade and started the sixth grade. Students in each grade were ranked based on academic performance each year and those who were ranked first through third were brought before the Emperor for awards. By grade eight, Melesse was appearing for the third time before the Emperor to receive an award. At the time the Emperor was trying to rebuild the armed forces and as the high achievers came before him, he would send the youngster to one of three groups after handing them their award – unbeknownst to them they were being selected for the air force, the police college or the Imperial Bodyguard academy. After receiving his award, Melesse was sent to the Air Force group but after the ceremony, and before he left, the Emperor signaled his aides to move Melesse to another group. The aides took the students' names and left. When school reopened, Imperial Bodyguard officers arrived to recruit. These were freshly minted second lieutenants from the Imperial Bodyguard first course and went from class to class to give presentations. They talked about Generals Montgomery, MacArthur and Rommel. Melesse recalled their uniforms were shiny, their belts, everything about them looked exceptional. All the students wanted to be soldiers in the end The previously chosen students were called outside, loaded onto Mac trucks and taken to the 3d Battalion Camp close by. Melesse said "we were like prisoners. We were put in a room. We couldn't go outside. Our families didn't know. That's how I joined the academy." Melesse said he arrived in Korea around *Sene* 21 or 22 (Ethiopian calendar), which translates to June 28 or 29 (Gregorian calendar), meaning he must have arrived with the second increment since the first increment arrived in late March or early April.[15]

Melesse said they were in the middle of the course at the academy and did not know anything about the Korean War but they would have occasional guest speakers who taught various topics including history to go along with their other military studies. Guest speakers from the American Embassy came with a 16mm projector and films about WWII battles with Japan and so on. After their presentation, they brought up Korea. They told the cadets, perhaps jokingly, if the war did not end soon, they might join the UN army and fight there as well. When the cadets got out of class, they started joking about going to Korea. Melesse said, "we didn't think it would happen. That was the first we got word of it. We didn't know anything about the Korean War or even Korea before then."[16]

At the time First Kagnew was in the Far East, the Ethiopian brass started to organize a new unit to replace it. Mengistu Neway had the Guard officers brought into an auditorium and called out the ones that would go to Korea. Melesse said they were not, strictly speaking, "volunteers." They were ordered to go to Korea. Even though the First Kagnew was in country, the replacement troops did not know much about the Korean terrain or what the fighting was like. They got occasional news from the radio but the information was not current. They just knew what awaited them was something difficult. They trained on how to attack up and down hills, on crossing rivers, and on the obstacle course. It was very tiring tactical training. The officers had to train for themselves and then train their troops and so they ended up doing the work two or three times. But in the end they became like brothers to their men.[17]

The second increment of the Second Kagnew group had received close combat, first aid and weapons training. Once a week, the battalion conducted field exercises with as many as 2,000 soldiers participating. Every Saturday, for two hours they turned out in formation and drilled bare feet accompanied by the Guard's one-hundred person band playing the Royal Halland Regiment's marching tune. The priest who was to accompany the troops to Korea also participated in close order drill and was eventually commissioned as a lieutenant.[18]

Their training complete, the troops gathered at *Jan Meda* to bid farewell to their Emperor. The next day, they got up early, shouldered their haversacks, and loaded up in trucks. The families did not know this foreign land their boys would soon be traveling to and separation was a big deal since families were close-knit. Melesse Tessema said, as he mounted the truck, his mother would pull him off the truck and then his father would pull him off the truck. Col. Mengistu Neway began yelling at him as his sister pulled his off the truck. There was a lot of crying. His relatives would hold him and not let him go. Their superiors yelled at the troops to load and started to hit them.[19] Since the same hysteria had played out with the First Kagnew's send off, the government tried to trick the families by telling them the troops would board the train at the main terminal at Legehar. Instead the soldiers were moved to Dukem (twenty miles south of the capital) and loaded on the train.[20]

Melesse Tessema said everything on the ship was clean, orderly and done on time. The troops assimilated western culture: how to sit at the table, how to pour tea, how breakfast was served. Since they had to be on the ship with other contingents such as Turks, Dutch and Greeks, the troops felt compelled to adapt to western culture. They had to learn how to hold their knives and forks, what food to eat with a spoon, how to butter their bread, and so on.[21]

The Second Kagnew Battalion, which would be at more than full strength (1,302 officers and men) by July 13, carried on with training. The men were given instruction in individual weapons, crew served weapons (heavy machineguns, mortars and 75mm recoilless rifles), distance judging and measuring, military sanitation, patrolling, scouting, squad in the attack, and night movements. Technical skills such as mine service, radio-telephone systems and map reading were also covered. They also participated in daily physical fitness. Even while training, elements of Kagnew Battalion were dispatched on numerous dangerous missions.

On July 4, a special ambush patrol from 1st Co departed at 2050. After trekking in the dark for more than an hour, it located the enemy and engaged it in a firefight that lasted only a few minutes and the patrol broke contact and continued to a secondary objective. When the patrol, returned to base around 0400 the next morning, it had three more men than it had at the start. This time they were not POWs. The patrol had picked up three US soldiers from George Company who had been missing. The Company G patrol had been ambushed by enemy troops employing concussion grenades and as the US patrol withdrew, the patrol leader noticed he was down three men, but had expected to find them back at base.

On July 6, 2014, 3d Co was ordered to conduct a special ambush patrol on Hill 358, which was nicknamed Hell's Gate. The patrol was to last from July 7 through July 9. The plan called for a capturing element of eight men to depart friendly lines on the night of the 7th. The supporting element of 15 men would depart a day later. The two units would get into position and remain under concealment in hopes of capturing some enemy troops. They were scheduled to return before dawn on July 9.

On July 7, the patrol leader checked the map overlays for known minefields. He also ensured counterintelligence measures were taken by searching his men and removing any division or regimental identification, personal papers, letters and billfolds. Having completed the pre-mission checks, the capturing unit, call-sign "Wekaw" departed at 2100. This group of eight men left the wire and hid for the

Kagnew pre-patrol. (US Army)

next 24 hours. The supporting element left on July 8 at 2050, with 12 men instead of the planned 15. The two groups linked up 40 minutes later and setup a horseshoe ambush.

At 0100 on July 9, the patrol leader sighted about 50 enemy troops approaching in two columns. The patrol leader ordered the enemy to halt. The lead enemy soldier responded by raising his hands as if to surrender. Two Kagnew men cautiously moved forward to apprehend him but when they got within 15 yards the enemy troops greeted them with concussion grenades and a 45-minute long firefight broke out. The enemy was supported by indirect fire from Camel's Back Hill (Hill 472). The friendly patrol was also supported by artillery and mortar fire. The patrol leader reported his situation and reinforcements were put on standby.

After suffering ten killed and nine wounded, the enemy withdrew in disorder. The patrol had suffered two wounded and was now getting low on ammo. It too withdrew and consolidated with the support element. After the patrol managed to evacuate one of the wounded, it sighted another group of 50 enemy soldiers coming from Hill 472. Fortunately the support element stopped them in their tracks with a wall of lead.

The enemy patrol reorganized and placed heavy fire on the patrol, while also removing his dead and wounded from the area. A platoon from 1st Co arrived to help. The reinforced patrol screened the area at

0300 discovering evidence of 15 KIA and nine WIA. They returned to friendly lines at 0445, having spent 56 hours in no-man's land.

On the night of July 17, Kagnew sent out four additional patrols in the vicinity of Camel Back Hill (Hill 472). 2d Lt. Melesse Tessema, who had just arrived in Korea four days ago and was platoon leader of 2d Platoon/4th Company, explained,

the places were named based on what they looked like. If it looked like a camel's hump, they called it camel hill. If it looked like a cow's yoke, they called it yoke. One placed looked like an alligator, they called it alligator. That's what we called them. We didn't know the Korean names.

The patrols were led by 1st Lts. Metaferya Ayele and Abate Gelano and academy mates, 2d Lts. Bekele Gebrekidane and Melesse Tessema. The patrols marched single file to their objective. The three officers took ambush patrols of six men each to three hills while 2d Lt. Bekele Gebrekidane positioned the remaining troops as a support element right in the middle. At 0240, one element of the patrol was advancing toward the hill when they were fired upon by an estimated 40 enemy troops. The patrol took cover and returned fire. It soon became clear to the patrol that they were being encircled by a numerically superior force. The other element of the patrol was simultaneously

Kagnew pre-patrol. (US Army)

ighting off an attack by an estimated 200 enemy in the vicinity of Hill 358. The enemy managed to separate and surround the different elements. Amidst bitter fighting, Melesse eventually linked up with his friend Bekele who by this point was badly wounded. Melesse gave him first aid and got him evacuated to the rear and then took the initiative and led his and Bekele's men. They were still being engaged by 50 Communists using burp guns, hand grenades, machineguns and 60mm mortars. The running battle continued until 0430, when friendly elements reorganized and eventually fought their way out of the encirclement to return to the MLR at 0515. The enemy suffered 40 KIA, 36 WIA, as well as an additional estimated 43 KIA and 54 WIA. The Kagnew patrol had two killed and seven wounded. Melesse and a few of his men were ordered back out to observe enemy activity and spent the next day and night on patrol until they were relieved by another unit. He said the others did more than him but this was one of the battles that gave a good name to the battalion. General Mulugeta Bulli and the Emperor sent letters of commendation to each of the officers.[22] Kimon Skordiles wrote that the Ethiopians suffered 11 KIA and two WIA. The Communists had 90 KIA and 130 WIA.[23] Casualty figures for the whole month were eight KIA and 15 WIA, but Skordiles wrote 11 KIA for this battle alone. Both Skordiles in his book, and Melesse during our interview, stated this battle occurred on July 8. However, US Army records do not show a patrol by 4th Company on that date and events matching the narrative were recorded on July 17.

On July 24, an ambush patrol from 3d Co, call sign "Nadew," departed at 2030 through George Company lines towards Hill 358. The platoon was led by 1st Lt. Telaye Wendemaghegnehu and got to its objective and started digging-in. Suddenly yellow and white flares were fired from the hill at 2330 and the patrol was immediately subjected to an artillery and mortar barrage. An estimated company dug-in on the hill opened up on the patrol and charged their position. "Observing that his men were disorganized and scattered by the surprise attack," Lieutenant Telaye left his position of cover "shouting words of encouragement and reorganizing an adequate defense force." The enemy attempted to wipe the Ethiopians from the hillside by raining "an overwhelming number of grenades down on the patrol." The patrol, however, fought ferociously and routed the attackers. They then formed a perimeter and prepared for what was to follow, but they would have to face it without their leader as Lieutenant Telaye was mortally wounded.

At some point during the fight, Pvt. Fekensa Geletu heard a cry for help from one of his comrades. "Disregarding all thoughts of personal safety," he charged towards the sound. There he found the patrol's radio operator tangled in telephone wire and in the hands of the enemy. He killed the would-be captors and rescued his friend. The two then rejoined the patrol.

A red signal flare was fired from Hill 472. That was the enemy's signal for directing enormous firepower consisting of mortar and artillery, followed by raking of the area with machineguns. Even though it might have felt like forever, the battle only lasted ten minutes in which the enemy suffered 36 casualties. Four Ethiopians were killed and six wounded. The Kagnew soldiers fought off and inflicted heavy losses on a numerically superior force which fought from prepared positions and had the element of surprise on its side. The patrol withdrew having recovered their wounded and one of the enemy corpses but not all of the Ethiopian dead.

Captain Workneh (S-3) and his radio op Pvt. Assefa Demissie were at an outpost when Capt. Hailemariam Lencho (3rd Co C.O.) came in and said he would take Assefa and go to recover the bodies. They got to the objective around 0300 but could not find the bodies and returned to friendly lines that night. They went back the next morning with a patrol consisting of two platoons of EEFK and one platoon of tanks to aid in the eventual recovery of the dead. All friendly troops closed on the MLR at 1015.[24]

Sgt. Gebreyohenis Ahmed was awarded the Bronze Star for Valor for exposing himself to hostile fire and directing the defense. Cpl. Berhanu Degaga assumed command of the patrol after Lt. Telaye and the platoon sergeant were killed in the initial attack. Following their example, he continued to direct the defense while exposing himself to enemy fire. Using a machinegun, he personally covered the evacuation of some of the wounded. His leadership was recognized with a Bronze Star Medal for Valor. Pvt. Mamo Abeda [sic], a medic, was awarded the Bronze Star for Valor for "disregarding his own personal safety, [moving] across open terrain under an intense artillery and mortar barrage to treat and evacuate wounded comrades." Lt. Telaye whose courageous actions inspired the patrol to resist defiantly was posthumously awarded the Silver Star Medal. PFC. Mamo Ayele was wounded in the initial attack but despite his wounds, he "held his ground" and "refused to abandon his position and continued his gallant stand until he fell mortally wounded." He was also awarded a posthumous Silver Star Medal. Pvt. Fekensa, who rescued his comrade from enemy hands, would die in combat on October 9, 1952. He was awarded the Bronze Star Medal for Valor – also posthumously.

Kagnew Battalion suffered eight KIA and 15 WIA in the month of July.

August 1952

By August 8, Kagnew Battalion, with 2d Platoon Tank Co, elements of 1st Platoon, Battery B, 15 AAA Aw Bn attached, relieved 2d Battalion on Line Missouri. A platoon from Item Company would also be attached to the battalion. In fact, throughout the month several US platoons would rotate in-and-out of Kagnew Battalion. The battalion suffered casualties while in position on the MLR and on the many aggressive patrols it dispatched. Sometimes the casualties received minor wounds, other times the wounds were devastating. Worst of all, it came down to pure luck.

The day the battalion got on the line, it suffered one killed and one wounded from artillery. On the 14th, two were wounded from machinegun fire; one man was shot in the head and the other in the foot. On the 19th, Love Company which was attached to Kagnew, suffered one wounded from machinegun fire. On August 21, a 3d Company soldier was hit by mortar fragments in the back and leg. On August 26, they had one wounded from incoming artillery. On the 28th, a 3d Company man on an observation post was shot through the neck by a sniper. On August 30, two more were wounded by mortar fire.

On August 31, 32d Regiment was relieved by 17th Regiment. The Ethiopian Battalion was attached to the 17th Regiment and would remain in position.

The Stars and Stripes reported that three Kagnew men, Pvt. Zelak Belai, Cpls. Wendemu Bayene and Birhanu Begaga were engaged in firefight deep in enemy territory. They formed a tight perimeter and caused the enemy to think he was facing a larger force by firing while constantly changing positions. Pvt. Zelaka was wounded twice but did not quit. They kept the enemy at bay for six hours until they could withdraw under cover of friendly artillery, leaving behind 30 enemy dead.[25]

September 1952

On September 1, the regiment moved into reserve around Chipo-ri and began preparing for an intensive two-week training. The first few days were dedicated to reorganization, maintenance of equipment and air attack countermeasures. Additionally, personnel started receiving training in the use and care of winter clothing. On September 5, Lt. Col. Asfaw held a ceremony at the Battalion CP to award medals to eleven of his men.

From September 22 through 24, the regiment relieved its sister unit, the Polar Bears, and moved into position on the division's right. Kagnew (with US tank and antiaircraft artillery units attached) relieved the Colombians.

On September 25, a 20-man ambush patrol from 4th Co led by Lt. Habtemichel was dispatched with the mission of capturing a POW. The patrol's call-sign was "Belew". It occupied its objective and at 2100 observed the enemy moving towards their position at platoon strength. The patrol opened fire and the enemy answered back supported by automatic weapon fire. After a seven-minute fight, an enemy squad approached from another direction supported by machinegun fire from Hill 459. The patrol broke contact and withdrew to another location where they received fire momentarily. The disciplined Ethiopians stayed hidden in their new position without returning fire. They had already inflicted five KIA and four WIA. Two of their own were slightly wounded.

On September 29, an Ethiopian patrol was attacked by a numerically superior force and the platoon leader was felled in the initial stage of the battle. Sgt. Maj. Tesfasion Gebryesus "moved forward through small arms and automatic weapons fire to evacuate his body. He then returned to the position and assumed leadership of the patrol successfully directing the defense against the hostile troops." Sgt. Maj. Tesfasion earned a Bronze Star Medal with "V" device for heroic achievement.

October 1952

On October 8, close to midnight a local security patrol from 1st Co observed an estimated 35 enemy and the patrol opened up with small arms and light machineguns. After a three-minute firefight, the enemy withdrew. The patrol did not inflict casualties but it did not take any either. Unfortunately, at 0200 a mine explosion left 1st Co with one killed and one wounded. The next day, 4th Co had one wounded from enemy mortar fire.

Starting on October 14, the division executed the first offensive action since the limited objective attacks more than a year ago in September 1951. The new offensive codenamed Operation *Showdown* called for US units to attack, seize, and defend "Triangle Hill" (Hill 598) and "Jane Russell Hill", while elements of the 2d ROK Division attacked "Sniper's Ridge" (Hill 580) simultaneously. The 32d Regiment supported the operation by conducting diversionary raids on Hill 419 and Hill 250.

Major Richard Hallock, who only arrived from the states a day before the operation commenced, was assigned as the S-3 for 1st Bn/32d Rgt. He felt the inaction from the previous months was

The winter uniform of the Kagnew Battalion was very necessary to protect troops from the harsh Korean weather. Indeed, this soldier is shown wearing several pieces of US combat clothing layered over each other, including a heavy wool blouse over the M1942 HBT uniform (which had supplanted all other models only during the final phase of the Korean War). Atop of these items, he added the M1943 winter jacket (widely copied for civilian use ever since). Instead of the M1 steel helmet, he is shown wearing a fur-lined cap, while boots were covered by gaiters. The M1936 canvas belt was used to carry a canteen and a bag for .30 ammunition for his M2 rifle (a semi-automatic version of the classic M1). (Artwork by Anderson Subtil)

Like that of many other international contingents in Korea, the summer uniform distributed to the soldiers of the Kagnew Battalion in Korea was that of the US Army. It included the M1947 HBT (Herringbone Twill) clothing and brown leather GI boots. The Ethiopians usually added the Imperial Bodyguard insignia on the collar, and sometimes also the badge of the 7th Division on their left shoulders. Head protection was provided by the M1 steel helmet, while other combat gear included the M1936 canvas belt, the 1942 first aid pouch, and an M4 bayonet knife for his primary firearm: in this case the .30 calibre M1 carbine. (Artwork by Anderson Subtil)

This Ethiopian Captain, shown as shortly after arrival in Korea, wore the traditional 'Safari' helmet and the Imperial Bodyguard uniform based on the British Army's 1937 battledress, but without the front pocket on the left thigh. The insignia on the collar is that of the Imperial Bodyguard, while the tab on the right shoulder reads 'ETHIOPIA' in capital letters. All troops in the Kagnew Battalion also wore epaulettes with metal tab with 'Kebur Zabagna' written in Amharic. Except for the rank insignia, the only other difference in markings between officers, non-commissioned officers (shown in the inset illustration), and enlisted men was that the officers wore a shirt, a tie, and a black belt surrounding the helmet brim. The canvas bag, black leather boots and gaiters also appear to have been based on British models from the Second World War period. (Artwork by Anderson Subtil)

The Willys MB ¼-ton 4x4 truck, best known simply as the 'Jeep', was probably the best-known US military vehicle of the 1940s and 1950s. Manufactured in large numbers it was a highly-mobile, all-terrain vehicle, used for a wide range of purposes. A number of jeeps were provided to the command staff and the military police element of the Kagnew Battalion during the Korean War. Some of these mounted the hefty 12.7mm Browning M2 machine-gun as shown here. As usual for this period, all US Army vehicles – including Jeeps assigned to the Kagnew Battalion – were painted in Forest Green overall. (Artwork by David Bocquelet)

Nick-named 'Gorilla', the 155mm M41 Howitzer Motor Carriage was a self-propelled artillery vehicle installed on a stretched chassis of the M24 Chaffee light tank, used extensively in the Korean War, and highly influential for the development subsequent US-made self-propelled artillery pieces. Highly mobile, they proved capable of evading enemy counter-battery fire. Nominally, M41s were operated by regiments consisting of up to six battalions, but only single battalions (each usually consisting of three batteries) were deployed during the Korean War. (Artwork by David Bocquelet)

The 155mm Gun Motor Carriage M40 was a self-propelled artillery vehicle consisting of the widened and lengthened chassis of the M4A3 Sherman tank, atop of which the 155mm M2 155mm gun was installed. Quite expensive, yet the heaviest- and longest-ranged self-propelled artillery piece deployed during the Korean War, it was nick-named the 'Cardinal'. The M40s were usually operated by artillery battalions assigned directly to Corps HQs, each of which consisted of a headquarters element and three batteries of four guns each. (Artwork by David Bocquelet)

Aman Andom

Despite Aman Andom's early dismissal from Korea, he was promoted to full colonel and became commandant of the military academy.[1] In 1954, his accreditation for military attaché in Washington D.C. was "informally rejected" by the US.[2] In 1956, he was promoted to brigadier and also spent some time in the Ministry of Defense as deputy chief of staff for the armed forces.

On the eve of the 1960 coup, he was CO 3d Division in Harar. Aman accurately predicted, intercepted and repulsed the Somali incursion into Ogaden, earning his the nick-name "Lion of the Ogaden" - but he was relieved of command for later disobeying the Emperor's order NOT to attack into Somalia.[3]

He was finally accredited as military attaché to the US from 1964 to 1965, and took advantage of his stay in Washington D.C. by earning a degree from Howard University. Aman retired from the military and served in the parliament where he remained an ardent reformist and outspoken critic of the Crown.[4]

Early during the unrest in 1974, he was named chairman of the council of ministers as well as minister of defense. He became chairman of the Derg as well as de facto head of state after the revolution. However, this judicious general of Eritrean heritage would not go along the Derg's extremism: he was killed in a firefight with Derg troops sent by Mengistu Haile Mariam to arrest him on November 23, 1974.[5] (US Army)

Asfaw Andargue

No information was found on Lt. Col. Asfaw Andargue after his time in Korea other than his trip to the Hague to receive the award from the World Veterans Federation.

Teshome Irgetu

The man who was appointed as CO of the First Kagnew Battalion after Aman – Lt. Col. Teshome Irgetu – was named governor of Kelem Awraja in Wellega in 1956.[6] In 1961, he led the Second Tikil Brigade in the Congo. He took command of the Ethiopian 2d Army Division in Eritrea sometime around 1966. In 1970, his convoy was ambushed by rebel fighters and General Teshome was killed. (US Army)

Desta Gemeda and Berkinesh Kebede

Desta Gemeda underwent airborne and commando training in Israel. As of 1960, he served as executive officer of the Imperial Bodyguard Hospital. He was detained and investigated because of the coup but cleared of any involvement.[7] Desta subsequently served as executive officer of the 6th Battalion in Congo: following the Kindu massacre, his unit took the city, disinterred the bodies for proper burial and brought peace to the area. After fighting against the Somalis during the Ogaden War and serving in the area for years, he was promoted to the rank of Brigadier General and assigned administrator for Dire-Dawa Awraja. In the 1980s, he served as governor of Sidamo, frequently protested the killing and detention of civilians, and finally demanded to retire. General Desta then worked for the World Food Program until this was shut down by the present administration.[8]

Nurses Berkinesh and Aster returned to work at the Imperial Bodyguard Hospital, where they were assigned to the medical and surgical departments, respectively. Subsequently, Berkinesh became an assistant matron at Haile Selassie Hospital (presently Yekatit 12 Hospital), before working as matron of St. Paul's 'Paulos' Hospital and then for the Ministry of Health and Chercos Clinic. She retired in 1992. After Korea, Berkinesh married General Desta and they raised four children and four grandchildren. This photograph was taken in 2012.[9]

Kebbede Guebre

Colonel Kebbede Guebre was placed in charge of the government of Assab (nowadays in Eritrea). In 1955, he was advanced in rank to Brigadier General and appointed the commander of the 3rd Division and Governor of Ogaden Awraja. Two years later, he was appointed the Chief-of-Staff of the Ground Forces, with the rank of Major General, replacing Mulugeta Bulli. After proving his loyalty during the 1960 coup attempt, he was promoted to Lieutenant General and then commanded all UN forces in the Congo. Upon his return to Ethiopia, Kebbede was made governor of Harar and then the Minister of Defence. He was detained and executed during the coup of 1974. [10, 11, 12, 13]

Mulugeta Bulli

In 1955, Mulugeta Bulli was advanced in rank to Major General and appointed Chief-of-Staff of the Armed Forces. Three years later, this extremely disciplined, hard-working and highly popular officer was appointed as Chief-of-Staff of the Emperor's Private Cabinet, and then the Minister of National Community Development, a year later. During the 1960 coup attempt, the conspirators took General Mulugeta hostage and tried to have him lend credibility to their cause by re-appointing him Chief-of-Staff Armed Forces. He was killed when forces loyal to the Emperor re-took the palace.

Woldeyohanis Shitta

After commanding the 3rd Kagnew Battalion, Colonel Woldeyohanis Shitta attended the Army Staff College in France. Around 1958, he became deputy commander of the Imperial Bodyguard. In 1960, he led the First Tikil Brigade in the Congo.[14] He was a brigadier general and ambassador to Yugoslavia during the 1974 revolution.[15] When asked about General Woldeyohanis, his radio operator, Tesfaye Woldeselassie, replied with typical Kagnew understatement, "He was a good leader."[16]

Asfaw Habtemariam

Lieutenant-Colonel Asfaw Habtemariam is known to have been appointed the Governor of Dire-Dawa Awraja, in Harar, in 1956.[17]

Bulcha Olika

Bulcha Olika served with the First, Second and Third Kagnew Battalions and later remained in the military. In 1976, he was drafted by the Derg to fight against separatist forces in Eritrea as a company commander in the *Abat Tor* (Elder's Army). He was later captured by the rebels and suffered a harrowing ordeal to get back to the capital. He retired as a captain.[18] This photograph shows him in 2012.

Melesse Tessema

Melesse Tessema who served with the Second Kagnew Battalion as a 2nd Lieutenant continued to serve with the military and rose in rank to that of a colonel. In addition to the US Bronze Star, he was decorated with a Korean Hwarang Medal, St. George Medal with two Palm Fonds, and Haile Selassie Military Medal with three Palm Fonds. More recently, he is the President of the Ethiopian Korean War Veterans Association, still very much the old colonel looking after his men as the shepherd watches over his flock. This photograph shows him as of 2012.[19]

Yilma Belachew

Yilma Belachew served as 2nd Lieutenant with the Second Kagnew Battalion and then with the Fourth Kagnew Battalion. After serving as editor of the Ethiopian Army newspaper, he retired as a captain – proud of his professional service but regretful for not having attained a higher rank. Recently, he worked as Vice President of the Veterans' Association. This photograph was taken in 2012.[20]

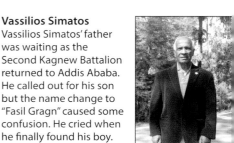

Vassilios Simatos

Vassilios Simatos' father was waiting as the Second Kagnew Battalion returned to Addis Ababa. He called out for his son but the name change to "Fasil Gragn" caused some confusion. He cried when he finally found his boy. Vassilios subsequently left the Guard but was later arrested for being of mixed race while not having proper documentation: taken to the same police station he had run away to as a child, he took care to get the paperwork straightened out and went to work for the Highway Department, for Ethiopian Airlines, and at the US Embassy in Addis Ababa. Later on, he was recognized as the top foreign national employee of the US Department of State in Africa and chosen as a finalist for the Foreign Service National of the Year Award.[21]

Wongele Costa

Wongele Costa remained in the military: after the 1960 coup attempt, he served seven years in Ogaden, eight in Eritrea and Tigray, six months in southern Ethiopia and then four years as an instructor at the Holeta Military Academy, producing many famous officers – including Mengistu Haile Mariam. He earned himself numerous decorations including the Haile Selassie Medal with Palm Fond, the Hwarang Medal with Gold Star, and a Belgian Medal. Upon his retirement, he was re-activated on Mengistu's personal request, and served as Chief of Instruction at the Holeta Staff College and Inspector of the Army: he finally retired as the rebel fighters entered Addis Ababa in 1991.[22]

Abebe Gebreyes

Abebe Gebreyes remained in the military where he served as instructor at the Harar Military Academy for 12 years, shaping many future officers. He underwent advanced infantry training and armor courses in the USA, at Fort Benning (GA) and Fort Knox (KY), respectively, and then went to the US Army Command and General Staff College in Fort Leavenworth (KS). Back in Ethiopia, Abebe was appointed the CO 3rd Division in Harar, then promoted to Brigadier General and appointed the Commander of the Central Command. The last few years of his active service he commanded all forces in northwestern Ethiopia, and then served as administrator for Gonder. He retired in 1990 and now lives in Los Angeles with his wife.[23]

Bekele Hora

Bekele Hora continued to serve in the Imperial Bodyguard and saw action with a mortar crew in support of the coup-plotters. He re-joined the military and served with the Third Tikil Brigade in the Congo, then in the Ogaden and later in Eritrea. He was there when General Teshome Irgetu was killed in an ambush, and retired in 1985 with the rank of Sergeant. When the Communist junta murdered his child, he joined the insurgency – just like he had done as a teenager after his father was killed by the Italian Fascists. Realizing the fight was going nowhere, he turned himself in and was imprisoned, but then won his freedom at the end of the Civil War in 1991.[24]

Tesfaye Woldeselassie

Tesfaye Woldeselassie spent six months recuperating from his wounds, returned to his unit and rotated back home at the end of their tour. After a one month furlough, all the members of the battalion including Tesfaye returned to duty with the Imperial Bodyguard and started training. Unfortunately, he had not completely healed and broke his bone again. He was sent back to the hospital and eventually discharged from the military with 25% disability but no pension. Tesfaye did not let that deter him. He finished the 12th grade and went on to work for various governmental offices rising to the level of director. This photograph was taken in 2012.[25]

Assefa Demissie(left) with Tadesse Gebrekristos (right)

Assefa Demissie of the Second Kagnew left the service around 1955 and then worked for Dire-Dawa Textile for 32 years. He subsequently moved to Addis Ababa and was instrumental in establishing the Veterans' Association. Thanks to his tireless efforts, it grew to about 700 members, but by 2012 was down to around 300, mostly due to age. Assefa was among the few veterans that recently paid a visit to Korea, where he was excited to see a flourishing Seoul instead of the desolate land from the early 1950s. He is a father of nine children from six women, and has 17 grandchildren.[26]

Major General John Hightower (left) with Lieutenant General Kebbede Guebre

John Hightower, who commanded the US 32d Infantry Regiment at the arrival of the 1st Kagnew Battalion, rose to the rank of major general and was later assigned as Chief of MAAG in Greece. This afforded him and Mrs. Hightower the opportunity to travel to Ethiopia in 1971. They were given a first class reception by their old friend Lt. Gen. Kebbede Guebre. They laid a wreath at the tomb of the dead of Kagnew Battalion as well as that of Lt. Gen. Teshome Irgetu. Maj. Gen. Hightower retired from the US Army in 1973. He passed away in 2001.

Harold Myers

It is believed the incident in Boise cost Captain Harold Myers an appointment as military attaché in Addis Ababa. Instead he was posted in Germany as an artillery officer. After the war "his ranks varied from officer to enlisted and back to officer depending on staffing needs." Last his family heard, a medical board had forced him into retirement because he was dying from a neurological disorder. The family was told that he got a retirement promotion to Lieutenant-Colonel before he passed away sometime in 1968. Following his father's advice, Myers' son proudly served in the armed forces – as a US Marine.[27] (Courtesy James Owings)

Richard Hallock

A 'product of his time' that 'used racist jargon', but 'whatever his prejudices, they in no way impacted how he viewed, and worked with, the Ethiopians', Richard Hallock had no doubt: '… the Ethiopian battalion was easily the best unit he came into contact with in Korea'.[28] Taking command of the 1st Battalion, 32nd Regiment in June 1953, Hallock became the youngest battalion commander in Korea. After the war, he remained in the military until becoming the first member of Secretary of Defense Robert McNamara's 'Whiz Kids'. He served at the Command and General Staff College in Leavenworth and sponsored a visit by two Ethiopian generals before retiring in 1967. Hallock amassed an impressive collection of decorations, including a Silver Star, a Purple Heart, and five Bronze Stars (four for valor) and was inducted into the Fort Benning OCS Hall of Fame. After running a successful business in consulting and real estate, he passed away in 1999.[29]

Orvar Nilsson

While in Korea, Orvar Nilsson met Nanna Weström who was serving as a nurse with the Swedish Hospital Unit. They got married in Ethiopia where Nilsson continued to serve as an instructor for the Imperial Bodyguard until 1953. He returned to Sweden and continued his military career. In 1964 he was assigned to the UN mission in Cyprus. When Lt. Col. Nilsson retired from the army, he was Sweden's most decorated soldier. He passed away in 2008 at the age of 89.[30] The Ethiopian veterans credit their Swedish instructors with providing rigorous training that kept them alive. (Courtesy CG Johanson)

Sten-Eggert Naucler

After his time in Korea, Sten-Eggert Naucler returned to Ethiopia. He went back down to captain and served in other UN missions in Egypt and later in the Congo where he led the Swedish Battalion under the overall command of Lt. Gen. Kebbede Guebre.[31] Col. Naucler retired from the military in 1963 and began work as chief of staff for a mining company in Liberia.[32]

Juan Raigoza

Juan Raigoza earned Purple Hearts both in WWII and Korea before retiring as a colonel. He was also awarded the Star of Ethiopia. He went on to teach high school math and Spanish literature for 17 years. In addition, he worked at a local Spanish language television show as co-host, newscaster, commentator and producer. He also ran for congress in New Mexico. Colonel Raigoza passed away in 2004.[33] During their first meeting, Lt. Col. Asfaw Andargue told Juan Raigoza, "You will always be our friend" and so Juan Raigoza remained to his death.[34]

Korean War Memorial in Addis Ababa, Ethiopia, as seen in 2012

Ethiopian Veterans of the Korean War in Addis Ababa, Ethiopia, 2012

Ethiopian Veterans of the Korean War in Addis Ababa, Ethiopia, 2012

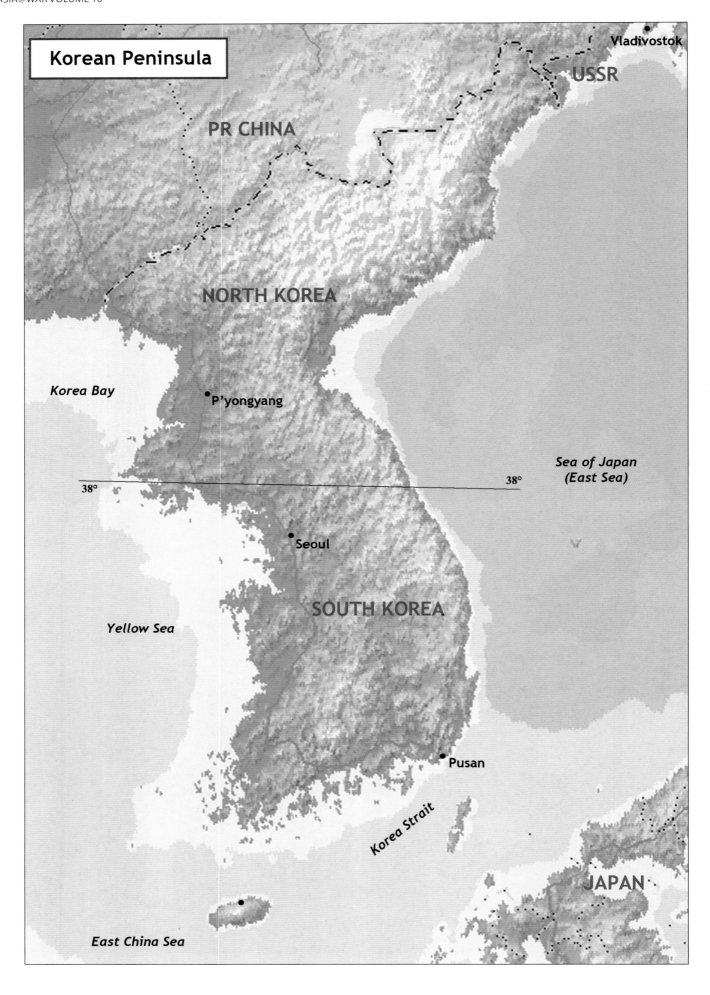

Korean Peninsula

Vladivostok

USSR

PR CHINA

NORTH KOREA

Korea Bay

P'yongyang

38°   38°

Sea of Japan
(East Sea)

Seoul

SOUTH KOREA

Yellow Sea

Pusan

Korea Strait

JAPAN

East China Sea

driven by the need to limit American casualties. According to Hallock, General Smith, the 7th Division Commander, "began planning for a 'limited action' attack designed to seize the initiative from the enemy…" Smith predicted he could take Triangle Hill in five days "with enough preparatory air strikes and massed artillery fire" with minimal casualties. Hallock assessed, "the hill possessed no great tactical significance except the Chinese observation points atop Hill 598 provided a bird's-eye view of the entire Kumwha valley." But when peace negotiations broke down on October 8, "local attack on positions like Triangle Hill took on strategic and political significance."[26]

Unfortunately, the planned air and artillery strikes had to be reduced. The main effort of Operation *Showdown*, which is also known as the Battle of Triangle Hill, was initially fought by two battalions from

Kagnew briefing. (US Army)

the 31st Regiment. However, they were beaten back after a sixteen-hour bloody battle, mainly due to intense enemy shelling. "The 31st suffered ninety-six KIA and 337 wounded, the heaviest casualties suffered by the regiment in the Korean War." The next morning, 1st Bn, 32d Regiment was sent into the fray and friendly units were able to gain some ground. After repulsing a counterattack early on October 16, three US battalions advanced abreast on the objective, taking heavy casualties under intense artillery bombardment. By evening, the Communists had been ejected from the objective with the exception of a small area on Hill 598 called Pike's Peak. Friendly units were ordered to dig-in for the night. That night, those troops were shelled mercilessly and attacked by two enemy battalions. In the afternoon of October 17, the battered 2d Bn, 31st Reg was relieved by 3d Bn, 17th Reg, whose elements eventually captured Pike's Peak. On the 19th, the enemy again counterattacked with six companies and re-took Pike's Peak. He then continued to attack friendly positions successfully until he depleted readily available troops.[27]

Instead of two battalions and five days of combat and 200 casualties, Smith had committed nine of his ten infantry battalions to the battle, suffered 2,000 casualties, and left the Chinese in possession of Pike's Peak. The battle for Triangle Hill was the largest and bloodiest of 1952.[28]

During Operation *Showdown*, on October 14, 2d Co dispatched a combat patrol tasked with inflicting maximum casualties on the enemy. The patrol, call-sign "Derb," was led by Lt. Admassu. It consisted of a fifteen-man assault group and support element at platoon strength. The homesick troops had chosen "*Sigga Wott*" (meaning beef stew) as their password. The patrol departed at 1850. At around 2105, it was engaged by an estimated 35 enemy in an exchange that lasted fifteen minutes. The patrol returned fire and called in artillery support causing the enemy to withdraw with two confirmed and an estimated

three killed. When Lt. Admassu returned to base, he was ordered to take his patrol back out and to contact the enemy. The patrol returned to no-man's land.

On the 19th, an enemy platoon probed the right flank of 2d Co in a fight that lasted sixteen minutes. Stiff resistance from friendly units ultimately forced the enemy to withdraw. The Ethiopians inflicted 14 casualties on the enemy to their one wounded. Kagnew was put on alert to counterattack and/or reinforce in case the enemy penetrated Hill 598, Jane Russell or Sandy.

That attack would not occur until the 23rd, when the enemy launched "the third and final" major counterattack after having received reinforcements. He was repulsed by the American defenders without the need for Kagnew reinforcements. On October 25, the ROK 2d Division relieved US 7th Division on the objective.

On October 23, elements of 4th Co under Capt. Belte Haille, were on a finger guarding a flank on Triangle Hill and US infantrymen on the crest. As usual, the Communist assault was preceded by a 15 minute artillery preparation. Then three companies of enemy from Pike's Peak charged the two Ethiopian platoons and got within 150 yards. One of the platoon leaders was wounded and forcibly evacuated. A sergeant and corporal successively assumed command until they too were wounded.[29][30]

Lieutenant Colonel Asfaw "left the safety of the command post and moved forward under an intense artillery and mortar barrage to observe [and direct] the action" personally. He ordered Sgt. Worku Wondemu, "renowned for his leadership among the men," to take command. Worku jumped into the fray and started encouraging and organizing the defenders, while also assuming the duties of the wounded radio operator.[31] "Realizing the gravity of the situation, Colonel [Asfaw] ordered all available headquarters personnel, including cooks, clerks, and drivers to reinforce the position." He ordered his men to hold the position "till you've fired your last bullet. Hold on till death."[32]

Asfaw then ordered Capt. Bekele Maleaku's 2d Co to reinforce 4th Co. When the Chinese tried to overrun the position again, Asfaw brought down indirect fire within twenty-five yards of the friendly position. The combined onslaught from the artillery and the small arms fire from the defenders forced the enemy to retreat after the sixth and final charge. Forty-five enemy were killed and 35 wounded.[33] [34]

Lieutenant Colonel Asfaw was awarded the Silver Star for his gallantry. Sgt. Worku was awarded the Bronze Star for Valor. Pvt. Araya Ekubayegezi, a medic, was awarded the Bronze Star for Valor for exposing himself to heavy hostile fire while administering first aid to his wounded comrades in the open. On his way back after helping evacuate these men, he "observed that the platoon was in danger of encirclement" so he took it upon himself to "move from position to position encouraging [the others] and directing" their efforts.

1st Battalion/32d Regiment records show a journal entry for October 29 which stated, "Bn CO mutiny at EEFK Bn at 1330." This is a peculiar notation as there is no other mention or explanation of the incident in official army records. No Ethiopian veteran has been able to shed light on it. On the American side Sgt. Irwin Braun recounted a similar incident. General Paul F. Gorman who as a 1st Lt. in 1st Bn/32d Rgt served as S-2 and S-3 during October 1952, vaguely referenced an incident involving a foreign contingent in his writing.

General Gorman wrote:

Just as an example, during one violent UN assault, the nine US battalions of an American division were thrown into the attack, and were being shot to bits by a rigid Chinese defense. On the third day of the battle, the division commander had only two battalions uncommitted. One of these was a US unit which had led the initial assault, and had lost 40% of its men and a great deal of its equipment. The other was a fresh, unused foreign battalion. The commander of the latter refused to allow his troops to enter the zone of action, for his unit was an elite group from a small country, and were it to be shot away, his career would be forfeit. Significantly enough, the US general acceded, and the battered American unit took up the assault once more.[35]

As stated earlier, the 7ID had committed nine of its ten infantry battalions during Operation *Showdown* but that operation began on October 14, so the third day would have been October 16. The incident referenced in the 1st Battalion, 32d Regiment records allegedly occurred on or about October 29. Furthermore, 7ID had another foreign battalion – the Colombian Battalion was attached to the US 31st Regiment.

Sergeant Irwin Braun of Brooklyn, New York, was studying graphic arts at New York City College of Technology when he was drafted. Based on his background as an artist he was assigned to the 32d Regiment S-2 section. He worked with the Ethiopian liaison officers at the front and even provided sketches of a Chinese held hill complex for Brigadier General S.L.A. Marshall during the general's visit to Korea.[36]

Braun stated, in October 1952, "some general got the bright idea that we outta take the Triangle Hill complex" in what could be the last UN offensive.

The 32 Regiment started to attack and before we knew it, the whole division was thrown into the attack. I was on Triangle Hill drawing enemy positions. The hill was captured by friendly forces then taken by the enemy and then recaptured by friendlies… and the

hill switched hands like that over two days. On one of the nights, everybody was being thrown into the battle: cooks, mechanics, etc. So Maj. Mitchell (Regimental S-3) called Lt. Col. Asfaw from the Ops bunker and ordered the Ethiopian battalion to counterattack. Asfaw replied that he would defend the hill to the death but will not counterattack. Maj. Mitchell hanged up the field telephone. He just turned to me and said, 'What do I do? I can't court-martial him.'[37]

Obedience to lawful orders is the bedrock of military discipline. But what if that order, despite being lawful, is tactically unsound or even unnecessarily costly? The system only works if subordinates' duty to carry out orders is balanced with the responsibility commanders have to ensure the sacrifices their orders entail are not gratuitous or excessive. Officers like Asfaw Andargue might have to question or even refuse some orders at the risk of their careers or even their lives since mutiny in a time of war is a capital offense.

General Anthony Zinni, former CINC of US Central Command, in his book *Battle Ready* discusses an officer's responsibility to speak truth to power. He points out how men who "bravely faced death on the battlefield" are sometimes "cowed and unwilling… to point out what is wrong." He wrote about "the chateau generals of World War One who sent hundreds of thousands of fine young men to useless deaths." [38]

Lieutenant General Gregory Newbold resigned from his position as Director of Operations (J-3) for the Joint Chief of Staff partly in protest to the US Defense Department's and Secretary Donald Rumsfeld's handling of the planning for the Iraq War. General Harold K. Johnson, who served as Army Chief of Staff during the Vietnam War, recounted sitting in his staff car on the way to the White House with his stars in hand contemplating resignation over the President's mobilization policy. He reattached the stars to his epaulet and carried out his duties. But he would later state, "I should have resigned." "It was the worst, the most immoral decision I've ever made."[39]

Sergeant Irwin Braun summed up the incident by saying,

At the time I thought maybe the Ethiopians had lost their nerve but now I know the Ethiopians were right. [Asfaw] was not going to waste his men on this battle. Maybe he had promised Emperor Haile Selassie that he would bring alive as many of his men as possible. But our officers did not have a problem sending their troops to die.[40]

The 2d ROK Division relieved the 7th Division, but could not hold the position which was ultimately taken back by the Chinese. Hallock did not blame the South Koreans for the loss as they had suffered 5,000 casualties on Sniper's Ridge and Triangle Hill, in addition to the 2,000 American losses. He concluded, "We probably would have lost it too… It can be defended only at prohibitive cost."[41]

In fact, the fighting in the Ethiopian sector had been so severe during the period of October 29 through November 3, the battalion was later awarded a US Presidential Unit Citation.

Private Germa Shibeshi who was manning a position during one of the enemy attacks on October 30 refused to take cover and "poured accurate, deadly rifle fire into the enemy ranks." Even after he was seriously wounded, he "refused evacuation and medical attention until the attack had been repulsed." Pvt. Tadesse Woldehana, on the other hand, "continually exposed himself to mortar and automatic weapon fire to care for and evacuate wounded comrades." Pvt. Demetu Aregayegn did his part by "maintaining communications with all parts of the battalion. Disregarding his own personal safety, [he] joined in the fighting and aided his comrades in repulsing the enemy until he was seriously wounded." All three were awarded Bronze Star Medals for Valor.

Second Lt. Robert F. Ensslin Jr reported to the 7th Division artillery in October 1952 and was assigned as a FO (Forward Observers) and was sent to an OP – a 4th Company, Kagnew Battalion position a mile in front of the MLR.[42] Ensslin met his first Ethiopian near the top of the hill. As he came around a corner in the trenchline, he was greeted by a bayonet leveled at his neck. The sentry realized who he was and backed off. Ensslin made an important observation. At their request, the Ethiopian troops had been issued the World War II bayonet, "which was a 14 inch bayonet which was considerably longer than what [US troops were issued]. And they just liked the bayonets. They liked their knives. They would sit around and sharpen them all day."[43] Bob

North Korean troops in winter uniforms. (via Tom Cooper)

Ensslin thought the Ethiopians were fierce fighters. He thanked his lucky stars that he was with them. He said, "I was important to them. They weren't going to let anything happen to me, because I was their artillery fire." He further spoke of how they did not have any prisoners taken. He said, "Well, it was just drilled into them that they didn't surrender.... And so the battalion was expected to die rather than come back in disgrace or rather than to surrender and become prisoners."[44] Ensslin said, "The Chinese didn't like to mess with them."[45]

October was an especially costly month for the 7th Division; it suffered more than 2,000 battle casualties between October 14 and 25. Kagnew started October with 1,248 men. During the month, they had four killed and 18 wounded. In addition, 185 soldiers were rotated out. On October 6, the USNS *General S. D. Sturgis* made a stop in Yokohama to pick up 21 medical evacuees and two days later stopped at Pusan to pick up the 185 rotatees going home.

November 1952

At 1840 on October 31, 2d Co observed two companies of Communist troops advancing toward its position. The company immediately began receiving small arms and automatic fire. That was followed by an intense artillery prep intended to soften 2d Co and 4th Co. Then came the assault by a battalion of Communist troops moving in three columns. The Ethiopians defended their position in a hand-to-hand battle that lasted an hour. While some enemy troops were able to penetrate inside the wire, most were repulsed. At 2330, after three unsuccessful assaults, the enemy broke contact but remained in the area placing sporadic harassing fire on friendly positions until 0030.

In the end, seven bunkers were destroyed with four Ethiopian troops killed and 19 wounded. Three US servicemen were also wounded. The enemy suffered 67 KIA and 50 WIA. The Kagnew's Heavy Weapons Company expended 187 rounds of 81mm mortar, 97 rounds of 60mm mortar, and 24,000 rounds of .30 cal and .50 cal ammunition. The 1st Bn, which was also supporting the Ethiopians, expended 800 rounds of 81mm mortar and 18,000 rounds of .30 cal

and .50 cal ammo. The regiment's sector was hit with more than 2,100 rounds of artillery and mortar.

The Regimental S-2 praised Kagnew for demonstrating "outstanding proficiency in the use of patrols to provide early warning and help break up enemy attacks on night of November 1-2." He elaborated, "On this night, the Ethiopians dispatched two patrols, one from 1st Company on the left and one from the 2d Company in the center. In addition a patrol from the Regiment I&R [Intelligence & Reconnaissance] platoon was placed in rear of enemy positions." Between 2015 and 2030, all three patrols reported enemy movement in the vicinity of Hill 400. The patrols were ordered to find the enemy's flank, and once the patrols replied with the information, the enemy was taken under artillery fire.

On November 1, at 2247, 2d Company was again the target of intense artillery prep. Two companies of Communists followed on the heels of the artillery and attacked the position. After 30 minutes of fighting, the enemy was repulsed. At 2325 another round of softening up started. This time it lasted five minutes. Again the enemy troops at company strength tried to swarm the defenders. But the friendly patrols, who previously called in effective artillery fire on the advancing enemy, came to the rescue. They provided the information to rain down more punishment on the Communists. Even though the enemy had made a slight penetration into 2d Co positions, "the weakened attackers were ejected at 2345."

At 2350 the enemy launched a three-pronged attack with a company in the center against the 2d Co area, and platoon on each flank [part of the attack might have been directed towards right flank of 1st Co], but the patrols continuously fed information to friendly artillery which halted the flanking units before they reached the friendly positions. The center column penetrated the 2d Co area but was promptly repulsed with bayonets. As the enemy was withdrawing at 0030, it was still receiving artillery fire that was being directed by friendly patrols which maintained contact. 1st Co and 2d Co continued to get shelled for a couple of hours after the engagement ended.

The Regimental S-2 who praised Kagnew for its "outstanding proficiency in the use of patrols… on night of 1-2 November" was Maj. Richard Hallock of New Jersey. Hallock was a 32-year-old paratrooper who had served in the 82d Airborne Division during WWII. After the war, he was personal aide to the top US officer in occupied Germany. He then served as a staff officer in the states before arriving in Korea in October of 1952. Hallock had pleaded for a field slot with a line unit. He got his wish and was made intelligence officer for the 32d Regiment, but his real desire was to command a battalion. In his capacity as regimental S-2, Hallock worked closely with the battalions in the regiment and was fond of the Ethiopians who he thought were "better than our US battalions." He became friends with Colonel Asfaw.[46]

Hallock explained the action in Korea, "[Troopers] spent the day hunkered down in the trenches and dugouts commanding the high ground. At night the war moved into the valleys where patrols hunted each other in no-man's land. The trick involved getting into the choice ambush positions before the other guys."[47]

There were five enemy probes of friendly positions in the 7ID sector in November. Three such probes were directed against the EEFK. On November 2, a 3d Co reinforced platoon supported by a squad proceeded to Hill 400. The patrol received fire 50 yards away from the objective. The platoon reinforced by the support element pressed forward and took the objective. The Ethiopians entered the Communist trenches and engaged the enemy in close combat. At 2111 the enemy was forced to flee from his own position and the hill was occupied by friendly forces. The enemy immediately counterattacked with an estimated two platoons up the north side of Hill 400. At 2116, the enemy fired one yellow flare from Hill 419 and an estimated 60 Communists counterattacked again. The two sides tangled again inside the trenches and bunkers. The patrol called in artillery support and began to withdraw. The enemy fired one green and one red flare from the north slope of Hill 400 and pursued the patrol with two separate elements moving down on either side of Hill 400. At 2130 the pursuers were stopped by the support element of the patrol using small arms, machineguns, grenades and mortar fire. The patrol counted five enemy KIA and seven WIA. However estimated casualties were believed to be heavy. Six bunkers were also destroyed on Hill 400. The Ethiopians had one KIA and three WIA. The company runner, Pvt. Bellete Tafesse, was awarded a Bronze Star Medal for Valor for breaking the cardinal rule of military service of never volunteering, by offering to go on several patrols and on this date engaging the enemy in hand-to-hand combat.

During the months of November and December, the enemy launched a series of brutal attacks on UN positions. They seized an outpost in front of US 3d Infantry Division on November 6. "Shortly after this success, the Chinese made an attempt to break through the defenses of… the Ethiopian Battalion. After a brief fire fight the enemy withdrew leaving 131 of his dead around the Ethiopians' positions."[48]

The battalion was planning to host a party in honor of the 22nd anniversary of the coronation of Emperor Haile Selassie. They invited the top brass including Lt. Gen. James Van Fleet (Eighth Army commander) and Maj. Gen. Wayne C. Smith (7th Division Commander). Neither Asfaw nor Hallock "thought much of their division commander" who was widely regarded as an officer unqualified for combat command and who had secured his position through political connections despite a background in logistics. The failure of Operation *Showdown* did not help his cause. The two friends – Asfaw and Hallock – decided to play a prank on Smith at the party. "Dick asked Asfaw to order his cook to make the serving [of traditionally spicy Ethiopian food] offered to Smith particularly

blistering knowing it would be an insult to the Ethiopians if the general never finished the plate. Meanwhile, the other members of the party would receive tamer versions." On the holiday, after some drinks, it was time for lunch. "Everything went better than planned. Even though Smith looked like something out of a cartoon—eyes spinning and smoke coming out his ears—he could do nothing but force down his liberal portion."[49]

On November 9, a platoon each from 1st Co and 4th Co departed MLR at 1835 with the mission of raiding targets in the vicinity of Hill 400. The support elements for both patrols were in position by 1920. Both assault elements slipped onto the objective. When 1st Co attacked, the enemy responded as if someone had kicked the hornet's nest. They poured out of the bunkers and engaged the patrol in the trenches. 1st Co blew up seven bunkers and started to withdraw but they discovered they were quietly surrounded by an estimated 80 enemy. The patrol fought ferociously to break out of the encirclement. After 20 minutes, the patrol managed to punch through. They withdrew toward 4th Co which was providing accurate covering fire. All friendly troops, including the four wounded, left together under cover of friendly indirect fire. The enemy suffered five KIA and an additional estimated four KIA and 25 WIA.

Between the 11th and 13th, 32d Regiment was relieved. The division transferred responsibility of this sector and Triangle Hill area to 25ID and went into Eighth Army reserve in Kapyong. Kagnew suffered nine KIA and 60 WIA in November.

December 1952

The Bayonet Division spent almost the entire month of December in Eighth Army reserve. It continued the training program initiated in November. Dwight Eisenhower, who had campaigned for the presidency of the United States partly on a platform of ending the war in Korea, won by a landslide. On December 2, 1952, the former five-star general and president-elect traveled to Korea to fulfill his campaign promise of observing the situation first-hand. Upon his arrival, he was greeted by honor guards from each foreign contingent. The Ethiopian honor guard was led by 2d Lt. Yilma Belachew who remembers seeing the president.[50]

On Christmas day the Ethiopians enjoyed a turkey and fixings flavored with hot sauce and peppers. They then held religious services followed by a traditional game of "*Genna*" – field hockey. Other UN contingents also passed the day by trying to bring a little bit of home to the frontlines.[51]

On December 26, the troops were moved to Sindang-ni by rail and trucks to relieve 2ID. The 7th Division assumed responsibility for a 12,000m front on Line Jameson across from elements of 38th and 47th CCF Armies, which consisted of a total of 12 infantry battalions supported by 15 artillery battalions.

On the night of December 29, the enemy hit an outpost of the Thai Battalion as they were waiting to be relieved by Kagnew. The Thais repulsed the attack. The next day, the Ethiopians were surely startled when an unidentified Asian male approached their position. It turned out to be a Thai soldier who had hidden in the bushes overnight after his position was overrun.

Kagnew had 74 officers, 18 warrant officers and 860 enlisted men. The battalion did not suffer any casualties during the month.

Juan Raigoza was a Mexican-American officer from Los Angeles who served as an infantry officer during WWII. During Korea he re-commissioned as an artillery officer and volunteered for service with the 7th Infantry Division. He reported to Brig. Gen. O'Meara, Commander of 7th Division Artillery sometime in mid-1952. Captain Raigoza joined the general at breakfast and asked for bacon, eggs and

Kagnew and US Military Police. (US Army)

Tabasco sauce. "O'Meara eyed him for a second and said, 'I know where I'm going to send you.'" [52]

When Captain Raigoza reported in to be the artillery liaison officer to the Kagnew Battalion, Lt. Col. Asfaw remarked,

"You're not American," after gazing at him for a moment.

"Sir, I'm American – we're from all over the world: Scandinavia, Europe, Africa, South America, Canada, Asia, Central America."

"But you don't look like an American. What nationality are you? When did you come to the States?"

"My ancestors came from Mexico at the turn of the century..."

"Ah – Mexico. Mexico is our friend. When the Italians invaded Ethiopia in 1936, Mexico was one of very few nations in the old League of Nations to stand up for Ethiopia and loudly protest the Italian invasion as aggression. They demanded the League take prompt action to stop the aggression. The Mexicans will always be our friends. You will always be our friend." [53]

Capt. Juan Raigoza was interviewed about his Ethiopian friends by Stars and Stripes newspaper on more than one occasion. When he was asked about their shyness, he replied, "They don't like to talk about their battles. They don't like the cold. And they don't like the Communists,' 'They are very good in combat,' he added with the pride of one who belongs to a crack outfit." He told the reporter to ask one of the officers why they are good and the Ethiopian officer who would not give his name said, "We don't like to have our names in the paper… Traditionally our soldiers defend their posts to the last drop of their life blood. When we fought at Triangle hill in the fall that was done many times." He added, "We also like to use bayonets. We are best at hand-to-hand fighting, and our men prefer it. Most of them have had five years' fighting experience during World II against the Italians in Africa." [54]

January 1953

At the start of the New Year the division was still defending Line Jamestown. In the Buccaneers' sector, 1st, 3d and EEFK Battalions were on the line with 2d Battalion in reserve.

On January 12, 4th Co was tasked with a raiding Hill 180 for prisoners. But that mission was re-assigned to 3d Co. At 1930, that 30-man combat patrol from 3d Co departed for the hill moving cautiously due to limited visibility. To make matters worse, Maj. Hallock (the regimental S-2) whose intel section had been intercepting Communist radio communications, determined the enemy was also intercepting radio traffic. At 2230, the raiding party reported closing within 200 yards of the objective with no contact.

The patrol arrived on the objective at 2310 and slipped into the enemy trenches. Twenty Communists immediately engaged the patrol. They fought hand-to-hand for 15 minutes. One of the Ethiopians was wounded and two Communists laid dead. When enemy reinforcements started rushing in from Hill 190, friendly artillery was

US Army troops on the 'Old Baldy' Hill, in 1952. (US Army)

called in to disperse them. Lacking reinforcements, the defenders on the hill retreated. With one of the enemy wounded in tow, the patrol withdrew from the hill having inflicted five KIA to their two WIA, and an additional 15 estimated KIA and 25 WIA. Unfortunately their prisoner died on the way. The patrol was ordered back to the objective but five minutes later that order was rescinded and the patrol started back to friendly lines.

In January, the enemy also signaled it was coming out of its defensive posture. A fifteen-man outpost on the right flank of 1st Company was probed around the same time. An enemy platoon was advancing towards the 1st Co position when it was detected by listing posts. The attackers were driven-off by artillery and mortars, but only momentarily. They returned in two platoon strength and engaged the outpost. The Ethiopian officers had fortunately reinforced the outpost with a platoon. The enemy penetrated the position and hand-to-hand fighting ensured. After two hours, the enemy was ejected by determined resistance. The Communists suffered an estimated 15 KIA and 18 WIA.

On the 20th, a ten-man combat patrol from 2d Co engaged an enemy force twice its size and inflicted an estimated seven casualties. The next night, a twelve-man patrol from 1st Co was also hit by a bigger force. The enemy withdrew with an estimated seven casualties. On January 23, a ten-man patrol from 2d Co engaged an enemy platoon in a 45-minute firefight. The enemy took the brunt of it with 12 casualties. Kagnew suffered two WIA.

On the night of January 24, a Kagnew patrol was tasked with raiding an objective. The assault element of a 2d Co platoon size patrol departed at 2111 for Hill 190. It started receiving enemy mortars from Hill 222 within minutes. Then ten minutes following the assault group, a support element left the wire. At the same time, the assault element of a 1st Co patrol set-off into no-man's land towards Hill 180. Sure enough, it started drawing machinegun fire from Hill 180 and Hill 185 but the patrol weathered the enemy barrage and started advancing on the objective.

The Communists fired a green signal flare from Hill 190 causing the 2d Co patrol to start being raked with small arms and automatic weapons fire from Hill 180 and Hill 190 as it moved forward. Meanwhile 1st Co reached its objective and engaged an unknown number of enemy in a 20-minute sporadic gunfight. 2d Co reached the objective at 2150 and swept the area without encountering any resistance. As fortune was smiling on 2d Co, she had turned her back on 1st Co. That patrol got hit by enemy reinforcements and an intense battle ensued. The two sides clashed in bloody hand-to-hand fighting inside the trenches. Eventually the enemy retreated with casualties, and all the patrol could find was destroyed trenches.

The Communists started dropping smoke on the hill and the astute patrol leader orders his men to get into defensive positions. At 2345, the 2d Co patrol started off toward Hill 180 to reinforce their comrades. As the two patrols completed the linkup at 0030, even more enemy reinforcement arrived and encircled the outnumbered Ethiopians. Then another fierce battle broke out. It lasted for 30 minutes. At 0250, 20 men from 3d Co arrived to reinforce the battered patrols and forced the enemy to break contact and withdraw.

As the three friendly elements were making their way back to the line, one group got lost. Maj. Hallock personally went up in a light aircraft to conduct an aerial reconnaissance. He directed the pilot to make several circles at extremely low altitude (between fifty to five hundred feet) in the vicinity of Pokkae. Despite his best efforts, Hallock was unable to visually locate the patrol but he managed to guess where they might be and although "he was prevented from signaling for fear of giving away their position to the enemy," he instructed the pilot to

call in a fire mission and smoke to cover their withdrawal". The plan stayed in the air "for forty-five minutes directing the fire mission— all the while taking small arms fire". The lost patrol eventually made its way back to American lines. Maj. Hallock was awarded the Air Medal.[55]

When the Kagnew patrols returned to the MLR at 0343, they reported one of their fallen comrades was left on the battlefield. At 0435, Maj. Kebede Tesema, the battalion X.O., asked for volunteers and organized a search party to rescue the missing man and personally led it back to the area where the previous night's fighting had taken place. He located the "body of the missing man on the forward slope of the enemy position." He directed his men to lay down covering fire and personally "advanced under a heavy concentration of enemy fire" to recover the body. Having maintained the Kagnew record unblemished, he led his rescue force back to friendly lines. He was awarded a Silver Star for his gallantry and leadership. After a brutal night of fighting, Kagnew had 4 dead and 18 wounded. The Communists had 16 KIA and an estimated 18 WIA.

On January 30, Kagnew was relieved at night by 2d Bn and went into regimental reserve. The battalion with an average strength of 936 (90 officers and 846 enlisted men) for the month, suffered six KIA and 43 WIA.

February 1953

In February the Bayonet Division started its second month of defense on Line Jamestown covering the left sector of I Corps. The 32d Regiment was on the MLR with Kagnew in reserve. However, the Ethiopian companies were attached to other units and put on the line.

On February 25, a platoon from 4th Co was ordered to raid Hill 180 to bring back a prisoner. The 30-man party left at 0500. Near the objective, ten men stayed behind to form a perimeter while the main assault force of 20 advanced. At 0620 the assault element arrived on the objective and after encountering no enemy, called up the support element. The two groups consolidated at 0630. Again, the support group set up a perimeter, while the assault element swept the east finger of Hill 180. The assault element was unknowingly advancing into a trap. The enemy waited until the Kagnew raiders got with 20 yards of their position before unleashing hell. Communists occupying nine bunkers estimated at platoon strength (40 men) opened up with small arms, three machineguns and threw grenades. The patrol fired back with everything.

At the same time the support group was taking machinegun fire from Hill 185 and called for help. A US tank on the MLR silenced the machinegun. An enemy mortar crew went into the open to rain down steel on the patrol. A keen forward observer placed friendly artillery which scored a direct hit. By this point the patrol had suffered one killed and ten wounded. The two elements consolidated but continued to receive all types of fire from different directions including Hill 177 and Hill 190. Friendly artillery was fired in response. Around 0700 the OPLR observed enemy reinforcements pouring in from Hill 204 to the rear slope of Hill 180. Again, artillery was directed with devastating effect. The force was scattered.

At 0715 the patrol was ordered to withdraw. It did so under friendly covering fire and a smoke screen at 0750. In all, more than 1,300 rounds were fired by friendly tank, mortar and artillery units. The enemy suffered 15 KIA and 16 WIA.

The next day, the Buccaneers were relieved by Polar Bears Regiment and closed on Line Wyoming. The Ethiopians were relieved by the Colombians. They had suffered two killed and ten wounded.

During February, the 7th Division dispatched a high number of reconnaissance and combat patrols. These patrols found the enemy to

Second Lts. Berkinesh Kebede and Aster Ayana, Ethiopian nurses.

...e increasingly aggressive in defending his positions. They also found ...t difficult to disengage after making contact as the enemy would ...ttempt to encircle them and/or pursue when they withdrew and there ...was even an increased sighting of enemy armor.

In mid-February, the UNC was informed the Third Kagnew ...attalion would arrive at Inchon sometime in late March or early April ...board the *Blatchford*. The Ethiopian government requested the 1,300 ...otatees and 80 remains be sent to Pusan for the *Blatchford's* return ...rip. The UNC objected on the grounds that the current battalion ...vould need to be retained for at least 40 days until the new battalion ...ompleted its training and got up to speed. In short, the current unit ...vould not be available for rotation until late May.

Colonel Mengistu Neway, the Operations Officer (G-3) for the ...mperial Bodyguard sent additional details about the Third Kagnew ...attalion. He confirmed all of the officers spoke English. About ten ...fficers and almost all squad leaders were Korean veterans who served ...vith the First Kagnew Battalion. The troops had undergone special ...raining given by Ethiopian officers who had experience in Korea. ...he training started with basic individual skills as well as technical ...raining with US weapons and communications equipment. It then ...rogressed to squad, platoon, company and battalion tactical training. ...he NCOs were put through an additional two-month course. Two

female military nurses would also accompany the unit.

Corporal Bulcha Olika of the signal platoon had served with the First Kagnew Battalion. He stayed in Korea partly through the deployment of the Second Kagnew and left for home with the hold-overs in July 1952. He would return to Korea in the spring of 1953 as a member of the Third Kagnew Battalion.

Lieutenant Desta and other officers had visited their wounded troops during trips to the rear area in Korea and while on R&R in Japan. They observed the men were having difficulties communicating with the hospital staff. The Ethiopians often had to resort to communicating with sign language, while other contingents had nurses, if not doctors from their own countries. Upon their return, the officers made suggestions to address this and other deficiencies in everything from how the troops dressed to how they were fed. Desta said their superiors were very receptive and took advantage of the experiences of the junior officers to improve the force. The veterans suggested that Ethiopian nurses be sent to Korea. After the idea was brought before the imperial government, it was decided recent graduates from the Ethiopian Red Cross Nursing School would be sent to Korea, if they were so wiling.

March 1953

By March 4, the 32d Regiment had been relieved from Line Jamestown and was in division reserve. After five days of rehabilitation, the regiment began a 12-day training cycle.

On Saturday, March 7, Captain Simu, and another captain from the battalion visited Col. Farnsworth. According to Farnsworth, the officer reported that the enlisted men of the battalion were extremely tired and their morale was low. The battalion had suffered heavy casualties and the men were required more frequently on patrols than before. The 40-day layover would have an extremely detrimental effect on the battalion. He reiterated the relief battalion was a fully trained part of regular Ethiopian ground forces and therefore should not require more than ten days or two weeks familiarization in Korea.

On March 16, the division requested the 32d Regiment staff to provide a tally of the Ethiopian Battalion's activities since coming on line. The regiment reported, Kagnew first came on line on June 3, [1952] and included the breakdown listed below:

Table 1: Activities of the four battalions under the US 32d Infantry Regiment

	Days On Line	Days In Reserve	No. of Combat Patrols	No. of Recon Patrols
1st Bn	149	137	141	172
2d Bn	156	130	133	160
3d Bn	132	154	175	171
Kagnew	150	136	152	110

This request was probably made in response to the discussion Col. Farnsworth had with the two Ethiopian officers. The command wanted to assess whether the battalion was carrying more than its fair share of the burden. However, it appears the workload and hazards were shared evenly by all four units.

On March 6, a 31st Regiment patrol intercepted an enemy battalion *en route* to attack Pork Chop Hill. During the ensuing engagement a high volume of ordinance was exchanged resulting in 56 enemy confirmed killed, 100 more estimated killed and another 100 estimated wounded. This was perhaps a prelude of what was to come.

Starting around March 20 and lasting for four days, the enemy commenced intense bombardment of the division front with the barrage heavily concentrated around Old Baldy. Then around 2100 hours on March 23, a reinforced enemy battalion attacked Old Baldy; Arsenal was attacked by two companies and Pork Chop was then attacked by a battalion.

The Colombian Battalion as part of the US 31st Infantry Regiment was in the center of the regiment's sector including the Old Baldy outpost. On the night of the March 23, the enemy launched a determined attack which raged all night and into the next day. Waves of reinforcements and supporting armor were sent in and made some progress but were ultimately halted. The main counterattack unit, 1st Bn/32d Reg, was reduced to a fighting force of four officers and 54 enlisted men. On March 30, the Eighth Army commander concluded "that it was not essential to the defense of the sector and directed that no attack to recover it would be executed." Maj. Hallock saw Old Baldy as "a meaningless piece of ground which no doubt will be ours again after suitable bloodletting." This abandonment of the Old Baldy position left the Pork Chop outpost severely exposed.[56]

On March 30, the Ethiopians relieved 2d Bn/17th Rgt and were attached to 17th Rgt.

On March 24, the Third Kagnew Battalion, which had been in training for the last ten months, was inspected by the Emperor and then passed in review. That afternoon the battalion began its journey to Korea by way of Djibouti.[57] The battalion commander was Lt. Col. Woldeyohanis Shitta. He was born sometime around 1918-19 in Cheha Wereda, Shewa Province. He was educated at L'alliance Francaise and *Lycée* Haile Selassie, two French schools in Addis Ababa. He was a cadet at Imperial Bodyguard academy in Genet and after graduation was commissioned as a first lieutenant. He was part of the small contingent sent to reconnoiter the pass at Termaber for a possible last stand against the Italian invaders. When that plan fell apart, he participated in the resistance for four months before being caught and imprisoned for three years and nine months. After liberation he served as a police lieutenant for a year and then returned to the Guard. He was promoted to lieutenant colonel in 1951.

Two 20-year-old female nurses: 2d Lts. Aster Ayana and Berkinesh Kebede would also accompany the battalion. The young ladies had attended the Empress Menen Girls' School and were part of a group of fifteen selected to attend the first nursing school established by the Ethiopian Red Cross Society. Starting in July 1949, the candidates were put through "probationary screening and examination." The nine who passed, attended a three-year nursing program. Right after graduation, Aster and Berkinesh were recruited into the Imperial Bodyguard and started their training under Lieutenant Desta Gemerda, the officer who had served with the First Kagnew and whose older brother was a member of *Tikur Anbessa*. The nurses received instructions in close order drill and pistol marksmanship. Their training was equivalent to that of the US Women's Army Corps (WAC) at that time. Berkinesh recalled there being 11 nursing candidates, even though an Ethiopian Ministry of Education publication stated 15 candidates. [58][59]

A huge crowd gathered in Addis Ababa to see the battalion off, both families and strangers. Berkinesh's family was there. Her grandmother was fretting, but her aunt told her that she was making history and that she should not miss this opportunity. Of course, being young, Berkinesh did not think much of it. She was just excited.[60] Sixty-seven officers and 1,205 men departed Djibouti on the USNS *Blatchford* on the morning of March 26. The nurses were immediately put to work with heat casualties and other illnesses aboard the ship.[61] An advance party consisting of Lt. Col. Woldeyohanis Shitta, (CO), Capt. Tesema Wakgira (S-3), Capt. Zaudie Istifanos (S-4) traveled by air to arrive in Tokyo on March 31.

On March 30, Lt. Col. Asfaw sent a letter to Eighth Army referencing

an earlier letter to the UNC Liaison Section. His frustration is evident as he wrote that the new battalion sufficiently trained in modern military operations and US weapons. He further asserted most of the key officers and NCOs were Korean veterans. He rejected the division plan to retain his battalion for five more weeks while the replacement battalion was trained. Asfaw wanted his unit to be relieved on Apr 24. He wrote, "Since I am the commanding officer of this voluntary force I have no intention to keep my troops more than 12 months in this war theater."

Asfaw's desire for the timely repatriation of his battalion was no extraordinary or unreasonable. The duration of distant campaigns has been an issue for soldiers and their families since ancient times and continues to be so to this day. In both Operation *Enduring Freedom* and Operation *Iraqi Freedom*, the length of combat deployments was a hotly debated issue in American political and military circles. During the height of both wars, Army servicemen were deploying for as long as fifteen months, much to the dismay of their families. In his book *Duty: Memoirs of a Secretary at War*, Secretary of Defense Robert Gates discussed his decision between extending the length of oversea deployments for US troops in Iraq and Afghanistan to fifteen month versus shortening the amount of time they spent at home between deployments. He wrote,

> This was the most difficult decision I would make in my entire time as secretary, difficult because I knew how hard even the one-year deployments were, not only because of the absence from family but because, for those in combat units… the fighting and the stress of combat were constant. There was no respite from primitive living conditions, the heat, and not knowing what the next moment might bring in terms of danger, injury, and death."[62]

During WWII the US Army rotated its troops as a unit. A group of soldiers would train, go into combat and move to the rear together as a cohort. The unit would get individual replacements to make up for combat losses usually while in the rear. In 1951, the Army adopted an individual rotation system based on points. A soldier earned four points for each month served in combat, two points for each month in the rear and three points for service in between (such as divisional reserve). By June 1952, an enlisted soldier was eligible to be rotated home with thirty-six points while an officer needed thirty-seven points. That meant the average American infantryman would spend nine months in a combat zone. Soldiers were so pre-occupied with calculating their points, it practically became the main pastime in Korea.[63]

The personnel policy was one of the biggest problems plaguing the Eighth Army according to Maj. Richard Hallock. In a letter home, he wrote, "Division and corps commanders are here for short periods;" many with non-combat arms backgrounds were there to get their "ticket punched." He added, "soldiers and officers' attitude all infected by rotation." He characterized the new captains coming into the regiment as "mostly court martial and/or reclassification bait and the lieutenants were newly-minted straight out of OCS or ROTC. Operation *Showdown* and the subsequent Operation *Smack* were dismal failures which resulted in needless casualties.[64]

In another letter Hallock wrote, "I have never seen anything like it. If I didn't know better I would conclude that the army is rotten to the core….certainly rotten in Korea." Hallock characterized the new regiment commander as "…chronically incapable of making decision—a complete middle-grade Pentagon administration type who appeared to have little interest in "the welfare of any [member of the regiment]." The futility of taking ground only to relinquish it after aving paid such a high cost was also corrosive to morale. No one including the Ethiopian battalion was impervious to these factors.[65]

The Second Kagnew Battalion arrived in Korea in two increments: ne group around early April and another in early July. Meaning, the roops would have been in Korea thirteen and ten months respectively. aced with such persistent requests from Lt. Col. Asfaw, the American rass decided to shorten the overlap and release the old unit as soon s practicable.

The battalion did not suffer any battle casualties for the month.

April 1953

At the beginning of April, the 7th Division was on Line Jamestown on he eastern flank of the I Corps sector. By April 2, the 32d Regiment vas on right side of the division sector with Kagnew Battalion in the enter of the regiment's sector.

The offensive activity of the division centered around dispatching ggressive patrols, until the enemy launched major but unsuccessful ttacks against three friendly MLR and OPLR positions starting on April 16 in what is referred to as the first Battle of Pork Chop Hill. The oss of Old Baldy in late March had left Pork Chop vulnerable. The ttacks were thought to have three primary motivations including: eizing and holding key terrain, discovering strength and location f friendly defenses, and to gain combat experience for green eplacements. Alligator Jaw, Pork Chop and Dale were the focal points of the enemy attacks. The most significant contact occurred between April 16 and 17, when Communist forces attacked outposts on Arsenal, Yoke and Upper Alligator.

Major Hallock observed Line Jamestown was "a mess. Fighting positions, constructed by a succession of tenants over a year and a half, occupied the bald hills like little fortresses. None had been laid out in any systematic fashion and most had horrible fields of fire." He noted deficiencies with the sandbagging, and the wire defense and called the outposts "death traps." Therefore, the CG, General Arthur Trudeau who was a combat engineer began an extensive rehabilitation of the 7th Division position. New fighting positions were constructed and existing bunkers were improved. Additionally, trench networks were widened and deepned.[66]

On the 16th, the *Blatchford* docked into the port of Pusan carrying Greek, Dutch and Ethiopian troops. They were greeted by Lt. Col. Woldeyohanis Shitta and liaison officers from the other two contingents. The Ethiopians again arrived clad in khaki shorts.[67] The two nurses were transported separately by car and given lodging. They stayed in Pusan for 26 days where they continued to provide care for the troops at field hospitals. They were then transferred to their permanent assignments; Aster went to the Tokyo Main Hospital while Berkinesh was assigned to the Tokyo Hospital Annex.[68]

The armistice talks in Panmunjom resumed in April 1953, after having been terminated in October 1952.

3

THIRD KAGNEW BATTALION

On April 21, the Third Kagnew Battalion (with 65 officers, 36 warrant officers and 1,165 enlisted men) arrived in the rear assembly area of he 32d Regiment sector, and the next day relieved the Second Kagnew on the MLR and OPLR positions. As the old battalion moved to the ear to prepare for its departure, the new battalion started gearing up. On April 24, it commenced a training program which was scheduled o end by May 9. The program would emphasize weapons training, specially with 81mm mortars, 57mm and 75mm recoilless rifles. They would also undergo instructions in small unit action, patrols nd raids. On the technical side, communications, especially the use f radios, would be covered.

Second Lieutenant Abebe Gebreyes was the commander of the 75mm recoilless rifle platoon in the Heavy Weapons Company of the Third Kagnew Battalion. The Heavy Weapons Company consisted of a platoon each of heavy machineguns, 81mm mortars and 75mm recoilless rifles. While the infantry companies had their own 60mm mortars and light machineguns, members of the weapons company were attached to the other companies to provide serious firepower.[1]

The 75mm recoilless rifle was a breach-loaded, direct-fire, crew-served weapon used in the Korean War, primarily as a bunker buster. It had an effective range of about seven kilometers. Members of the Third Kagnew trained with it in Ethiopia under the direction of the First Kagnew veterans. Lieutenant Abebe's platoon was assigned four such weapons per the TO&E, but they would sometimes crew six or seven such weapons including pieces assigned to a specific sector of the front.[2]

Abebe Gebreyes was born in 1921 in Addis Ababa. To address a shortage of leaders during the post-war era, government officials went around the schools and without taking the students' wishes into account started conscripting young men into the officer corps. They took Abebe and about 10 of his friends from Arbegoch School and enrolled them into the second cadet course at the Imperial Bodyguard Academy. After completing the three-year course, Abebe was retained as instructor for the third cadet course. That allowed him to further develop his military skills. He and his peers still in Ethiopia expected to eventually go to Korea since two battalions had already seen action. After a one-year stint at the academy, he was selected for the Third Kagnew Battalion and began training as a unit. The First Kagnew Battalion which had rotated home by then was busy passing on the costly lessons learned on the Korean battlefield to the new battalion on deck.[3] Early on during familiarization training in Korea, a hand grenade explosion injured 2d Lt. Abebe in the knee. He was evacuated to a mobile hospital unit where the fragments were removed. He made a full recovery and return to duty in eight days.[4]

On April 25, Lt. Col. Woldeyohanis Shitta, who arrived at the front around April 5, officially took charge of Ethiopian combat forces in Korea. That day and the next, the CG visited the Ethiopians to see off the departing troops as well as welcome the new ones.

Casualties for the month were four wounded in action.

On April 26, the two sides returned to the negotiating table at Panmunjom, ending six months of silence. They agreed to an exchange of sick and wounded prisoners, resulting in the repatriation of 6,670 Communists and 684 UN personnel under Operation *Little Switch*.[5]

Also on April 26, the *Blatchford* sailed from the Far East carrying the Second Kagnew Battalion.

The Second Kagnew Battalion was greeted in Addis Ababa with huge fanfare. They disembarked at the Legehar train station and paraded through the city sweating all the way up Churchill Road

Private Gabremicail Tumebo visiting the UN after losing a leg in Korea, May 1953. (UN photo)

and around to the Imperial Palace. Crowds filled both sides of the streets and waited in anticipation. Just like when they left, relatives were pulling on them and calling their names along the way. They were brought into a large hall at the palace where the Emperor went around and spoke to every single person. He would ask, "Why don't you eat? Don't you like this food (Is this not agreeable)? Try this." Melesse Tessema said the Emperor already knew which individuals had done something special and had studied them and he would go to that person and hug them around the neck and say, "You did this… you're a hero…" After the banquet, the soldiers collected their medals and went home.[6]

From what he was told, Wongele Costa was born around 1933. He had an Ethiopia mother and a Greek father whom he never met and had two younger brothers who died at an early age. As a result of some general unrest in Addis Ababa, he was sent to live with an uncle in Sululta approximately 40km from the capital. One day, a young Wongele was struck by lightning and was given up for dead and almost buried. But the family decided to wait and see and he made a miraculous recovery.[7]

Upon returning to Addis Ababa, he progressed through traditional church schooling and later Tafari Makonnen School. He then attended Tegbareid for three years earning and received his diploma from the Emperor's hand. He was then recruited into the Imperial Bodyguard cadet school, took the entrance exam and passed. He was commissioned a second lieutenant after completing the second course.[8] When the Third Kagnew Battalion was initially organized, Wongele was not selected as a member. Fortunately for him, when one of the platoon leaders could not go, he was chosen to replace him and was assigned to lead 1st Platoon, 2d Company.[9]

After the Third Kagnew arrived at the front, 2d Company, including

2d Lt. Wongele, had spent a night with elements of the Second Kagnew in the trenches for some quick on-the-job training. The next day they briefly went to the rear and soon returned to the frontline position to assume responsibility for that sector.[10] Second Lieutenant Wongel was the first member of the Second Kagnew to be assigned a mission He was ordered to conduct an ambush patrol. He did not believe h was picked for any particular reason, just that he had the first platoon in the company. He said, "This was our first time in war. We were s young, every time a bullet was fired, we thought it was going to hi us."[11]

Heavy clouds cast a dark blanket over the front on the evening o April 28, greatly reducing visibility. Despite the unfavorable weathe conditions, at 2000, 2d Lt. Wongele and his 20 soldiers started th descent into enemy territory, walking single file, hand-in-hand, t ensure no one got lost or separated. Exhibiting incredible speed an strict radio discipline, they reached their objective at the Alligator' Jaw 4,000 yards away by 2018.[12]

Wongele then split his men into two. An assault group of ter armed with nine M1s and one carbine took the high ground on hill 30 feet above the valley floor. Each man carried four grenades The group also had one radio, one sound powered phone and flare for communication. Cpl. Raffi Degene was in charge of this group.[1 Wongele then organized a support group of seven men where an irrigation ditch, which was protected by a dirt bank a foot above th ground, made a wide V. He placed "three men faced north on the righ of the turn and four men faced west to left of it." The group was armed with thee M1s, two BARs, two carbines and forty grenades. Cpl. Tiggu Waldetekle was left in charge of the support group.[14]

Wongele placed himself along with his runner and two aid mer halfway between the assault and support groups and was linked to both by phone and with his superiors by phone and radio.[15] Fo six and a half hours, they waited quietly only breaking their silence when Wongele made the hourly report by radio to the company "Everything negative."[16] At 0300, Waldetekle saw his men on the left "pointing vigorously out into the enveloping darkness with their rifles It was the signal that they detected enemy movement." He crawled to them and saw a "clear silhouette standing not more than 20 yard beyond the ditch."[17]

Waldetekle backtracked along the ditch to his patrol leader anc pointed with his rifle. Wongele sent Private Tilahullninguse to signa Degene and his men. The alerts were made at a crawl and withou a sound. Waldetekle crawled back to Wongele again "gesturing stil more vigorously with the rifle" to point out additional Chinese moving in the same direction.[18] "Using hand signals, he told Tilahullninguse to unpin a grenade, crawl down [a shallow gully that ran toward the ditch] and toss a bomb into the enemy group." He hoped to inflic damage on the enemy without giving away his true position and possibly capture a POW.[19]

Tilahullninguse got within 15 yards of the nearest Chinese and tossed his grenade. As it exploded, by its light, Wongele Costa could see about twenty of the enemy lying flat and with weapons pointed straight toward his support group. As darkness settled, the Communists opened up on the support group in the ditch with grenades, rifles and submachineguns. "Before Wongele Costa had time to shout an order, the left wing of the support group had joined the fight full blast, three rifles and the BAR."[20]

Only the support group men on the left wing had line of fire on the enemy and were exchanging fire. Wongele quickly raised the assault group on the sound power phone and told them, "Don't move! Don't fire! Now send a man down to the right flank of the support and give them that same message." Wongele turned to Tilahullninguse and his two aid men and said, "Follow me!" He and his three men crawled to Waldetekle's position pausing every few feet to fire at the enemy.[21]

They jumped into the ditch and filled gaps left by casualties. Waldetekle's right arm was blown off when a grenade bounced off the bank and struck him above the elbow. Without a peep, he passed the BAR to Pvt. Yukonsi with his left hand instructing him, "Fire, and keep it low" and continued to give orders. "Yukonsi triggered the weapon for only a few seconds. Then a burp-gun burst hit him in the left arm, shredding it from wrist to shoulder. The BAR was still in working order. Yukonsi handed it to Tilahullninguse without a word, then collapsed in the ditch unconscious from loss of blood." "On the extreme left of the line, Pvt. Mano Waldemarian took three bullets through his brain but, in the frenzy of the action, no one saw him fall."[22] Wongele Costa ordered the two aid men to take over the grenading as he fired his carbine at full auto into the enemy. The firefight lasted another fifteen minutes with the Ethiopians gaining fire superiority.[23]

A messenger from the assault group crawled down with word from Lt. Col. Woldeyohanis Shitta who was asking, "Shall I send help?" The patrol leader replied, "Tell him no. Tell him I can hold this field with my own men" and resumed defending the position.[24] After they realized they were no longer taking enemy fire, 2d Lt. Wongele called a cease fire. Silence fell on the battlefield again. The patrol took stock of their ammo to learn both the BAR and carbine were empty and the aid men were out of grenades.[25]

Wongele requested a flare from the 48th Field Artillery Battalion and received illumination rounds over his position. He recalled the light making everything very clear and shadows growing as tall as trees. He looked to his rear and saw fifty Chinese troops deployed in skirmish order advancing toward the assault group.[26] Wongele got on the radio and directed artillery fire on the enemy. The rounds arrived in thirty seconds and landed on target smashing the enemy formation. Those who weren't killed or wounded, fled. Even in the dark, Wongele noticed one of his automatic weapons was not firing and sent a soldier to investigate. The soldier, Pvt. Mamo Waldemarian, was found dead with rifle in hand. Wongele Costa crawled over and returned carrying the body and then kept up and even increased the artillery barrage as the enemy tried to reorganize.[27]

Exhibiting remarkable discipline, "Degene's men neither shifted position nor fired a shot… Wongele Costa and assistants had long since returned to their position between the two groups. The aid men had tourniqueted and quieted the wounded. They would have to last it with the others."[28]

At 0430 Colonel Shitta ordered the patrol to withdraw. They counted 22 enemy KIA and estimated at least as many WIA. They closed

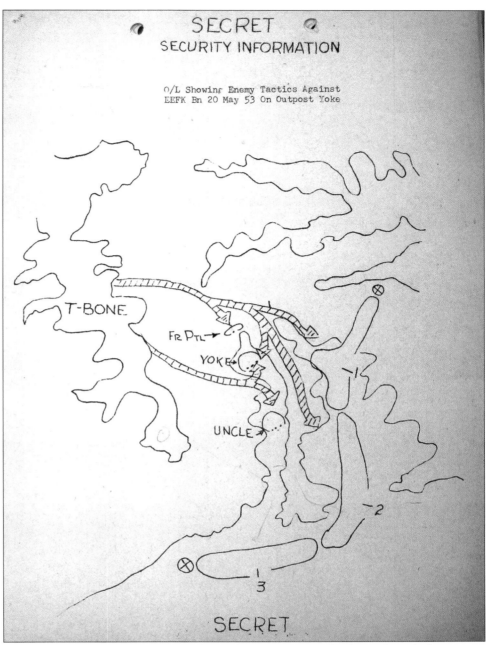

A US Army map depicting the CCF tactics for attack on the Outpost Yoke, during the night from 19 to 20 May 1953. (US Army Historic Division)

on friendly lines at 0535 carrying their dead and wounded. S.L.A. Marshall wrote, "They still looked fresh in the full light of a lovely dawn." Marshall further pointed out this remarkable achievement was by a unit which was getting its first taste of combat.[29] The patrol was debriefed by Marshall as soon as it returned to friendly lines. Wongele attributed his patrol's success in large part to American fire support. He said, "US artillery can shoot at the exact point you request. I asked for them to fire illumination flares to check if the enemy was in the area. The flare made everything clear. We would have been wiped out had it not been for the American artillery."[30]

On the last day of the month General Clark, CINC-UNC, wrote Colonel Woldeyohanis to welcome him to his command. He wrote,

The valor and courage of the Ethiopian soldier is well known to all of your comrades in arms as well as to the enemy… I am fully confident that your regular troops will carry on the splendid combat record of Colonel Asfaw's battalion and will successfully discharge the mission with which His Highness Haile Selassie has

A US Army map depicting patrolling action of the Ethiopian troops around the Outpost Yoke, on 29-30 May 1953. (US Army Historic Division)

When three Communists suddenly ran into an abandoned bunker, assistant squad leader Cpl. Mastin Goangul gave chase hoping to toss a grenade inside. As he approached, the three men came back out. Goangul's rifle jammed so he bayoneted one and "held off the others until several Kagnews came to his aid." He rejoined the patrol with a piece of his ear shot off. In the end, friendly artillery cleared a path back to friendly lines. PFC James Gill, an observer-radioman, said, "While the Chinese were attacking us, the Ethiopians kept howling and yelling to make the Reds think there were more of us. They're smart fighters, these Ethiopians."[31]

On May 2, the division adopted a three-regiment front with two battalions on line and the rest in regimental reserve and division reserve. On May 19, 1953, the Ethiopians were on a ridge on the 7th Division right flank on the MLR. Seven hundred and fifty meters forward of the ridge, were two entrenched outposts named Yoke and Uncle which were barely large enough to be garrisoned by a platoon. The job of the platoons was to screen the main position from attack and to bait the enemy into position for US artillery.[32] Outpost Yoke was manned by 1st Platoon (reinforced)/3d Company. The Officer-in-Charge, 2d Lt Bezabihi Ayele, had 56 men under his command. His second in command was Sgt Maj. Awilachew Moulte.

There was also a 15-person patrol from 1st Company operating in no-man's land. It was led by 2d Lt. Zenebe Asfaw who was tasked with capturing prisoners and inflicting damage on the enemy. The patrol left around 2300 and reached a concrete irrigation ditch about 700 yards north of Yoke. The ditch was located at the intersection of three trails and made a right angle that pointed towards the Northwest. 2d Lt. Zenebe deployed his men in the ditch with one BAR on each flank.[33]

At 2350, 2d Lt. Zenebe observed an enemy pointman in front of his position. Five minutes later he saw an estimated two enemy platoons amass 300 yards to his front near the scout. He couldn't open fire because he hoped to take a prisoner. Nor could he alert other friendly units because his comms were out. "He spat in disgust at a technical failure which, seen in retrospect, was clearly a blessing in disguise." "So he crawled along the ditch cautioning his men to maintain silence and retain fire until he gave the word."[34]

Starting at 0015, the enemy bombarded the Ethiopian MLR, Yoke and Uncle with mortars and artillery. The MLR and Yoke received around 500 and 50-60 rounds respectively over the next hour. 2d Lt. Bezabihi placed his men on alert for the assault that was sure to follow.

At 0125, Zenebe observed three groups of enemy moving in his vicinity. One company of Chinese was advancing on his left flank toward 1st Company while another company was advanced single file on his right toward Yoke. A third group came directly toward the patrol. "He was in the middle of a Communist battalion launched

charged you.

May 1953

On May 1, a 1st Company combat patrol was in no-man's-land when the patrol's nine-person assault force heard enemy soldiers imitating bird calls. The patrol leader 2d Lt. Berhanu Abaye said, "It sounded as though there were two forces moving up on either side of a finger to our front." The enemy flashed a light towards the friendly troops to draw their fire. Berhanu told his men to hold. When the Communists got to within 15 yards, he called for illumination flares and caught them in the open. The Ethiopians rained down grenades. But to their credit, the Chinese continued the charge. The Ethiopians in turn greeted them with fixed bayonets. As the enemy was about to overrun them, Lt. Berhanu ordered his group to withdraw and join the rest of the patrol in the defensive positioned 50 yards back. The Chinese pursued and encircled the patrol, which started tossing grenades down the slope onto the enemy. An American forward observer with the patrol got on the radio and ringed their position with artillery fire.

in a general attack. Its grand deployment was in the shape of an M and the V-shaped body advancing on his ditch was simply a sweep that tied together the two assault columns."[35]

The group advancing toward the patrol was led by five men who were 15-20 yards in front of the main force. When these enemy soldiers who had not seen the patrol, which was perfectly hidden in the ditch, got within ten yards, "The patrol leader yelled '*Tekus*' (open fire)." The patrol opened up and killed the five. The patrol continued to fire and throw grenades at the rest of the enemy troops. Rifle fire from each flank took the V in enfilade. The two BARs accounted for another dozen casualties. The enemy withdrew and attempted to execute its favorite move. One group tried to pin down the patrol while other tried to outflank it. Zenebe's comms had come back to life. He radioed, 'The enemy came. I stopped them. Now they surround me. I want artillery on White Right,"

Gen. and Mrs. Mark Clark, Lt. Col. Asfaw Andargue and Ethiopian liaison officers on liberation anniversary in Tokyo, May 5, 1953. (US Army)

and directed artillery onto the enemy on their flank. Even faced with insurmountable odds, he chose to target enemy units heading towards his brothers at the outposts. The Ethiopians on Yoke heard the faint sounds of a firefight, but they had no idea the patrol was engaged.

The enemy fired three red flares at 0155. This was probably the signal to lift the artillery and initiate the ground assault on Yoke. The defenders heard a noise coming from the left rear and opened up with small arms on ten enemy troops coming up the slope. "2d Lt. Bezabihi Ayele, commander of Yoke, heard the fire and told Sgt. Maj. Moulte to '*Beirta*' (stand by)." As he proceeded to the sounds of the battle to personally lead his men, he was killed by a Chinese grenade.

At this time, two groups of enemy started firing on 1st Company and 2d Company positions from 300-400 yards using machineguns and small arms. Another group also fired on Outpost Uncle from 100 yards away. The Ethiopians were also fighting off about 20 Communists who were attacking Yoke from the rear. Cpl. Ayalew Shibishi reported to Sgt. Maj. Moulte that "Lt. Ayele had been killed, and he had killed the Chinese soldier who threw the grenade." Moulte assumed command and went to the rear area where the fighting was taking place. He saw his men engaged in hand-to-hand fighting with the enemy in bunkers and trenches. "A machinegun, [Browning Automatic Rifle (BAR)] and six men with M-1s and carbines were keeping the enemy off the southwest side of the position." When the machinegunner Pvt. Kassa Misgina got wounded and his gun jammed, he handed his machinegun off, stepped out of the bunker and engaged the enemy in a grenade fight. At this time, five more Ethiopians were wounded by grenades.

After the enemy reached the trenches from south and southwest, another group attacked from southeast. The Ethiopians left the relative safety of their bunkers and fought from the trenches to keep

their position. The Communists were able to penetrate only about 15 yards in, as far as the 60mm mortar positions where two crewmen were wounded by grenades.

Captain Berehanu Tariku, 3d Company CO, was in an outpost with his forward observer when he received a request for "VT on position" from Yoke. The message was passed up to the Lt. Col. Woldeyohanis Shitta and resulted in artillery support for the defenders. Friendly units on Uncle also assisted Yoke by raking the Chinese with machinegun fire from the rear.

Realizing his men on Outpost Yoke were in peril Capt. Berehanu "disregarding all thoughts of personal safety" dashed forward to join his men in defending the position. "During a lull in the fighting, he personally evacuated three dead and 13 wounded soldiers under heavy artillery fire. [He] remained with his men…" He earned his second Bronze Star for valor after having earned his first Bronze Star with the First Kagnew Battalion on September 12, 1951. Capt. Tesemma Wakgira, S-3, was also in the defensive position and noticed the enemy infiltrating the area. So he "quickly organized squads and supervised them in the [counterattack]." After artillery was called in, he went into the barrage "to assure that all hostile personnel had withdrawn." He too was awarded a Bronze Star.

The brutal fight on the outpost lasted an hour. "At 0300 as an estimated enemy company withdrew down the north finger of Yoke directly into Lt. [Zenebe's] patrol which was still in position. The patrol opened fire on the enemy when they were 50 yards away and continued to fire for ten minutes. The patrol was nearly out of ammunition, and called for more artillery and mortar fire on the Chinese. The artillery and mortar fire dispersed the enemy…"

The patrol was then tasked with screening the battlefield for prisoners. By 0430 the patrol counted 44 KIA and took one prisoner.

Later one more prisoner was found by another screening patrol. Sgt. Maj. Ayele Kassa, Sgt. Bekele Selassie, Pvt. Aderaw Alamirew who were operating in front of the [MLR] as a member of a six-man screening patrol were fired on by an enemy soldier hiding in a ditch. All three advanced forward through the fire and took him prisoner. They were each awarded a Bronze Star Medal for Valor. Total casualties for the Communists were 45 KIA counted, 50 estimated KIA, 130 estimated WIA, and two POWs. Three Ethiopians were killed and 13 wounded. Sgt. Maj. Ayele Kassa was the member of First Kagnew who with the help of Cpl. Kebe Defair had captured a Chinese POW washing himself by the river.

Due to the sheer intensity of the attack, Colonel Woldeyohanis Shitta took personal command of the defense by directing all of the battalion's supporting weapons. He even "requested and adjusted artillery fire, at one time bringing barrages on his own position." Throughout the battle the colonel "was in view of the enemy and was fired on numerous times." He earned a Silver Star Medal for his actions. The citation credited his presence in the area and his clear thinking under heavy enemy fire as being a source of great inspiration to his men. He "radiated" encouragement.

The President of the Battle Records Board, Lt. Col. Acuff, praised the defenders on the outpost and Lt. Zenebe's patrol for their outstanding performance. The regiment concluded the patrol carried out explicitly its mission of inflicting heavy casualties on the enemy. It was also credited with disrupting the enemy attack by blocking one of its axes of advance and by calling in accurate indirect fire on enemy positions. Not only did the patrol withstand what the enemy dished out, it also weathered approximately 4,000 rounds of friendly shells that came in right on top of its position without a single casualty.

The After Action Report prepared by the 7th Division Battle Records Board listed enemy KIA as 44. S.L.A. Marshall wrote there were 110 dead Chinese and estimated four times as many wounded, "effectively eliminating one Chinese Battalion."[36]

Marshall further lauded the patrol, "As a feat of arms by a small body of men, it was matchless. No other entry in the book of war more clearly attests that miracles are made when a leader whose coolness of head is balanced by his reckless daring becomes attended by a few steady men. Victory came not because of the artillery but because [Zenebe] Asfaw believed in it, willed it, then planned it."[37]

Private Bekele Hora was an infantryman in the 2d Squad, 3d Platoon, 3d Company of the Third Kagnew Battalion. He was born in Guder Wereda in Ambo Awraja. During the Italian occupation, a *banda* (collaborator) burned his family's home with all their possessions and hanged his father. A 12-year-old Bekele grabbed a Belgian carbine and joined his uncle in the resistance and fought as a patriot for one-year. After liberation Bekele was placed into government service because of his combat experience. He joined the Guard sometime in 1950.[38]

Bekele said "the Chinese attacked us as soon as we got there because they thought they [we] were just kids." It was more likely that the Chinese who had up to date intelligence knew there were green troops in the line and wanted to test their mettle. The Communist troops overran the position and hit two bunkers. The Ethiopians at the outpost, including Pvt. Bekele Hora, engaged the Chinese with bayonets. Bekele summed it up by saying, "a lot of ours were killed and we killed a lot of theirs." When the outpost reported its dire situations to the Americans by field telephone, Col. Woldeyohanis said, "No, let

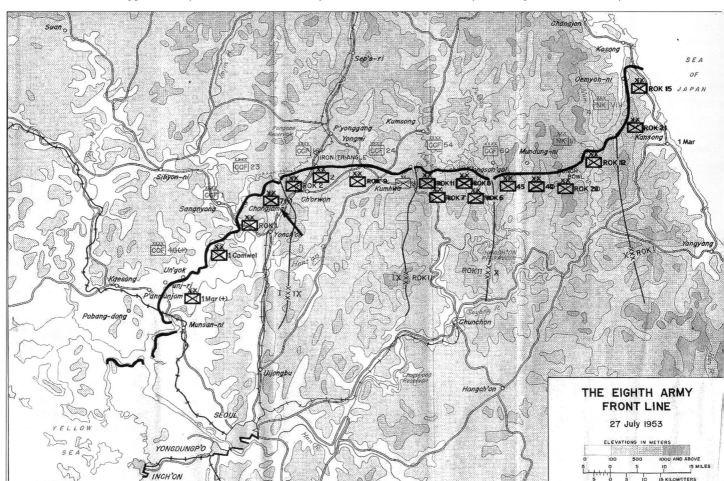

Front lines of the 8th Army as of 27 July 1953. By this time, the 7th Division was re-deployed further west, along with Kagnew Battalion, close to the Chongjamal. (Hermes, Walter G. *Truce Tent and Fighting Front*. Washington D.C.: Center of Military History, United States Army, 1992, p. 476)

Newly arrived Ethiopian troops being served coffee by the American Red Cross, June 29, 1954. (US Army)

Woldeselassie had preceded him into the military and gave him some guidance. Tesfaye went to *Jan Meda* along with the other recruits, where they were evaluated for military bearing and education. Tesfaye had completed traditional church education as well as 4th grade formal education. After passing a test he became a member of the "youth company."[42]

He later took the Signal Corps test and became a radio operator. Since he was a little bit older and taller than the others, he was selected to serve in Korea with the Second Kagnew. Tesfaye said a rifle never left his hands since childhood. He knew the *demotfore* and *minishire*, but now he started training with new American weapons like the M1, carbine, and machineguns. After finishing all the necessary training and pre-deployment screening including immunization, the unit was assembled at *Jan Meda*. The Imperial Bodyguard brass came for an inspection. Tesfaye's older brother, Deresse Woldeselassie, who by now was a sergeant major and acquainted with Col. Mengistu, asked to go to Korea in place of his little brother.[43]

Sgt. Maj. Deresse left with the Second Kagnew Battalion while LCpl. Tesfaye stayed behind. It appears the Imperial Bodyguard was not devoid of a sense of humor. Two months later Tesfaye was added to the roster of the Third Kagnew Battalion. He once again stood in formation for another inspection at *Jan Meda* with the other Guardsmen headed to Korea. The troops then started marching to the palace for a lunch reception.[44] They returned to *Jan Meda* after lunch, loaded onto "boisterous" Mac trucks and headed to the train station where the entire population of the capital came to see them off with songs and tears. Again, they were greeted at each stop by the local citizenry.[45]

As the Ethiopian positions were getting hit on May 19, Tesfaye who was normally assigned as the radio operator for the battalion commander had volunteered to man the radio for a forward observer. As the two men drove to the front, their jeep hit a mine and flipped. Tesfaye was seriously wounded on the left shoulder and got carried out on a stretcher. He spent the next two or three days in and out of consciousness as he traveled from the MASH to hospitals in Korea and eventually the Tokyo Army Hospital Annex.[46]

them fight and hold on all night." All night long, the men fought to hold their position alongside their officers while clutching their dead and wounded comrades. At 0600 the next morning, Mamo Haptewold and Zenebe Asfaw came with their platoon. The outpost had lost five dead.[39]

Amidst the pitched battle, 20-year-old Lance Corporal Tesfaye Woldeselassie and an American artillery liaison were rushing to the front in a jeep to serve as forward observers.[40] Tesfaye was born in Shewa Province, Woliso Awraja, Tulubolo Wereda, Berebere Mender. He came from a long line of warriors. His father was a captain in the resistance, while two of his brothers fought against the Italians in the southern campaign and later joined their father. A young Tesfaye had witnessed their deaths at the hands of the Fascists. In fact, of his seven brothers, only one never served in war and even his father-in-law died on the field. Tesfaye tearfully said he and his family begrudge the Italians to this day.[41]

It was these atrocities committed against his family and his country that convinced him to join the military. His older brother Deresse

He would eventually spend three months in the hospital. He said he received great treatment; everything, including food was plentiful. Patients from different countries were in the same ward, but he never experienced any racism. He recalled being cared for by American nurses regularly and Ethiopian nurses while making their rounds. He said they not only worked tirelessly to treat the physical wounds, but the emotional and psychological scars as well. They encouraged the soldiers to be active, interact and do things like play checkers. They also wheeled out the patients at night so they could watch movies.[47]

At the end of the three months, Tesfaye was given 15 days leave before returning to his unit. By then, the fighting would stop. He would spend another six months preserving the fragile peace in Korea.[48]

On May 29, the Ethiopians were sent out on another patrol. Lt. Mamo Haptewold and 11 enlisted men from 1st Co plus one American from the I&R Platoon left at 2014. They were in position lined up

Delegates from the USA (left) and North Korea (right), signing the Korean Armistice Agreement in Panmunjom. (US DoD)

behind a rice paddy wall by 2045. Another patrol composed of five men from I&R Platoon led by a Sgt. Davis was sent out 300 yards west of the Lower Alligator Jaw. This patrol was 800-1,000 yards north of Lt. Mamo's patrol. It was tasked with capturing an enemy wounded or straggler returning from contact with the Ethiopian patrol.

The Ethiopian patrol had its first enemy sighting around 2315 with an enemy squad on their flank moving towards Yoke. They Ethiopians held fire because the enemy, walking in a stream bed 75 yards away, offered a less than ideal target. Instead, they radioed 1st Co which in turn alerted Yoke. Around the same time, Sgt. Davis' patrol observed two small enemy units crossing the Lower Alligator Jaw and called artillery on them. Another group was seen 200-300 yards to their front and they heard another group in a drainage ditch behind them. At 2356, Sgt. Davis called artillery all around his position.

At 2330, a friendly position near Yoke was attacked by Communist forces. After a three-minute fight and having killed one friendly soldier, the enemy was chased off by artillery and mortars. As the enemy forces withdrew they were ambushed by the patrol. The enemy again broke contact.

It was quiet again until 0050 when two enemy squads retreating back to their MLR ran right into the rear of Lt. Mamo's patrol. The patrol opened up on the enemy when they got within 20 yards. The Communists charged through the patrol throwing hand grenades. In the wake of the attack, all 14 men of the patrol were either killed or wounded. The survivors had to fend off another assault when they were hit with grenades from close range. After a 10-15 minute firefight the enemy withdrew to about 100 yards away.

Lieutenant Mamo gathered his casualties into a small perimeter and started looking for the two radios the patrol had brought with it. He found one radio destroyed by a grenade. As he started searching for the second radio, a wounded Communist soldier tried to throw a grenade at him. Mamo got him first with a grenade. At 0105, he fired a green flare requesting reinforcements and continued to search for the radio. At 0117, he found the radio and made contact with 1st Company. His situation was grim because he only had four men other than himself who were able to fight. He gave his sidearm and three grenades to one man and placed him to the front. He then placed a man on each flank.

A member of the patrol, Cpl. Taddesse Wolde had, on his own initiative, ran back 500 yards towards Yoke, yelled for help and returned to his comrades all before his commander noticed. The patrol kept seeing enemy

Ethiopian troops celebrating their New Year, September 11, 1954. (US Army)

troops about 100 yards away and called artillery. The patrol leader radioed the company checking on the reinforcements and continued to walk the artillery in closer to his position. When word got to Lt. Col. Woldeyohanis Shitta, he ordered reinforcements to aid the patrol and also sent a platoon to reinforce 1st Company.

Lieutenant Zenebe Asfaw, who led the extraordinary patrol on the night of May 19, was on alert. At 0125 he and his small force of 12 men left the MLR and linked up with the patrol at 0140. The two officers quickly conferred and set up a perimeter. Five minutes later the Chinese attacked again with small arms and grenades. What remained of Lt. Mamo's patrol and the reinforcements fired back and repulsed the enemy. Lt. Mamo joined in with a BAR he picked up on the battlefield but it cost the Ethiopians three more wounded from Zenebe's group. They administered first aid as best they could and radioed back to the company for extra litters to evacuate their mounting casualties and requested another round of artillery cover. All was quiet again by 0151. The I&R patrol also received small arms fire and mortars. They observed 12-15 enemy troops withdrawing after their encounter with the Ethiopians, "each man was carrying, dragging or assisting a wounded or dead enemy soldier over the tip of the Lower Alligator Jaw." They directed artillery on the retreating Chinese.

Seven more Ethiopians arrived from Yoke with litters at 0318. They shuttled eight litter cases, five walking wounded and three dead under harassing small arms fire from the enemy who was positioned in a riverbed 100 yards away. Mamo who was also wounded in the battle, refused to leave until all his men had been evacuated. The last of the troops returned to the MLR at 0430. Later, the I&R patrol screened the area where the Ethiopian action took place. However, they did not find any enemy dead or wounded because the Chinese had policed the battlefield. The enemy suffered 15 KIA, 15 WIA counted, and an additional estimated ten KIA and 20 WIA.

Sgt. Ishete Amenu was part of Lt. Mamo's patrol. Sometime during the battle, he lost an arm to hostile fire and despite the "intense pain" and "suffering from a loss of blood," Sgt. Ishete "hurled hand grenades and consistently remained in the thick of the fighting, encouraging and inspiring his comrades" to kill many of the enemy, until he was "mortally wounded when the enemy completely encircled the patrol."

In March 1952, 22-year-old Pvt. Gabremicail Tumebo lost a leg in Korea in a booby trap explosion. While he was hospitalized at a Tokyo hospital, he was cared for by US Army nurse Lt. Sonny Le Glaire. When Pvt. Gabremicail found out there was a shortage of artificial limbs in the Far East, he refused to leave without one. He returned home only after Nurse Le Glaire promised she would send a prosthetic limb to him. She even offered to pay for it herself but was told it would be practically impossible to fit a prosthetic remotely.[49]

Pvt. Gabremicail, the son of a retired military man, was visited both by Emperor Haile Selassie and Brig. Gen. Mulugeta Bulli after returning to Addis Ababa. Pvt. Gabremicail had been a soldier since the age of 16 and hoped the artificial leg would be good enough to allow him to remain in the Imperial Bodyguard.[50] The World Veterans Federation and the American Veterans Committee arranged and paid for his trip to the US and for his prosthetics in their effort to get equally high standards of medical care to all UN combatants. He walked with an imperceptible limp while visiting UN Headquarters in New York. Through an interpreter he said, "He wanted to see the UN because, directly or indirectly, it had taken him to Korea."[51][52]

The Ethiopian nurses were also hard at work providing care not only to their countrymen but to all UN servicemen. One time, Nurse Berkinesh had two majors in her ward – an Ethiopian and an American. The latter kept passing gas and did not think much of it,

but since this was taboo in his culture, the Ethiopian officer thought the American was doing it out of disrespect. He finally had enough, jumped out of bed and tried to strangle the man. Berkinesh and other staff came running in, broke them apart and explained this was normal.[53]

Nine Kagnew soldiers were killed and 47 wounded in the month of May.

Foreign Secretary Aklilou Habte Wolde and General Mulugets Bulli arrived in the US on March 30, 1953, to negotiate contracts for US bases in Eritrea as well as Ethiopia's request for military assistance. They met with Gen. John Hull (Vice CoS, US Army), Lt. Gen. Lemnitzer (former C.O. of 7th Division, and at the time of the meeting, Dep. CoS, US Army), and other representatives from the Army and State Department.[54]

First on the agenda was the terms of America's continued use of Radio Marina in Asmara, Eritrea. Radio Marina was a communications base built by the Italians and commandeered first by the British and then the US. Minister Aklilou lobbied for military assistance on the same basis as Greece and Turkey – a "Mutual Defense Treaty" and not "reimbursable assistance." He had been instructed by the Emperor to clear up a $4.5-million invoice for 12,000 rifles and reminded the group that small arms retained by Kagnew Battalion were charged at 30% of their original cost. He closed by stating that the Imperial government had to show its citizens "results" for the goodwill extended to the US. The Americans saw Gen. Mulugeta Bulli's assignment to this mission as a not so subtle reminder of Ethiopia's contributions in Korea. The Undersecretary of State wrote to his counterpart at the Pentagon to request Ethiopia be made eligible for "grant military aid" which would allow the US to provide the arms free of charge by paying for them from $26-million earmarked for military assistance in the Near East. After some back-and-forth, five-million dollars in military aid was fast-tracked and signed by the President by mid-May. Subsequently the two countries reached an agreement on US basing rights for Radio Marina. However, much of the detail was kept secret as "to avoid any obvious link between the base and aid agreement." The US also agreed to send a Military Assistance Advisory Group (MAAG) to train Ethiopia's armed forces.[55]

On May 28, Brig. Gen. Mulugeta Bulli left the US and arrived in Tokyo. The next day, he met with General Mark W. Clark (CINC-UNC). During his time in Tokyo, he also visited Ethiopian patients at army hospitals. LCpl. Tesfaye Woldeselassie who was recuperating from the injury he received when his jeep hit a landmine recalled the visit. The Ethiopians were a bit of a novelty and entertained more than their fair share of visitors, especially US Army brass who would stop by for a cup of tea or a frosty brew. They were overjoyed to see their own commanding general, and thought, "Our commander loves us this much."[56]

On June 2, Gen. Mulugeta arrived in Seoul and called on Gen. Maxwell Taylor and Eighth Army. The next day, he was greeted by a 7ID honor guard. He then visited Kagnew Battalion's forward command post where he was briefed on the tactical situation. He then went to the frontline and inspected the 4th Co bunkers and observed enemy positions. That afternoon, he returned to the rear for an award ceremony honoring eight Americans and seven Ethiopians.[57] Maj. Hallock was invited as a guest of honor and personally presented with the Haile Selassie Medal with Palm by General Mulugeta.[58]

The general's visit was a surprise to most of the troops including 2d Lt. Wongele Costa, the half-Greek platoon leader whose exploits were chronicled by S.L.A. Marshal. The young officer was fearful because he expected to get court-martialed for the casualties his platoon suffered. Instead he and his men were awarded the Haile Selassie Medal with

Palm device. He would later receive the ROK Hwarang Medal with gold star and a Belgian decoration.[59]

June 1953

The division continued to defend the MLR on the right flank of the I Corps sector during June. The enemy appeared to have scaled back his activity with reconnaissance patrols focused around Pork Chop during the first seven days, with raids widely scattered across the OPLR and probes on Dale, Pork Chop, Yoke and Uncle.

On the evening of June 4, Outpost Yoke was occupied by Lt. Workneh Mako and 58 men. Around 2118 Lt. Workneh reported to Capt. Fisiha Gebremariam, commander of 4th Company, that his men were in a firefight. He then radioed each of his squad leaders for a report. He also requested artillery flare and shot 60mm flare to illuminate the area. The squad leaders informed him the Chinese were attacking both sides of Yoke. He immediately pulled back his men guarding the outer perimeter and told them 30 enemy soldiers were within 150 yards of Yoke. He radioed again and requested flash fire (pre-arranged defensive artillery barrage around a position) on Yoke at 2130.

Capt. Fisiha, who was already at the outpost, took command and started directing the placement of automatic weapons. He then "discovered that communication with the supporting artillery had been knocked out by heavy enemy fire" so he "voluntarily moved back to the rear through a heavy barrage of hostile fire until he contacted the artillery liaison officer and gave him the proper coordinates for the targets." He then raced to the outpost to rejoin the fight.

A combat patrol of fifteen men from 1st Company had departed the MLR at 2010. Lt. Col. Shitta ordered the patrol to move from its current position 700 yards northeast of Yoke to a new position east of Yoke. They got in position at 2211.

The Chinese set up machineguns on the north finger of Yoke and on the west side near the valley floor. Then the enemy tried to assault Yoke from the east and west employing hand grenades and small arms fire. The flash fires requested by Lt. Workneh poured in for the next twelve minutes. When the artillery lifted, everything was quiet. At 2145, the enemy scored a direct hit on the Yoke Command Post resulting in one killed and two wounded. It also knocked out both wire and radio comms.

At 2148 friendly aircraft started dropping flares. Although they weren't receiving reports from Yoke, friendly forces in the area provided assistance when enemy activity was sighted on Yoke's flanks. Anytime small arms or grenades were heard or seen near Yoke, the tanks on the MLR and the 81mm mortars behind the MLR fired on each side of yoke. The 60mm mortar at Outpost Uncle was also firing flares, in addition to the .50-cal machineguns and BARs raking the hillsides.

At 2204, Lt. Workneh reported by radio that the enemy was dragging its dead away from Yoke. For the next hour the enemy maintained sporadic fire on the outpost as it evacuated its casualties. By 2300 all communications with Yoke was lost. The enemy assaulted Yoke one last time at 0335 after setting-up two bases of fire with machineguns 150 yards to the front and 150 yards to the rear. Under covering fire, a small group of enemy started to move up on the west side of Yoke. Lt. Workneh directed his men on the west side to open fire on the advancing enemy, forcing them to retreat.

At 0300, Capt. Tesemma Wakgira (S-3), along with Cpl. Phillips from the tank company, his driver, and one bodyguard, left for Yoke with a radio hoping to re-establish comms. An hour later the small band arrived at Uncle. Capt. Tesemma took ten more men from there and proceeded to Yoke. They arrived at 0430 and began evacuating the wounded and dead.

A recon patrol from 1st Co departed at 0430 and observed the aftermath of a battle: CCF first aid bandages, trails where the bodies were dragged over the grass, grenades, belt and bangalore torpedos. During the night, Yoke was hit with approximately 30 rounds of artillery and mortars. Two bunkers were destroyed. One man was killed and seven wounded on Yoke. One more was killed and another wounded on the MLR and one wounded from a 15-man patrol dispatched by 1st Company in the vicinity of Yoke. Enemy casualties were ten KIA and 12 WIA.

The battalion's total losses for the month were two killed and sixteen wounded. Capt. Fisiha Gebremariam was awarded a Silver Star Medal.

July 1953

The 7th Division started the month of July on the MLR with all three regiments on the line. The 32d Regiment had the right sector with 1st Bn and EEFK Bn on the line. During the month the division would sustain one major attack and repulse several probes with heavy losses on the enemy's side.

On July 6, the Chinese kicked off the Second Battle of Pork Chop Hill when they attacked 17th Regiment's positions around Pork Chop, Snook and Arsenal. The division commander ordered the 32d Regiment C.O. to relieve 3d Bn with Kagnew Battalion which had been in regimental reserve. If elements of 17th Regiment failed to dislodge the enemy, the Ethiopian battalion would be required to either counterattack or relieve friendly units. The Ethiopians completed the relief by the early morning hours of July 9. After days of bloody battle under monsoon rains, on July 9, it was decided to relieve all units on Pork Chop by 3d Bn, 32d Rgt.

On July 10, the 32d Regiment including EEFK was relieved on the MLR and OPLR positions by the 14th Regimental Combat Team, and the 32d in turn relieved the 17th Regiment with 3d Battalion, 32d Regiment occupying Pork Chop. The Communists continued to mount ferocious attacks which UN forces repulsed before initiating their own counterattack. On July 11, the commanding general decided to abandon Pork Chop Hill and withdrew from the position after suffering 74 KIA, 877 WIA and 148 MIA. The Communists paid an even bigger price with 4,400 casualties. In the end 2d Bn and EEFK held the MLR with the other two battalions of the regiments forming the reserve.

Irwin Braun, the intelligence sergeant from Brooklyn, New York, recalls sometime in June or July 1953, at 0200 the field telephone rang and "the Orange Battalion" reported Chinese playing music at the front [as part of their psychological warfare]. "Orange" was the code name assigned to Kagnew for radio communication. Sgt. Braun relayed the same message to division but forgot to use their code name. A little bit later his phone rang again. This time it was Division HQ because General Trudeau wanted the name, rank and serial number of the person who relayed the message and had identified a friendly unit by name. A lieutenant in the bunker overheard the exchange and told Sergeant Braun that he'd be a private by morning. Luckily, that didn't happen. Of course, the Chinese didn't need any help identifying opposition units, because "they knew everything about us."[60]

Braun said 5.7-million guys were drafted during the Korean War, of those, only 1.7-million served in Korea. The rest served in places like Europe, Hawaii or in the US, which compared to Korea was like paradise. He said, "I never understood how I was one of the 'lucky' ones that were sent to Korea." [61] It should be noted there were 5.7-million US Service members during the Korean War. Of those, 1.5-million were drafted per the US Selective Service System.

On July 27 at 1000, after two years of intermittent negotiations, the

Korean Armistice Agreement was signed by representative of the UNC and the Communists (NKPA and CCF). Lt. Col. Woldeyohanis Shitta and other United Nations delegates attended the ceremony. Gen. Clark wrote to Woldeyohanis, "I feel that after almost three years of fighting and sacrifice by the contingents of the United Nations Command it is only fitting that you should be present at the conclusion of hostilities in the field."

Forty minutes after the signing, the 7th Division received orders to cease-fire effective 2200 that evening.

The Ethiopians were excited to hear the good news. Pvt. Bekele Hora remembers the troops celebrating with traditional ululation. He said they were happy because the fighting had been heavy and costly. "The enemy was determined. And a lot of our friends were killed or wounded. If it was not for the cease fire, we would have had no hope." Bekele added, "We were thankful it was over."[62]

Second Lieutenant Wongele Costa had not expected the fighting to stop but he was happy to hear the news. There had been heavy fighting all along the front until the cease fire because both sides were attempting to seize key terrain before a final agreement permanently established the DMZ. After his triumphant patrol, two of his academy classmates were involved in serious fighting, another officer from his course was killed after his outpost was overrun. He said, "The soldiers accepted it. It was better than dying."[63]

Lance Corporal Tesfaye Woldeselassie, who had suffered serious injuries when his jeep struck a landmine and was hospitalized at the time of the signing, echoed the same sentiment. He said, "There was bitterness because [the enemy] had hurt us previously. But we got them back for that, so the news was well received. I was glad to hear of the armistice."[64]

Second Lieutenant Abebe Gebreyes and his 75mm recoilless rifle platoon were in the vicinity of Pork Chop when the cease fire was announced. He said they did not have news radios or other means of knowing, so they only found out when the battalion told the company which in turn told the platoon. Abebe recalled, he just did what his superiors said. He did not have any opinions at that time. He was more concerned about the logistics of their withdrawal.[65]

Melesse Tessema who was now back home after serving with the Second Kagnew was also happy. He thought there is nothing greater than peace. The young officers now in Ethiopia missed their friends, especially those from the same cadet course. He said they didn't get enough of each other. "The First Kagnew left five months before we finished our course… when we went there, they came back… when we got back, the ones that were here left. We wanted to get together when the war ended. We were happy."[66]

The relief was equally shared by the Chinese. The enemy was seen "celebrating the ceasefire with small gatherings and parties" and showed no "signs of fear that the armistice would be broken."

Despite the elation, the Armistice was only a military agreement between military commanders for the cessation of hostilities and not a peace treaty. The day the Armistice was signed at Panmunjom, representatives of the 16 nations which contributed troops to the UNC met in Washington to declare their support of the armistice agreement and threatening that the consequences for a future breach of the armistice might not be confined to Korea.[67]

Over the next 72 hours, the 7th Division relocated artillery and support elements to a new position. Then on July 30, between 0500 and 1650, "the main body of troops and covering forces" conducted a tactical withdrawal to their new position behind the Demilitarized Zone (DMZ). The area wasn't completely vacated until 2000 as work parties were salvaging equipment from the old MLR. The 17th and 31st Regiments were placed on the line, while the 32d Regiment with

Kagnew attached went to division reserve.

At the end of the war Kagnew's strength stood at 1,185. The battalion had suffered 2 killed and 9 wounded on the last month of the war.

August 1953

From August 1 until August 16, the division occupied a sector on the post-armistice main battle position. It was tasked with maintaining readiness for immediate combat, carrying out the terms of armistice, and conducting training. The 32d was in division reserve and worked hard to salvage useable material from the DMZ. The enemy was observed doing the same: removing supplies from the DMZ and constructing defensive positions to the north. Enemy work parties and vehicles operated boldly in the open until mid-month when the enemy took corrective action and the sightings decreased. On August 16, 7ID was relieved by 25ID from the DMZ and finished it move to I Corps reserve by August 18. The 32d Regiment initiated a training program in preparation for a more robust 20-week training program slated to commence on November 1.

After the Armistice

During the September, the division was in I Corps reserve. The 32d Regiment was engaged in preparing a defensive position along Line Kansas. The four battalions including Kagnew were assigned a sector and constructed fortifications for a period of three weeks followed by five days of rehab. There were no reports of enemy activity in the division's sector. During this period two language instructors were assigned to provide English lessons to the Ethiopians. Lt. Col. Woldeyohanis opted to enroll just the enlisted men, since his officers already had a working knowledge of English. The division also initiated a winterization program.

On November 18, 1953 the World Veterans Federation named the "Unknown Soldiers of Korea" as the recipient of that year's peace award. Two individuals from the two nations which received the least recognition were chosen to share the symbolic award: the five-year-old daughter of a Dutch soldier killed in action and Lt. Col. Asfaw Andargue.[68]

Just as the troops went on R&R for a change of scenery, Nurses Berkinesh and Aster requested to go to Korea to visit the troops. They wanted to be around more of their countrymen and speak their own language again. They were undoubtedly a welcomed sight for the war weary troops. The young ladies were then given a one-month furlough by the Emperor to visit Siam (present-day Thailand). The nurses had seen it on the way to Korea and thought it would be a great place to visit. The second time around they were unimpressed and only stayed two weeks.[69]

On February 4, 1954, members of the Kagnew Battalion went to train on the regiment's confidence course. While Pvt. Abebe Desalegn and a few other Ethiopians were taking a break and warming themselves on a nearby fire built by an American corporal, one of the soldiers noticed a 60mm mortar shell in a box burning in the fire. He immediately alerted his comrades in their native tongue but the American corporal did not understand the warning and remained by the fire. Knowing the round would cook-off at any moment, Pvt. Abebe Desalegn, left his position of cover "without regard for his personal safety and started to pull the American away from the fire." After he managed to get the corporal "to a position of relative safety, the shell exploded, knocking them to the ground." The corporal was slightly burned. Private Abebe, however, suffered severe burns to his face and was wounded by shrapnel.

Private Abebe Desalegn was subsequently awarded the US Soldier's

Medal for "distinguishing himself by heroism not involving actual conflict with an enemy." The award is higher than the US Bronze Star Medal.

Even though combat operations had ceased, the men kept up their physical conditioning. They completed a nine-mile march with a full field pack in two hours. When they finished, one of their officers boasted that the men could march another nine miles in the same time.[70]

On June 21, 1954, His Majesty the King of Belgium issued three royal decrees awarding twelve decorations to six members of the Kagnew Battalion "for Exceptional War Services" in Korea. They were 1st Lt. Zenebe Asfaw, 2d Lt. Mamo Haptewold, Sgt. Maj. Awlachen Mulat, Cpl. Tadesse Wolde, Pvt. Tega Mengistou, and Pvt. Yzaachew Delelegn. The Ethiopian liaison section had also nominated Capt. Lenchio Hailemariam and 2d Lt. Abera Gulilat, but it is not certain whether they were awarded.

4

FOURTH KAGNEW BATTALION AND FIFTH KAGNEW COMPANY

Lt. Col. Asfaw Habtemariam, Capts. Tefara Waldetensye (S-3) and Zewde Bilala (S-4) departed Addis Ababa by air on June 14 and arrived in theater on the 16th to effect another relief. For both Capts. Tefara and Zewde this was their second tour in Korea, having already served with the First Kagnew Battalion. Tefera had commanded 1st Co and was critically wounded in battle. He along with Desta Gemeda and another officer had serenaded a Japanese crowd while on R&R in Tokyo. Zewde had been the executive officer for 4th Co.

Lieutenant Colonel Asfaw Habtemariam was born in Harar around 1917. He attended L'alliance Francaise School and joined the Imperial Bodyguard in 1930 or 1931, possibly as an enlisted man. It appears he underwent three-years of military training. Skordiles wrote that Asfaw was sent to Switzerland for anti-aircraft weapons training, but this was not mentioned in the brief biography provided to the UNC. He fought at the Battle of Maychew before spending all five years of the occupation fighting as a patriot. After liberation, he was commissioned as a first lieutenant in the Imperial Bodyguard. By 1946, he was a captain and administrators of the Imperial Bodyguard cadet school.

The Fourth Kagnew Battalion consisting of 80 officers and 957 men which left Djibouti on June 10, aboard the *Blatchford* arrived in Korea on June 30, 1954. *Abba* Ariaya was the unit chaplain. Their medical officer, Maj. Hans Rasch, arrived in Tokyo by air on July 8. The battalion had trained for five months in Ethiopia in individual skills and small unit tactics.

On July 7, a parade was held for the departing Third Kagnew Battalion. More than 600 members of the 32d Infantry Regiment passed in review. Three army planes flew overhead and dipped their wings in salute. The regiment presented them with a large silver bowl and fourteen cups "in remembrance of our association as comrade in arms and in appreciation of your gallant combat record." Maj. Gen. Edmund B. Sebree, 7th Division Commander, awarded a posthumous Silver Star Medal to Sgt. Eshete Amenu, the soldier who kept fighting even after he lost an arm during the battle on May 29, 1953.[1]

On July 9, another parade was held for the battalion. This time 1,600 men from the 7th Division passed in review after Eighth Army commander Gen. Maxwell Taylor tied a Distinguished Unit Citation battle streamer to the Kagnew guidon in recognition of the May 29 action.[2]

On July 15, the Third Kagnew Battalion left for home aboard the USNS *Eltinge* with 60 officers and 1,078 men. Seventeen were patients from Yokohama and Tokyo Army Hospitals. The bodies of their comrades who had made the ultimate sacrifice were also onboard. The Ethiopians left the theater of war, as they had done many times in battle, with their dead. The two nurses traveled by air and rejoined the

battalion in Djibouti.

Both 2d Lt. Wongele Costa and LCpl. Tesfaye Woldeselassie remember the train stopping because the tracks were washed out or otherwise damaged. Another train was brought to the other side of the broken track and the troops had to transfer the caskets of their fallen comrades to the new train.[3][4]

The veterans arrived in Addis Ababa on August 5, 1954. LCpl. Tesfaye remembers being greeted by the Emperor, *Ras* Abebe Aregay (Minister of Defense) other military and public officials. The air was filled with ululation.[5] The Emperor told them,

Your valourous deeds on the Korean battlefield marked an important trend in current events which the world followed in amazement – that you were able to have won the distinction which only famous warriors deserve." He added of the martyrs, "we reverently welcome your remains and lay them where your names and your bravery shall never be forgotten, just as We solemnly wished you farewell when We dispatched you to the Far East for the purpose of defending world peace.[6]

Afterwards, the returning troops followed the Emperor to the Imperial Palace where they passed in review and were honored at a luncheon. Wongele Costa remembers eating rich, fatty beef and drinking the local honey mead – *Tej*. Even though the food was great, their minds were with their families. Some participated in traditional martial boasting *Fukera* calling themselves "*Yante Ashker*" (Your Servant).[7]

Lieutenant Colonel Woldeyohannis was awarded the medal of the Order of Menelik II while other officers were awarded Medals of the Order of the Ethiopian Star. All others were presented with Korean War service medals. The troops then turned-in their rifles and hailed newly imported "kurkur" scooter-taxis to take them home to their families. Strangers on the streets grabbed to kiss them on the cheeks.[8]

Wongele Costa's mother had gotten word that he was killed in Korea, so she did not go to greet the battalion but his uncle went to the parade to see for himself. He spotted the half-Greek Wengele who had very light complexion.[9]

The bodies of the fallen were escorted by an honor guard and entombed at Selassie Church (Holy Trinity Cathedral).

Back in Uijeongbu, Korea, a Stars and Stripes reporter accompanied a handful of Kagnew men for an extraordinary event. Four soldiers and a supervising captain gathered in a quonset hut to record music for a Tokyo radio station. They were Tekola Meren on the clarinet, Kassa Tessama on the kirar, Tesfaye Sahlu playing tambourine and Aberra Yemer on the masinko and accordion. After a few attempts at different Ethiopian folk music the captain cut in, "They will do one more. They will do the railroad song." He turned and told the men, "*Allem alle*!" As the group stared belting out the tune, the captain explained, "It means the train is vanishing. In Ethiopia there is only one railroad. It runs between Addis Ababa and Djibouti. They sing of a fellow who says goodbye to his sweetheart. He travels from Addis Ababa to Djibouti. It is a short way. Then he will go to war." When the song ended the captain remarked, "It is a long way from [Djibouti] to [Uijeongbu]."[10] The song "*Allem alle babooroo*" credited to Kassa Tessama would become the unofficial Kagnew anthem.

At the end of March 1955, the US MAAG in Addis Ababa was informed by a representative of the Imperial Bodyguard that Ethiopia was considering replacing the current battalion in Korea with a rifle company.

In April, Col. Mengistu Neway approached the American attaché Col. Townsend "informally as a friend" to gauge his reaction to Ethiopian troops being pulled from Korea. Mengistu cited the financial burden of maintaining a battalion in the Far East and reports that the Greeks and Turks would soon be pulling out their troops from Korea in June or July. The US itself had withdrawn two divisions in April. He floated the idea of maintaining an alert battalion in Ethiopia for immediate deployment to any UN operations in any part of the world. Furthermore, Ethiopia would maintain liaison officers at hot spots in the Far East.

Col. Townsend was instructed to inform the US ambassador to Ethiopia but he also told Col. Mengistu that he personally thought "it was important both militarily and psychologically for Ethiopia to retain a battalion in Korea." He also stated that "as historically, Ethiopia was a champion of principle of collective security, that other nations were observing carefully her action." He didn't have an easy answer as to why Ethiopia should keep a contingent in Korea if Greece and Turkey pulled out however.

The next day, the Pentagon clarified that the Turks were only rotating and the Greeks reducing their force. Later, the State Department told the Embassy in Addis that the US desired for the coalition to maintain the status quo. The US was also opposed to the Commonwealth reducing their combined forces to battalion strength. The Belgians were withdrawing; the Filipinos were leaning that way; the Greeks were drawing down to a battalion and the Turks hadn't indicated either way. The Department of State, the Army, and the Joint Chiefs of Staff were all extremely concerned about what appeared to be the imminent disintegration of the United Nations Command. It was requested that the ambassador directly remind the Emperor that the UNC was the first instrument for collective security established under UN and that Ethiopia should appreciate this principle.

On May 11, Foreign Secretary Aklilou Habte Wolde informed the ambassador of the Emperor's decision to send a reinforced rifle company.

The Fifth Kagnew marched past in front of the Imperial Palace right around noon and boarded the train from Addis to Djibouti in the evening of June 6. Ras Abebe Aregay (Minister of Defense), General Mulugeta and other officials saw them off. The unit arrived in Korea aboard USNS *General R.L. Howze* on June 29 at company

Ethiopian troops undergoing gas training, June 1, 1955. (US Army)

Lt. Col. Asfaw Habtemariam greeting Capt. Yohannis Meseker and the Fifth Kagnew, June 29, 1955. (US Army)

strength with 16 officers and 231 men. Capt. Yohannes Meseker was in command. This was his second tour of duty in Korea having served as a staff officer with the First Kagnew Battalion. After the colors were passed to him at a division review and change of command ceremony on July 8, Capt. Yohannes commented, "I feel a deep sense of pride and pleasure in accepting these combat colors which have passed through four years of service in peace as well as war." The company assumed responsibility on July 9.[11]

The *Howze* departed Inchon carrying the Fourth Kagnew Battalion on July 12 or 13 with 81 Ethiopian officers and 929 men as well as the five Korean students. The Emperor planned to return these orphans to their homeland after they receive an education either in Ethiopia or at a foreign university. Aboard the ship were also Greek and Thai soldiers headed home. This departure reduced the ground contingent of these three countries to one rifle company each.

According to UNC records, 109 remains of Kagnew's dead were shipped home presumably with the Third Kagnew Battalion. It is unclear if that was all of the Ethiopian dead up to that point or if any additional remains were left in the Far East for some reason.

Lt. Col. Asfaw Habtemariam hands the colors to Capt. Yohannis Meseker during the farewell ceremony, July 8, 1955. (US Army)

Lt. Col. Asfaw Habtemariam presenting a plaque to a US officer, July 10, 1955. (US Army)

Even with the war being officially over, it appears the Fourth Kagnew also suffered additional casualties. Lt. Col. Asfaw Habtemariam requested the remains of Sgt. Maj. Desta Deyas and Pvt. Asefa Degefa be disinterred from the UN Cemetery at Tanggok for shipment home with his rotating battalion. That seems to be in addition to the remains of Sgt. Belehu Yigeletu (who was disinterred on June 18, 1955). It does not appear these men are included in the tally of Kagnew martyrs.

Despite General MacArthur's warning that "there's no substitute for victory," the United Nations eventually accepted a stalemate. In the subsequent years South Korea has seen tremendous prosperity, while the North remained a hermit kingdom with its people living in complete ignorance and abject poverty.

To this day, the four-kilometer wide, Demilitarized Zone acts as a buffer between the two sides. The DMZ is fenced, electrified, sealed with an estimated one million landmines and guarded by a large number of North Korean soldiers on one side and US and ROK troops under UN control on the other.[12] The tension gets even more palpable at the Joint Security Area (JSA) in Panmunjom, where ROK troops face-off against their North Korean counterparts. Between them stands a North Korean officer facing north to stop would-be defectors in a tacit admission that all might not be well in the Democratic People's Republic of Korea.

A ten-person Military Armistice Commission (MAC) composed of five officers from the UNC and five from the Communists was tasked with monitoring the situation at the DMZ as well as investigating any violations of the Armistice. Until 1991, the ranking UNC member was a US major general. The others were two ROK generals, one British general, and one officer rotated among the other UNC member nations which still had representatives in the Far East as part of an Advisory Group. The MAC averaged 12 meetings a year from 1953 until 1991, when the Communists withdrew from the process.[13]

UNC Headquarters including the MAC relocated from Tokyo to Seoul in 1957.[14] But despite the Armistice still being in effect, life at the DMZ was neither quiet nor safe.[15] For instance in 1968, more than 100 US and ROK soldiers were killed and 200 wounded by the exchange of gunfire along the DMZ.[16] Just in one year (1974), the UNC charged the Communists with 4,985 violations of the agreement while the KPA/CCF charged the UNC with 22,079 violations. A majority (76% and 78% respectively) involved identification infractions (i.e. – failure to wear armbands in the DMZ). The remaining charges involved allegations of weapons firing in the DMZ, heavy weapons in the DMZ agent infiltration, and air violations.[17]

The Ethiopians showed their commitment to collective security by keeping a liaison group of two officers and one NCO as part of the UNCMAC Advisory Group. The constant finger pointing and circular discussions at the MAC meetings must have taken a toll on the personnel, because sometime in the 1960s the Ethiopian government requested to withdraw the group citing "boredom and general dissatisfaction with the situation." This paralleled the sentiments of other UNC member nations.[18]

In June 1975, Lt. Col. Teshome Abenbe [sic] informed the UNC the Ethiopian liaison group composed of him, Maj. Tesfaye Eshete and their admin sergeant was being recalled home.[19] At the time, no official notification was given by the new Marxist government in Ethiopia and no replacements were sent. Thus ended the Ethiopian involvement in Korea.[20]

5,720,000 Americans eventually served in the armed forces at home and abroad during the time of the war, of those 1.7 million were deployed to Korea. UN troops numbered around 166,000 of which about 110,000 were from Commonwealth nations. Ridgway noted,

"Catering to all the particular preferences, in food, in clothing, in religious observances – gave our service and supply forces a thousand petty headaches."[21] He was right. Just feeding the international coalition was a tremendous undertaking as food was not only sustenance but a comfort item. "Ask frontline foxhole soldiers from 17 countries what they would like for supper and the chances are the reply would be home cooking." But in the absence of home cooking, US Quartermasters had to cater to the dietary needs and restrictions of the various contingents. The Turks could not eat pork but requested more lamb and bread. The French and Greek wanted more olive oil. For the ROK it was dried cuttlefish, and for the Brits, tea and scones. The Thai, Puerto Ricans, Greeks, Turks, Filipinos and later the Colombians and Ethiopians all requested additional rations of hot sauce. And so on and so forth.

On Wake Island, when General Omar Bradley, Chairman of the Joint Chiefs, asked about United Nations troops, "…are not some of them more trouble than they are worth militarily?" MacArthur

1st Lt. Amare Checkol holding an Ethiopian Christmas Mass for Fifth Kagnew, January 6, 1956. (US Army)

responded, "They are useless from the military point of view and would probably never see action. From the political point of view, they give a United Nations flavor."[22]

MacArthur could not have been more wrong. Despite the logistical

Officers of the Fifth Kagnew, January 19, 1956. (US Army)

A B-26B Invader light bomber of the 425th Bomber Wing, US Air Force, releasing bombs over North Korea, on 29 May 1951. (US Air Force)

challenges faced in fielding a multi-national force, their necessity on the battlefield, as well as, in the political arena cannot be overstated. The allies contributed relatively smaller forces, usually at battalion or brigade strength, and as such could afford to send their best soldiers from crack units. The Turks fought a bloody rearguard action in the wake of the Chinese intervention. Casualty figures were so high, the Turkish government fell under tremendous pressure from opposition parties. Both the French and the Greeks played a critical role in Operation *Roundup* and subsequent actions. The French commander took a voluntary demotion from lieutenant general to lieutenant colonel in order to lead his country's forces. A Filipino armor captain was posthumously awarded his nation's Medal of Honor after personally killing at least 60 enemy soldiers and risking his life to rescue one of his soldiers. The Commonwealth troops were the first to join the war on the UN side after the US and continued to fight ferociously in many of the early battles including their valiant stand at Gloster Hill. The New Zealand frigate *Hawea* spent the longest time at sea and accounted for the deepest penetration into enemy territory. And of course, the Ethiopians. American officers who fought alongside them, like Maj. Hallock, Capt. Raigoza and Capt. Myers, swore they were the best troops in Korea.

A U.S. Army Chief of Staff said, "No braver or finer troops ever fought in Korea. They were never driven from the battlefield. They returned as they went out – all together – whether they were living or wounded or dead."[23]

In *Pork Chop Hill*, S.L.A. Marshall wrote,

…of all the troops which fought in Korea, the Ethiopians stood highest in the quality of their officer-man relationship, the evenness of their performance under fire and the mastery of techniques by which they achieved near perfect unity of action in adapting themselves to new weapons during training and in using them to kill efficiently in battle.

He further praised their adaptability,

They couldn't read maps but they never missed a trail… They could take over U.S. Signal Corps equipment and in combat make it work twice as well as the best-trained American troops… The information which they fed back by wire and radio was far greater in volume and much more accurate than anything coming from American actions.

He decried their lack of "a good press" and dubbed them the "Unknown Battalion." With Richard Hallock's goading, he dedicated two chapters of his book to their skill and daring.[24]

However, in 1962, while testifying at a senate investigation on US troop performance, Marshall said the Turks "were never really as good as their reputation." He also said "the same was true of the Ethiopian troops' record."[25] This was a confounding statement as the Ethiopian record was in some part based on glowing reviews of Kagnew troops in his book. Marshall perhaps got too carried away in downplaying the achievements of the foreign troops while defending the American GI who was taking unfair flak for exaggerated accounts of "bug out fever" during the early days of the war. It is also worth noting that Marshall's work has been called into question over the last few decades both by veterans and academics.

Most Kagnew members reported positive interactions with white American troops despite wide-spread racism in the US with parts of the country still under Jim Crow. The issue of race was always

This detonation was caused by B-26B bombers of the US Air Force when they hit a warehouse in Wonsan, in 1951. (US Army)

simmering below the surface starting with General Mulugeta Bulli's discussion with US representatives in Addis Ababa about not wanting his men to experience any discrimination, to Colonel Kebbede's request for the investigation of the treatment of Ethiopians on R&R. The US government took precautions to ensure the allies did not feel discriminated against. When Sgt. Maj. Mamoushet Goshime and Sgt. Molla Kebede toured the US, they were sent to northern states and not the south. Fortunately, there were no documented major incidents. Time and time again US personnel indicated they viewed the Ethiopians favorably and perhaps even differently than African-Americans. This differentiation was probably based as much on prevailing biased attitudes and racism toward African-Americans as it was on the positive impression made by the Ethiopians. The proud Kagnew soldiers would not allow themselves to be degraded and even went as far as to request they get classified not as "Negros" but as "Ethiopian" on Army paperwork – an option not available to their African-American comrades.

Melesse Tessema of the Second Kagnew said you did not see any racism on the battlefield. That was a place of war, suffering and death. No matter what your citizenship, you had a spirit of collaboration and camaraderie. We actually made a lot of friends. Maybe when you went to Tokyo on R&R, you might see it from some of the whites.[26]

Juan Raigoza recounted an incident where he accompanied an Ethiopian captain on R&R in Japan. The two met other American soldiers at a restaurant for dinner when one of the Americans said, "He didn't sit down at a table with niggers." Capt. Raigoza angrily told the American,

Let me tell you, you stupid son-of-a-bitch, this man is one of our allied soldiers. He's a hell of a proud fighter, and a damn good one, as they all are – while you sit on your ass here in Japan and make those remarks. That's an insult. You can cause a diplomatic incident. You either sit down with us or get out. I'll take this all the way to Eighth Army if I have to.[27]

Korean War casualties just in the first year of fighting were 430,000 Chinese killed or wounded, and 16,200 captured. Additionally, 360,000 North Koreans were killed or wounded and 145,000 captured. The total for the whole war would exceed two-million Communist military casualties. It is estimated that one-million South Korean and two-million North Korean civilians were killed, wounded or went missing. Scores more were displaced.[28]

The Korean War cost United Nations forces over 559,000 casualties, including approximately 94,000 dead. The United States suffered 36,516 killed, 103,284 wounded and 7,245 captured. During Operation *Big Switch*, which lasted from August to December 1953, a total of 75,823 Communists and 12,773 United Nations personnel (including 3,597 Americans) were repatriated to their homeland. Approximately 46,000 former Communists were allowed to stay in South Korea or go to Taiwan. 347 UN personnel, including twenty-one Americans defected to the Communists.[29]

It was impossible to determine exactly how many Ethiopians served

A dramatic sequence from a gun-camera film, showing a train in North Korea under low-altitude attack by US fighter-bombers. (US Air Force)

in the Korean War due to the incomplete nature of the official records available. The records that are available show great discrepancies. *The Korean War Almanac* states a total of 3,158 Ethiopians served in Korea. But it also states, incorrectly, the battalion had 566 missing in action.[30] *Korean War Order of Battle: United States, United Nations, and Communist Ground, Naval, and Air Forces, 1950-1953* states a total of 3,518 troops served during the war (meaning until the Armistice).[31] According to the Ethiopian Korean War Veterans Association President, a total of 6,037 Kagnew troops served in Korea.[32] In his thesis for the Naval Postgraduate School, citing an unpublished manuscript from the Ethiopian Ministry of Defense, Col. Haile Araya Amdemichael wrote "341 officers and 5,696 NCOs, totaling 6,037 troops" served in the five successive units.[33] The same problem arose when trying to provide an independent tally of those wounded or killed in action.

Remarkably, of the twenty-two United Nations members that participated in the war, Ethiopia is the only nation which did not have a single soldier missing or captured. They even recovered the bodies of their fallen from the battlefield. When asked about the absence of Ethiopian POWs, Bekele Hora of the Third Kagnew Battalion, whose home was burned and his father hanged by *banda* during the Italian occupation, said,

We were naive… we were uneducated. We were in a hurry to kill the enemy with no regard for our own lives. We were told if you think you'll be captured, kill yourselves. Don't get taken prisoner. Don't disgrace our name. Remove all your papers, eat them if you have to. For us it was dishonorable to retreat; it was dishonorable to even get shot in the back.[34]

As a bi-racial member of Kagnew Battalion, Vassilios Simatos was admonished by the Second Kagnew Battalion S-3, Capt. Workneh, not to become the first to be taken prisoner. He was told not to sully their name and threatened with court-martial.[35]

Melesse Tessema of the Second Kagnew Battalion said the Americans felt Kagnew soldiers were never taken prisoner because we were uncivilized. He got the impression they felt civilized people did not want to die, so they were willing to surrender. But the Ethiopians did not have that mentality and disagreed with the Americans over this. He said "we would rather die than surrender." He added,

another reason for us not surrendering stemmed from our impoverished tactical training. The Americans had lots of weapons and wasted lots of ammo. We felt we had to kill an enemy with each bullet. If we could not kill, we would not shoot. This was our tradition. Our training did not make it possible for us to surrender. When we attacked, we would give specific instruction on where to go and the squad leaders would help us officers keep track of our men. We pre-planned what to do and where to place our wounded. So we attacked together. We defended together. Surrender was shameful, so we were careful."[36]

One of Melesse Tessema's experiences during his time in Korea illustrates Kagnew's commitment to ensuring no one got left behind. One time, after a pitched battle, his unit took the objective and was subsequently ordered to withdraw. When they got back to friendly lines, they noticed they were down a man. At daybreak Melesse started scanning the area of the battle with binoculars and saw something right in front of the enemy position. The battalion X.O., Maj. Kebede, ordered 2d Lt. Melesse to recover the body. Melesse returned to the field with three of his men. He then took up a position and directed two soldiers with radio wire tied around their waist to crawl to the area where he saw the suspicious object. After they confirmed it was their fallen comrade, he had them tie the wire to the dead man's leg. They then pulled the body from a distance in case

2nd Lt. Alemu Ghebremariam dressed as a traditional Ethiopian warrior, January 7, 1956. (US Army)

the enemy had booby trapped the body with grenades. Melesse said, "that is how we made sure we recovered the dead. Rather than having someone missing or taken prisoner, we would die to bring him back."[37]

Yilma Belachew of the Second Kagnew Battalion, who was reassigned to Capt. Workneh's S-3 section after a successful patrol, attributed their feat mostly to divine intervention. He said, "It is God's work… It doesn't mean someone is a coward just because he got taken prisoner or that someone is brave just because he did not." He recalled how even an American general [William Dean] was captured by the North Koreans while fighting gallantly. He said, "Ethiopians are courageous; it is the courage we inherited from our fathers, but there is no other magic to it." "Even our dead were not taken. We've had to call tanks and crawl on our bellies into enemy territory to retrieve the bodies." When asked whether rumors of Communist atrocities against prisoners spurred him and his men to fight harder, he replied he did not hear such rumors, but quipped, "Nothing good comes of being taken prisoner."[38]

Abebe Gebreyes, the 75mm recoilless rifle platoon leader with the Third Kagnew Battalion offered his take. He said, no, it wasn't luck, "There was a reason we were not taken prisoner." He explained,

Americans naturally were used to comfort and happiness, they were not accustomed to suffering. When they got into a bad situation, they would surrender so as not to lose their life. We on the other

hand did not have a life of comfort and enjoyment. We just knew to do what we were told. We chose death over surrender which was shameful for us. But after all, we are human beings. We might be afraid just like everyone else. Anyone can be fearful, but one has to overcome that fear. That is what makes you a soldier – it is not anything else.[39]

In living up to these examples, the battalion suffered 536 wounded and 122 killed. Inscribed on the tombstone of the 300 Spartan dead at Thermopylae is the epitaph, "Go tell Sparta, stranger passing by, that here obedient to their laws we lie." The same could be said of the martyrs of Kagnew Battalion who gave their lives for King, Country and the tenets of collective security.

The human toll of war cannot be measured only in the number of men killed and wounded in action. There were also non-battle casualties. There were vehicle collisions, training accidents, cold weather related injuries and countless other hazards. Some of these injuries were life-altering. For example, one soldier was seriously hurt when supplies were air dropped onto the Kagnew positions. Another was injured by a rocket which dropped from a crashing airplane. Abebe Desalegn was severely burned by exploding munitions.

Of course, any discussion of casualties would not be complete without mention of perhaps the most courageous type of soldier – the medic. These men braved hostile fire to provide first aid to wounded

Gen. Lemnitzer with Ethiopian Liaison Officers on the anniversary of liberation, May 5, 1956. (US Army)

Maj. Gen. Lemnitzer presented forty-eight Ethiopian awards to members of the First Kagnew on behalf of their Emperor. As for foreign awards, Kagnew members earned many individual awards from the governments of the United States, South Korea and Belgium. Kebbede Guebre, Teshome Irgetu, Asfaw Andarge, and Woldeyohannes Shitta received the US Legion of Merit. The Ethiopians earned at least nine US Silver Star Medals, forty-two Bronze Star Medals for Valor, forty-one Bronze Star Medals for Meritorious Service and one Soldier's Medal. From the Republic of Korea, they received at least seven decorations. Six Ethiopian servicemen were awarded a total of twelve Belgian military decorations. Two additional men (Capt. Lenchio Hailemariam and 2d Lt. Gulilat Abera) were at least nominated for similar Belgian awards.

The Ethiopians from the Emperor on down were committed to getting the most out of their involvement in the Korean War. Haile Selassie used every opportunity to secure

comrades, often without the ability to fight back as their rifles were still slung over their shoulders and their hands clutching a stretcher or bandage. While some were decorated for their heroics, most went unrecognized because the extreme hazard they faced every day was considered par for the course. Before the arrival of the two nurses, members of Kagnew were billeted at army hospitals and did their best as interpreters.

Kagnew's medical platoons were usually headed by European doctors. Very little is known about these men. Maj. Hans Erman served as battalion surgeon for the First Kagnew from May 4, 1951 through June 21, 1952. Maj. Erman left the Saar (present-day Germany) in 1934 and had previously served with the British Army as a physician during WWII.[40] It is believed he had become a citizen of Ethiopia. Once in Korea, he supplemented his section of ten medics with six additional men recruited from the infantry battalion and re-trained for their new roles before the units moved to the front.[41] Another doctor, Maj. Hans Rasch joined the battalion around November 1952, replacing Maj. Friedrich Von Caprivi. Maj. Rasch again served with the Kagnew Battalion starting on July 8, 1954. Records show Von Caprivi was back in the Far East around October 1954. These men provided next level care at field dressing stations before the casualties were evacuated to MASH Units or Hospitals. Both Dr. Hans Rasch and Dr. Erman were awarded the Ethiopian Order of the Star of Honour in 1954.

The First, Second and Third Kagnew Battalions were all awarded US Presidential Unit Citations. It is undetermined how many Kagnew soldiers received Ethiopian decorations for valor and/or meritorious service. For instance, on one occasion 7th Division commander

better training and equipment for his fledgling armed forces. He ensured the military was up to modern standards by first retaining British, then Swedish and lastly, after much lobbying, US advisers. He sent the successive battalions to Korea knowing they would receive modern training as well as real combat experience. He tried to do the same for his air force by requesting to send pilot-trainees to Korea. He ensured the veterans returned with their individual small arms once their tour was over. He was able to secure at least five-million dollars' worth of weaponry from the US to equip a division. By 1955, Ethiopia would send 42 men to the US for training including: 34 army officers, two enlisted men and six Imperial Bodyguard officers. By the 1960s, that number would mushroom to 4,000.[43]

But this came at a cost to Haile Selassie and his administration. His former adviser John Spencer wrote the Emperor came under heavy local criticism "after the number of casualties gradually became known." Minister of War Ras Abebe Aregai "was falsely accused of having embezzled funds allegedly provided by the United Nations for the Ethiopian contingent in Korea."[44]

The troops did not waste this opportunity either. Upon arrival in Korea they underwent intense training at the United Nations Reception Center and continued to train hard every time the battalion went into reserve. They inspected equipment, toured facilities, asked questions and learned any chance they got. Some officers attended special courses like Nuclear, Biological, Chemical (NBC) Warfare indoctrination, tank familiarization, airborne training and so on. For the enlisted men, there was driver training, vehicle maintenance training, as well as gas training including exposure to tear gas. Yilma

Capt. Yohannis Meseker handing Christmas donations to an orphanage, January 7, 1956. (US Army)

Belachew described his military experience in Korea as priceless. He said he got to apply the theory-based training he received at the Imperial Bodyguard academy. Other veterans echoed his sentiment.[45]

The troops even enrolled in English classes. They took advantage of reading programs offered by the US Army and the Red Cross; *Riders of the Purple Sage* and *Sunset Pass* were among the favorites. Some who arrived illiterate, left Korea having learned how to read and write, at least in their own language. This was not unique to the Ethiopians as US troops took advantage of similar opportunities to earn their high school diplomas.

A dark room was set up for those who enjoyed photography. They organized a band, put on plays and participated in athletics – soccer being the most popular. In 1956, the 32d Regiment's "Buccaneers" soccer team made up mostly of Ethiopians went undefeated. The men also played volleyball and competed in track & field. Competition was fierce, but so was sportsmanship. The officers often joined in. Lt. Col. Asfaw Habetmariam commented, "The only way to uphold the high spirit and close cooperation which makes the Kagnew Battalion the fighting unit it is, is the close association between officers and their men."[46]

Amidst the heavy fighting, the division also took some time for philanthropy. The Bayonet participated in a reforestation program which collected 6,000 pounds of chestnuts that were later presented to the ROK. Operation *Santa Clause* was also kicked-off in hopes of providing some Christmas spirit for Korean children in the division's area. The approximately $10,000 raised by division personnel in the winter of 1952 was used to purchase gifts and essentials for an American style Christmas for the children of Pochon-Gun and Chunchon-town. Kagnew battalion donated $1,879; that was more than any other unit. Kagnew Battalion raised $1,425 for the I Corps Children School program at another fundraiser in July 1953. The newspaper wrote, "They have as much generosity as fighting skills…"[47] The Fourth Kagnew Battalion donated 500,000 hwan to the Greek Orthodox Church and Orphanage in Seoul.[48]

Second Lieutenant Yilma Belachew led an honor guard for President Eisenhower. Second Lieutenant Abebe Gebreyes also had the opportunity to lead an honor guard on several occasions during American or UN holidays. It was necessary that representatives of the battalion, usually a squad from his 75mm recoilless rifle platoon, carry the Ethiopian flag at ceremonies.[49]

Kagnew members enjoyed United Service Organization (USO) shows along with the rest of the US Army. During his time in Korea, Abebe Gebreyes and about 9,000 men from the 32d Regiment turned out to see a performance by a famous blonde American actress and singer. Even though he could not recall her name, Abebe remembers having to use binoculars because he could not see the star from where he stood in the back of a huge crowd. He said, "The Americans were excited. But we did not care because this was new to us." He later learned this woman was involved with President John F. Kennedy. Records show Marilyn Monroe had visited Korea as part of a USO Tour in 1954.

EPILOGUE

Upon inking a 25-year lease for Radio Marina in Asmara in 1953, the US renamed the base Kagnew Station. The communications hub was the most reliable link to the Near East as well as the Pacific and at times handled communication between continental US and forces in Korea.[1]

In 1955, Col. Mengistu Neway was made acting commander of the Imperial Bodyguard. The next year he was promoted to brigadier general and officially took over the division.[2]

General Mengistu had a younger brother named Germame who was educated in the US and considered to be a "radical". In 1960, while the Emperor was abroad, the two brothers initiated a coup d'état in hopes of bringing much needed reform to their beloved country. They were joined by Kagnew veteran Workneh Gebyeou (former operations officer of the Second Kagnew Battalion and wearer of the Bronze Star) after Korea, when the Emperor sought a military man to head the domestic intelligence program as Chief of National Security, Mengistu Neway recommended Capt. Workneh who was rapidly promoted to lieutenant colonel.[3][4] The two brothers used the Imperial Guardsmen, many of whom were unaware of their true intentions, to take control of the city and arrest several high ranking officials, including members of the royal family, the prime minister and General Mulugeta Bulli. However, the conspirators failed to arrest all the key figures. Ground Forces Chief Kebbede Guebre, the Air Force Chief, the Minister of Defense and others worked together to quash the rebellion using the Imperial Army and Air Force.

As forces loyal to the Emperor re-took the palace, some of the hostages, including Maj. Gen. Mulugeta Bulli were killed by gunfire. Lt. Col. Workneh took his own life. Brig. Gen. Mengistu became a fugitive until he was caught, tried and hanged for his crime. Maj. Yohannes Meseker, who as a captain had commanded the Fifth Kagnew, was also killed in the firefight.

On June 30, 1960, the Republic of the Congo, which had been a Belgian colony, won its independence. As the country descended into chaos, local strongman Moise Tshombe declared the resource rich province of Katanga independent. The Congolese government requested United Nations military assistance and Opération des Nations Unies au Congo (ONUC or the United Nations Operation in the Congo) was authorized by the Security Council.[5]

Haile Selassie, the most prominent African leader of his time and ardent proponent of collective security, offered to send troops. He designated the unit "Tikil Brigade" ("*Abba Tikil*" being the name of his charger and consequently his *nom de guerre*). While the expedition was commanded by an Ethiopian brigadier general, the combat brigade was led by Korean War veteran Col. Woldeyohanis Shitta (Third Kagnew Battalion C.O.). The brigade was drawn from the Imperial Army and Imperial Bodyguard which contributed two battalions each. Many Kagnew veterans would end up serving in the Congo.[6]

On August 27, 1960, a US Air Force cargo plane with five US airmen and two Canadians landed in Stanleyville. Congolese soldiers and civilians forced the servicemen off the plane and beat them mercilessly. The Congolese also seized almost a dozen men from a nearby UN office. Ethiopian troops waded into the fray and rescued some of the victims at the airport and the other hostages. Five Ethiopian officers were credited with saving these lives and awarded the US Legion of Merit. The recipients included two Kagnew veterans

After the end of the Korean War, the Ethiopian armed forces – including the Imperial Bodyguard – returned to their routine, peacetime duties. This photograph shows the training of artillerymen in the early 1960s. (Albert Grandolini Collection)

Two close-up photographs showing the crew manning a US-supplied M1A1 75mm Pack Howitzer. (Albert Grandolini Collection)

Col. Woldeyohanis Shitta (C.O.) and Capt. Aster Ayane (Nurse).[7] One of the rescued Americans gave an account of how Capt. Aster fought her way through the frenzied mob to get to him.[8]

Ethiopia sent a total of four brigades consisting of fourteen battalions, in addition to air force units. Many Kagnew veterans served in high profile positions, including Lt. Gen. Kebbede Guebre who commanded all United Nations forces from April 1962 until July 1963.[9] The Second Tikil Brigade was commanded by Col. Teshome Irgetu.

On May 18, 1968, Emperor Haile Selassie became the first African head of state to visit Seoul: a day later, he attended the unveiling of a monument near the city of Chunchon honoring the service of Ethiopian troops.[10] Minister of Defense Kebbede Guebre also visited the monument five months later.[11]

As the number of educated Ethiopians continued to grow, so did the frustration at the imperial government over perceived authoritarianism, corruption and mismanagement. The situation was exacerbated by a severe drought in certain parts of Ethiopia. The Emperor who was once seen as a champion of progress was seen as an impediment. In January 1974, a mutiny at a remote military outpost was quietly settled without any punishments. Soon other military units, the police, students, taxi drivers and unions submitted demands, demonstrated, mutinied and striked. This resulted in the resignation of the cabinet. The Emperor replaced the prime minister and all but two former cabinet members were arrested. Still, none of the radical agitators or participants were punished.[12]

In late June 1974, the creation of the Coordinating Committee of the Armed Forces, Police, and Territorial Army was announced. The Committee, known as the "Dergue" or "Derg," was composed of three

Col. Mengistu Neway.

General Kebbede Guebre, ONUC Force Commander in Congo, August 1962. (UN Photo)

members each from the forty police and military units in the country. The 3d Division in Harar was represented by Major Mengistu *Haile Mariam*.[13] The end of June 1974 also saw a second wave of arrests of government officials. On July 22, the new prime minister was removed. On September 12, the Emperor was deposed. On November 23, sixty notables among the nobility, politicians, bureaucrats and senior military were summarily executed.[14] The Emperor was killed on August 27, 1975.

The Derg adopted communism and fell in with the Soviet bloc. Later *Mengistu Haile Mariam* emerged as the head of the Derg and appointed himself president of the country.[15] Relations with Pyongyang improved during this era, culminating in the deployment of hundreds of North Korean "military advisers, an array of small arms, ammunition, and other materiel" beginning in 1985. North Korea provided Ethiopia with an interest-free loan for the construction of a shipyard, in addition to paying for the training of a 20,000-person commando unit.[16] The country suffered decades of civil war and economic stagnation until a coalition of rebel groups overthrew the Derg government in 1991.

The Guard

After the Korean War, the Imperial Bodyguard underwent substantial modernization not just in tactics, operations and equipment, but culturally as well. Young Ethiopians were sent abroad for education through the patronage of the Crown already since earlier, but Korea represented the first time thousands of them travelled overseas: indeed, it turned them into nation's ambassadors to the World. They

Nurse Aster Ayana (left) with Nurse Zenawit Ayele in Leopoldville, Congo, Jan 1960. (UN photo)

were intelligent, proud, courageous, and above all else, modest. For all their ferocity in battle, they were quick to smile and had a certain boyish charm. These qualities endeared them to everyone they came across. When they returned home, they brought back a level of worldliness. Their involvement in Korea would pay dividends.

During the attempted coup in 1960, the masterminds kept a large majority of the Guardsmen in the dark as to their real intentions. Furthermore, two of the Guard battalions were at that time serving in the Congo. Most were eventually cleared of any wrongdoing but the act was still billed as an Imperial Bodyguard undertaking. The unit's reputation was blemished and it lost the confidence of the Emperor.

As the 1974 Revolution reached its crescendo, the Guard commander, Maj. Gen. Tafesse Lemma, was arrested by the Derg. The division was disbanded and the Korean War veterans were maligned by the Marxist regime for waging war against fellow Communists. Most of the remaining veterans retired with meager pensions and faded into obscurity. Lt. Tadesse Gebrekristos, who served in the First Kagnew Battalion, recalled being told by the Imperial government, "Complete your mission and we will repay the favor," but he said the veterans did not get anything when they returned from Korea. When they brought their complaints before the Marxist junta, they were threatened with death.[17] Proving once again, "A nation that fails to honor its heroes, soon will have no heroes to honor."

The post-Derg administration took a more neutral, if not favorable, stance towards the veterans. Many, including Col. Melesse Tessema, Lt. Tadesse Gebrekristos and Sgt. Bekele Hora, are appreciative of the opportunity they were given to preserve their history and to associate freely, not to mention the plot of land they received to erect a monument and build a museum which stands tribute not just to Kagnew Battalion, but to all who served in the Ethiopian armed forces.

General Desta Gemeda feels, "Korean veterans (in Ethiopia and elsewhere) did not receive much recognition." He said, at least for the Ethiopian veterans, "It is the Korean people, not their government, that have recognized these sacrifices. The Korean people have tried to repay the debt." Following a state visit by President Lee Myung-bak, the ROK government announced in 2012, that it would start paying pensions to these veterans.[18]

Many of Kagnew members spent a lifetime in service of their

Congolese child and Ethiopian soldier, March 1963. (UN Photo)

A rare view of a M41 Walker Bulldog light tank of the Imperial Ethiopian Army, together with a long row of support vehicles, as seen during an exercise in late 1960s. (Tom Cooper Collection)

country. They started before the Italo-Abyssinian War and continued to serve during the invasion, occupation, and ultimately, in post-liberation. Some transferred back-and-forth between the Imperial Bodyguard, the Imperial Army and the police force. Guardsmen were detailed to provide basic training to the Imperial Ethiopian Navy in its infancy. For the officers, their leadership skills were put to use as governors-general, administrators and bureaucrats. The enlisted men made enormous contributions in all aspects of Ethiopian society, including television, music, sports, and commerce. Tesfaye Sahlu, also known as "*Ababa* Tesfaye," entertained and educated generations of Ethiopian youths. Kassa Tessema who composed the Kagnew anthem "Allem Alle Babooroo" became a music legend. Two world-famous marathoners Abebe Bikila and Mamo Wolde were members of Kagnew Battalion.

Those still living are now in their 80s and 90s: most are surprisingly strong for their age. They have not lost their military bearing. They walk everywhere, out of habit and partly necessity, and they walk far. Vassilios Simatos still regularly hikes Mount Entoto and walks thirty miles from Addis Ababa to Debre Zeit (Bishoftu).

Urban Legends

A lot of folk lore and orientalism has been attached to the battalion's history. One of 7th Division's veterans wrote,

> The Ethiopians were the Emperor's Bodyguard. Huge men. Tall, thin runners. They were famous in the division because their commander wouldn't let them take ammunition on patrols. Bayonets. Knives. They used the rifle as a club but no shooting. They couldn't hit anything anyway. Gun fire makes noise and calls attention to where you are. 'Get out there and bring me back the ears.' I gather they literally did that. I never had any personal experience with them in that sense, so I can't testify to it but that was the rumor.[19]

The Ethiopians conserved ammo and they were adept at hand-to-hand combat, but it is quite a stretch to suggest they did not take ammunition on patrols because the countless patrols where they engaged the enemy in gun battles are well-documented.

Some US veterans have given accounts of Ethiopian troops collecting body parts as trophies and engaging in cannibalism. One US veteran who served in Korea starting in October 1952 (during the time of the Second Kagnew Battalion) recounted a story where an Ethiopian patrol returned to their company commander and reported engaging the Chinese in a firefight and killing the enemy patrol. The commander did not believe their story, so he sent them back out. The patrol went back out to the area of the previous firefight and brought back the ears of the Chinese dead in a handkerchief as proof.[20]

Another veteran who served in Korea around November 1951 (during the time of the First Kagnew Battalion) told a similar story. An Ethiopian patrol sent to capture prisoners returned with the ears of the enemy dead. He said their furious commander, sent them back out the next day with instruction to bring live prisoners. Yet another US veteran said each soldier was promised a palace and maiden for a wife if they fought well and survived. He added, "it was rumored they were collecting casualty ear tips to send home to substantiate their claims of courage in combat."[21]

The Ethiopian Korean War Veterans Association categorically denies any such assertions. But at least one Kagnew officer attributed the cannibalism myth to a practical joke played by members of the First Kagnew Battalion. The story goes, members of an Ethiopian patrol crawled up to a Chinese corpse within sight of the enemy, took out a knife and pretended to slice off chunks from the body. Then they

Ethiopian Korean War Medal. (Author's Collection)

started munching on some raw beef they took out of their own pockets. Soon Chinese officers were warning their men not to get captured by Ethiopians. General John Hightower recounted to his family, "The Chinese told the North Koreans the Ethiopians were cannibals to make them fight harder. When the Americans brought in a prisoner he would be grinning and asking for chocolate. When an Ethiopian brought one in he would be yelling and begging for mercy."[22]

Captain Yilma Belachew said the battalion had its supporters as well as detractors and attributed such tales to those who might not have liked them for some reason. He commented,

> Ethiopia is an honorable country. Not just our modern soldiers, but even our fathers and grandfathers were under orders by [their Emperor] to bring back prisoners alive and unharmed. That is where we learned it. We were taught to do the right thing. Maybe the [Chinese Communists] told their men these things to deter them from surrendering.[23]

Colonel Melesse Tessema commented,

> …some thought we were savages because we did not surrender. They told such tales to highlight that we were uncivilized. But we learned about the Geneva Convention at the academy and we instructed our soldiers about this before we went to the battlefield. Once someone surrenders, he is no longer an enemy. Of course you can tie his hands so he does not escape and you can cover his eyes so he does not recon your camp in case he escapes. There was nothing we could do if the prisoner even refused to give us his name. We did not cut off ears or noses.[24]

In fact, mutilation of corpses was relatively uncommon in mainstream modern Ethiopia. In earlier times, weapons and other loot were fair game, but cannibalism was beyond taboo. The Kagnew troops, who were mostly devout Orthodox Christians, strictly adhered to dietary restriction of the Old Testament. They had to be given special permission by the head of the church just to break their

Imperial Bodyguard Badge. (Author's Collection)

won much renown. When the Ethiopian battalion went to Korea, it inherited this name. Go and see it, try it… introduce our country."[25]

A New York Times clipping quoted in a State Department cable seems to have captured the true essence of Kagnew Battalion. They were extolled as, "tough fighting men respected by allies and foe for fearless but noble natural soldiers… Many an American has said he would rather be out on patrol with them than any other troops. On leave in Tokyo they spend time going to museums, sight seeing and listening to opera." They were and still are "generous to a fault."[26]

In his farewell speech before Congress, General MacArthur stated, "Old soldiers never die, they simply fade away." But their deeds, especially in the case of Kagnew Battalion, live on.

fast or consume US rations. Even then, some balked. They would not eat pork. When they were served lobster for Christmas, they tossed it in the garbage.

In 1936, when the last Italian soldier succumbed to his wounds after *Tikur Anbessa's* daring raid at the airfield, the young Ethiopians buried him with full military honors. The proper treatment of prisoners of war was in fact explicitly stated in their constitution.

As outlined in a letter issued by Col. Kebbede on May 29, 1951, even autopsies were forbidden "for religious reasons" and "for psychological effect" on the troops who desired their bodies remain "repose and respected according to [their] religious rule." Two exceptions were granted by the Ethiopians after Damasia Tousua died in March 1953 at the Tokyo Army Hospital of unknown causes and Sium Ayele's sudden death in June 1953.

Several meanings, both literal and symbolic, have been ascribed to the term Kagnew. Some have said it means "to make order out of chaos," "never caught," or "always winner." "*Abba Kagnew*" was the war horse and *nom de guerre* of *Ras* Makonnen – one of the Ethiopian generals who played a critical role in defeating the Italians at Adwa in 1896. He was also Emperor Menelik's first cousin and more importantly Emperor Haile Selassie's father. It was also the name of the airplane used by Haile Selassie during the early days of the Italian invasion. The Ethiopian military mission to the Congo was named Tikil Brigade after Haile Selassie's *nom de guerre* "*Abba Tikil.*" It stands to reason the Korean battalion was named primarily in honor of *Ras* Makonnen.

According to the Amharic-English dictionary, "Kagnew" means to scout, survey, investigate or reconnoiter. Ethiopian Korean War Veterans Association president Col. Melesse Tessema agreed with this literal translation but explained further. He said the main reason for naming the unit "Kagnew" was because of *Ras* Makonnen. During the Battle of Adwa, the *Ras* who commanded the vanguard arrived at the Italian position at Amba Alagi. Despite Emperor Menelik's instructions to go there and wait, he chose to fight and took that position after much bloodshed. Thus, the meaning of "Kagnew" is not to "overthrow," but "as *Abba Kagnew* did, to try it, to see it… what is at that place? Because of his deed on that battlefield, *Ras* Makonnen

Notes

Introduction

1. Armed Forces Information & Education Division. Office of Secretary of Defense. *A Pocket Guide to Korea* (Washington D.C.: Government Printing Office, 1950), pp. 4-5.
2. James F. Schnabel, *Policy and Direction: The First Year* (Washington D.C.: Center of Military
History, United States Army, 2001), p. 9.
3. Matthew B. Ridgway, *The Korean War* (New York: Da Capo Press, 1986), p. 1.
4. Schnabel, pp. 24-28.
5. Roy E. Appleman, *South to the Naktong, North to the Yalu* (Washington D.C.: Center of Military
History, United States Army, 1992), pp. 13-16.
6. Schnabel, p. 39.
7. Truman Library. *State Department Overview of Korean Situation*, June 28, 1950. (Truman Library. Web).
8. Appleman, pp. 24-30.
9. Ibid, pp. 31-33.
10. Truman Library. *Memorandum of Conversation, June 25, 1950*. Web.
11. Harry S. Truman, *Memoirs, Vol. 2: Years of Trial and Hope* (Garden City: Double Press, 1956), p. 333.
12. Miller Merle, *Plain Speaking: An Oral Biography of Harry S. Truman.* 1974. (New York: Berkley Publishing Corporation, 1974), pp. 200.
13. Appleman, pp. 6-8.
14. Truman Library. *United Nations Security Council Resolution, June 25, 1950*. Web.
15. Truman Library. *Notes Regarding Blair House Meetings, June 26, 1950*. Web.
16. Truman Library. *State Department Overview of Korean Situation, June 28, 1950*. Web.
17. Appleman, pp. 110-112.
18. Ibid, pp. 266-487.
19. Joint Staff, J-7. *Planner's Handbook for Operational Design, Version 1.0.* (Suffolk, Virginia. 7 Oct. 2011). D-11-D-12. Accessed 20 Feb. 2017. Web.
20. Truman Library. *Substance of Statements Made at Wake Island Conference, October 15, 1950*. Web.
21. Appleman, pp. 622-651.
22. Ibid, pp. 768-770.
23. Schnabel, p. 235.
24. Richard W. Stewart, *American Military History Volume II, The United States Army in a Global
Era, 1917-2008.* (Washington D.C.: Center of Military History, United States Army, 2010), p. 235.
25. Richard W. Stewart, *The Chinese Intervention, 3 November 1950-24 January 1951* (Washington D.C.: Center of Military History, United States Army), pp. 9-12.
26. Appleman, pp. 14, 33.
27. Stewart, *The Chinese Intervention*, pp. 15-16.
28. Ibid, pp. 18-19.
29. Ibid, pp. 16-20.
30. Ibid, pp. 22-26.
31. Ibid, p. 20.
32. Ibid, pp. 27-28.
33. John Miller Jr., Owen J. Curroll, Margaret E. Tackley. *Korea 1951-1953* (Washington D.C.: Center of Military History, United States Army, 2010) pp. 13-25.
34. Stewart, *American Military History Volume II*, pp. 236-238.
35. Truman Library. *Memorandum, "The MacArthur Dismissal", April 28, 1951.*
36. Truman Library. *Transcript of General Douglas MacArthur's Address to Congress, April 19, 1951.*
37. General Staff (Intelligence) Headquarters Troop in the Sudan. *Handbook of Western Italian East Africa Volume I* (Khartoum, 1941), p. 3. (*Handbook* hereafter)
38. *Guidebook of Ethiopia* (Addis Ababa: The Chamber of Commerce, 1954), pp. 14-15. (*Guidebook* hereafter)
39. Ibid, pp. 15-16.
40. *Handbook*, p. 5.
41. Ibid, p. 6.
42. Ibid, pp. 7-8.
43. Ibid, p. 9.
44. Ibid, pp. 9-10.
45. *Military History Volume I* (Haile Selassie Military Academy. Harar). pp. 132-133. (*Military History Volume I* hereafter)
46. *Handbook*, p. 14.

47. *Guidebook*, pp. 20-22, 28, 42, 314, 344.
48. Thomas P Ofcansky, Laverle Bennette Berry, and Library of Congress. Federal Research Division. *Ethiopia: A Country Study.* (Washington, D.C.: Federal Research Division, Library of Congress: U.S. Government Printing Office, 1993), p. 273. (Ofcansky & Berry herafter)
49. Ibid, p. 282.
50. Ibid, p. 273.
51. "The Imperial Guard." *Ethiopian Review*, Vol. II, No. 23 (Addis Ababa: Ethiopian Press and Information Office. Sept.-Oct. 1945), p. 7.
52. Eric Virgin, *The Abyssinia I Knew* (London: Macmillan and Co. Ltd, 1936). pp. 119-124.
53. Viveca H. Norberg, *Swedes in Haile Selassie's Ethiopia, 1924-1952. A Study in Early Development Co-operation.* (Uppsala: Uppsala Offset Center AB, 1977), pp. 136-138.
54. Benito Mussolini, *My Autobiography* (New York: Charles Scribner's Sons, 1928), pp. 188-194.
55. *Handbook*, p. 16.
56. *Military History Volume I*, pp. 132-133.
57. Bahru Zewde. *A History of Modern Ethiopia 1855-1974* (Athens: Ohio University Press, 1991) p. 154.
58. Anthony Mockler, *Haile Selassie's War* (New York: Random House, 1984), pp. 67-68.
59. Bob Woodward, "The High Command." *The Washington Post*, 9 Apr. 1989. Web.
60. Mockler, p. 77.
61. *Military History Volume I*, pp. 139-140.
62. *Yekedamawi Haile Selassie Tor Temehert Bet Birrawi Iyobel* (Asmara: Kokel Tsbah, 1952 EC), pp. 64-72.
63. Ibid, pp. 68-72.
64. Tadesse Mecha. *Tikur Anbessa be Me'erab Iteyopeya.* (Asmera: Corriere Eritrea Printing, 1951).
65. *Yekedamawi Haile Selassie Tor Temehert Bet Birrawi Iyobel* (Asmara: Kokel Tsbah, 1952 EC), pp. 100-102.
66. Ibid, pp. 106-108, 112.
67. Ibid, pp. 112-124.
68. *Foreign Relations of the United States, Diplomatic Papers, 1937, Volume II* (Washington D.C.: U.S. Government Printing Office, 1954), pp. 679-680.
69. *Yekedamawi Haile Selassie Tor Temehert Bet Birrawi Iyobel* (Asmara: Kokel Tsbah, 1952 EC), pp. 124-126, 146-158.
70. *Handbook*, p. 17.
71. David Talbot, *Ethiopian Review* (Addis Ababa: Ethiopian Press and Information Office, 1945), pp. 2-5.
72. United Nations. *History of the United Nations.* Web. Accessed 26 Jul. 2015.
73. United Nations. *Charter of the United Nations.* Web. Accessed 26 Jul. 2015.
74. William Z. Slany, John A. Bernbaum, Joan M. Lee, Carl N. Raether, Charles S Sampson, Paul Claussen, David W. Mabon, Lisle A. Rose, David H. Stauffer *Foreign Relations of the United States, 1951, Volume V* (Washington D.C.: U.S Government Printing Office, 1982), pp. 1240-1241.
75. D. Damte Assemahegn, *Tekilena Serawitu* (Addis Ababa: Commerce, 1950 EC), pp. 337, 339.
76. Ibid, pp. 339-340.
77. Ibid, p. 346.
78. Ibid, pp. 349-350.
79. Ibid, p. 350.
80. Norberg, pp. 199, 216.
81. Ibid, p. 227.
82. "Zena Mewael." *Berhanena Selam*, Vol. 37, 21 Meg. 1939 EC. Amharic Edition.
83. Stewart, *American Military History Volume II*, pp. 206-214.
84. Office of the Under Secretary of Defense (Comptroller). *National Defense Budget Estimate for FY 2016* (March 2015), p. 246.
85. Stewart, *American Military History Volume II*, p. 121, 211.
86. Schnabel, p. 43.
87. Stewart, *American Military History Volume II*, p. 121, 211.
88. Schnabel, pp. 40, 53.
89. "Command: Old Pro." *Time*. 31 Jul. 1950. Web. Accessed 17 Feb. 2018.
90. Schnabel, p. 53.
91. Douglas MacArthur, *Reminiscences* (New York: McGraw-Hill, 1964), p. 327.
92. Harold Martin. *Soldier: The Memoirs of Matthew B. Ridgway* (New York: Harper 1956), p. 191.

Chapter 1

1. United Nations Archives. S/1555. Cablegram Dated 2 July 1950 From the Vice Minister of Foreign Affairs of the Government of Ethiopia Addressed to the Secretary-General Concerning the Security Council Resolution of 27 June 1950 (S/1511). 3 Jul. 1950.

2. William J. Fox, *History of the Korean War: Inter-Allied Co-operation During Combat Operations* (Fort Leavenworth: US Army Command & General Staff College, 15 Aug. 1952), p. 3.
3. John H. Spencer, *Ethiopia at Bay: A Personal Account of the Haile Selassie Years* (Hollywood: Tsehai Publishers, 2006), pp. 219-220.
4. United Nations Archives. S/1896. Letter Dated 2 November 1950 from the Minister for Foreign Affairs of Ethiopia to the Secretary-General in Reply to the Secretary-General's Cablegram of 14 July 1950 (S/1619) Concerning the Security Council Resolution of 25 and 27 June, and 7 July 1950 (S/1501, S/1511, and S/1588). 10 Nov. 1950.
5. Ibid.
6. Abebe Woldetensaye. *Kehasena Tor Serawitu*. (2000 EC), p. 39.
7. National Archives and Records Administration. Group 59 – Central Foreign Policy Files, created 7/1/1973 – 12/31/1979. U.S. Department of State. Electronic Telegrams. "Appointment of New Chief of Staff." 5 Jul. 1974.
8. Charles Dumas. "Into Battle: Ethiopians Join Fight after Final Training." *Pacific Stars and Stripes*, 28 Aug. 1951, p. 9.
9. National Archives and Records Administration. Group 59 – Central Foreign Policy Files, created 7/1/1973 – 12/31/1979. U.S. Department of State. Electronic Telegrams. "Appointment of New Chief of Staff." 5 Jul. 1974.
10. Orvar Nilsson, *Med Ethiopiska Bataljonen i Korea*. Unknown publisher/date.
11. Desta Gemeda. Personal Interview. 16 Mar. 2012.
12. Ibid.
13. Ibid.
14. Bulcha Olika. Personal Interview. 23 Feb 2012.
15. Ibid.
16. Ibid.
17. Ibid.
18. Desta Gemeda. Personal Interview. 16 Mar. 2012.
19. Ibid.
20. Bulcha Olika. Personal Interview. 23 Feb 2012.
21. Mercogliano, Salvatore R. Korea: The First Shot (Military Sea Transportation Service in Korean War). www.usmm.org. Web. Accessed 25 Jul. 2015.
22. Nilsson, Med Ethiopiska Bataljonen i Korea. Unknown publisher/date.
23. Ibid.
24. Desta Gemeda. Personal Interview. 16 Mar. 2012.
25. Fox, p. 151.
26. Dumas, p. 9.
27. Fox, p. 35.
28. Dumas, p. 9.
29. Fox, pp. 34-35.
30. The National Archives (TNA). Records of the Foreign Office. FO 371/96785. Military Attaché's Annual Report on the Ethiopian Armed Forces, 1951. 1952, p. 13.
31. *Bayonet: A History of the 7th Infantry Division* (Tokyo: Toppan Printing Company, 1952), p. 8.
32. John M. Hightower and Jane Hightower, *From Sand to Stars: A Soldier's Story* (Heah Tur Genesis, Augusta, GA, 2012), p. 123.
33. Hightower, Jane. Personal Interview. 17 Nov. 2011.
34. Hightower and Hightower, pp. 116-117.
35. Hightower, Jane. Personal Interview. 17 Nov. 2011.
36. Hightower and Hightower, pp. 9, 133.
37. The National Archives (TNA). Records of the Foreign Office. FO 371/96785. Military Attaché's Annual Report on the Ethiopian Armed Forces, 1951. 1952, p. 12.
38. Kimon Skordiles, *Kagnew* (Tokyo: Radio Press, 1954), p. 47.
39. Dumas, p. 9.
40. "Four Ethiopians Win Bronze Star Medals." *Pacific Stars and Stripes*, 2 Sept. 1951, p. 6.
41. Desta Gemeda. Personal Interview. 16 Mar. 2012.
42. Ibid.
43. *Metasebya* (Addis Ababa: Finfinne, 1999 EC), pp. 239-241.
44. Desta Gemeda. Personal Interview. 16 Mar. 2012.
45. Ibid.
46. Skordiles, p. 63.
47. *Bayonet*, p. 37.
48. Robert Miller. "Ethiopians Win Hill as Slinging Bayonets Send Enemy Fleeing." *Pacific Stars and Stripes*, 24 Sept. 1951, p. 2.
49. *Bayonet*, p. 37.
50. Truman Library. The President's Day, October 24, 1951. Truman Library. Web.
51. Ibid.
52. James Owings. Personal Interview. 10-12 Nov. 2011.
53. Ibid.
54. Ibid.
55. Ibid.
56. Hightower and Hightower, p. 136.
57. Hightower and Hightower, p. 137.
58. *Yekedamawi Haile Selassie Tor Temehert Bet Tarik* (Addis Ababa: Commerce, 1950 EC), p. 215.
59. "Ethiopia Gets Wounded Men." *The Baltimore African-American*. 6 Nov. 1951, p. 15.
60. The National Archives (TNA). Records of the Foreign Office. FO 371/96785. Military Attaché's Annual Report on the Ethiopian Armed Forces, 1951. 1952, p. 13.
61. *Le'ul Makonnen Haile Selassie: Mesfine* (Harar: Artistic Publishing, 1957), pp. 63-64.
62. "UNRC." *Pacific Stars and Stripes*, 20 Dec. 1951, p. 8.
63. Hightower and Hightower, pp. 142-143.
64. The National Archives (TNA). Records of the Foreign Office. FO 371/96785. Military Attaché's Annual Report on the Ethiopian Armed Forces, 1951. 1952, p. 12.
65. Bemebratu Gebeyehu. Arayanet. (Addis Ababa, 2012), pp. 4-5, 17-18.
66. Yilma Belachew. Personal Interview.
67. Ibid.
68. Vassilios Simatos. Personal Interview. 27 Feb. 2012.
69. Ibid.
70. Ibid.
71. Ibid.
72. Ibid.
73. Ibid.
74. Ibid.
75. "Ethiopians Korea Bound." *Pacific Stars and Stripes*, 13 Mar. 1952, p. 2.
76. Yilma Belachew. Personal Interview.
77. Vassilios Simatos. Personal Interview. 27 Feb. 2012.
78. Murray Fromson, "Elite Battalion." *Pacific Stars and Stripes*, 29 Mar. 1952, p. 6.
79. *Yekedamawi Haile Selassie Tor Temehert Bet Tarik.* (Addis Ababa: Commerce, 1950 EC), p. 181.
80. Assefa Demissie. Personal Interview. 6 Mar. 2012.
81. Yilma Belachew. Personal Interview.
82. Ibid.

Chapter 2

1. Yilma Belachew. Personal Interview.
2. "Ethiopian Group Leaves on Rotation." *Pacific Stars and Stripes*, 24 Apr. 1952, p. 7.
3. Le'ul Makonnen Haile Selassie: Mesfine (Harar: Artistic Publishing. 1957), pp. 64, 66.
4. Desta Gemeda. Personal Interview. 16 Mar. 2012.
5. George Buttery, "Ethiopians Mark Independence." *Pacific Stars and Stripes – Korea Edition*, 8 May 1952, p. 6.
6. Yilma Belachew. Personal Interview.
7. Ibid.
8. Ibid.
9. Ibid.
10. Ibid.
11. Ibid.
12. Vassilios Simatos. Personal Interview. 27 Feb. 2012.
13. Ibid.
14. Ibid.
15. Melesse Tessema. Personal Interview. 22 Feb. 2012.
16. Ibid.
17. Ibid.
18. Orvar Nilsson, *Korea – Avlosning: Ethiopienbrev av Orvar Nilsson*. Unknown publisher/date.
19. Melesse Tessema. Personal Interview. 22 Feb. 2012.
20. Ibid.
21. Ibid.
22. Ibid.
23. Skordiles, p. 93.
24. Assefa Demissie. Personal Interview. 6 Mar. 2012.
25. "3 Ethiopians Hold Reds Through Night, Kill 30." *Pacific Stars and Stripes – Korea Edition*, 29 Aug. 1952, p. 6.
26. Daniel Crosswell. Unpublished Manuscript on Biography of Colonel Richard Hallock.
27. Ibid.
28. Ibid.
29. "Ethiopians Keep Positions From Enemy on CO's Order to 'Hold on Till Death.'" *Pacific Stars and Stripes – Korea Edition*, 12 Nov. 1952, p. 6.
30. Untitled. *Nevada State Journal*. 24 Oct. 1952. p. 1.
31. "Ethiopians Keep Positions From Enemy on CO's Order to 'Hold on Till Death.'" *Pacific Stars and Stripes – Korea Edition*, 12 Nov. 1952, p. 6.
32. Ibid, p. 6.
33. Ibid, p. 6.

34. Untitled. *Nevada State Journal.* 24 Oct. 1952. p. 1.
35. Paul F. Gorman, *Cardinal Point: An Oral History – Training Soldiers and Becoming a Strategist in Peace and War* (Combat Studies Institute, 2010-2011), p. 71. Web.
36. Irwin Braun. Personal Interview. 1 Dec. 2011.
37. Ibid.
38. Tom Clancy, Tony Zinni, and Tony Koltz. *Battle Ready* (New York: Berkley Books, 2005), pp. 425-426.
39. Bob Woodward, "The High Command." *The Washington Post.* 9 Apr. 1989. Web. 17 Feb. 2018.
40. Irwin Braun. Personal Interview. 1 Dec. 2011.
41. Crosswell.
42. Robert F. Ensslin, Jr. Collection (AFC/2001/001/41587), Veterans History Project, American Folklife Center, Library of Congress, pp. 3-4
43. Ibid, pp. 5-6
44. Ibid, pp. 6-7
45. Ibid, p. 7
46. Crosswell.
47. Ibid.
48. Miller Jr., et al *Korea 1951-1953*, p. 274.
49. Crosswell.
50. Yilma Belachew. Personal Interview.
51. Robert Udick. "U.N. Troops Plan for Christmas." *Pacific Stars and Stripes*, 19 Dec. 1952, p. 6.
52. Bill McWilliams, *On Hallowed Ground: The Last Battle for Porkchop Hill* (Berkley Caliber, 2004), pp. 171-172.
53. Ibid, p. 172.
54. PFC Deswysen, "Modest Ethiopians Show Bravery, Honor In Combat." *Pacific Stars and Stripes* – Korea Edition, 13 Jan. 1953, p. 7.
55. Crosswell.
56. Ibid.
57. Orvar Nilsson. *III. Bataljonen.* Unknown publisher/date. p. 88.
58. Berkinesh Kebede. Personal Interview. 16 Mar. 2012.
59. *Imperial Ethiopian Ministry of Education Yearbook 1949-1951* (Addis Ababa: Berhanena Selam, 1952), p. 189.
60. Berkinesh Kebede. Personal Interview. 16 Mar. 2012.
61. Ibid.
62. Robert M. Gates, *Duty: Memoirs of a Secretary at War* (New York: Alfred A. Knopf, 2014), p. 58.
63. John S. Brown, *Years of Stalemate July 1951-July 1953* (Washington D.C: Center of Military History, United States Army. Web. 25 Jul. 2015), p. 27.
64. Crosswell.
65. Ibid.
66. Ibid.
67. "3 Nations Land New Troops in Korea Port." *Pacific Stars and Stripes*, 17 Apr. 1953, p. 5.
68. Berkinesh Kebede. Personal Interview. 16 Mar. 2012.

Chapter 3: Third Kagnew Battalion
1. Abebe Gebreyes. Personal Interview. 24 Dec 2013.
2. Ibid.
3. Ibid.
4. Ibid.
5. Brown, p. 29.
6. Melesse Tessema. Personal Interview. 22 Feb. 2012.
7. Wongele Costa. Personal Interview. 5 Mar. 2012.
8. Ibid.
9. Ibid.
10. Ibid.
11. Ibid.
12. S.L.A. Marshall, *Pork Chop Hill* (Nashville: The Battery Press, 1986). (Special Collections Department, University of Texas at El Paso, El Paso, TX.), pp. 141-142.
13. Ibid, p. 142.
14. Ibid, p. 142.
15. Ibid, p. 143.
16. Ibid, p. 143.
17. Ibid, p. 143.
18. Ibid, pp. 143-144.
19. Ibid, p. 144.
20. Ibid, p. 145.
21. Ibid, p. 145.
22. Ibid, p. 145.
23. Ibid, p. 146.
24. Ibid, p. 146.
25. Ibid, p. 146.
26. Wongele Costa. Personal Interview. 5 Mar. 2012.

27. Ibid.
28. Marshall, p. 147.
29. Ibid, p. 147.
30. Wongele Costa. Personal Interview. 5 Mar. 2012.
31. "Outnumbered 7 to 1 Ethiopians Stun Red Attackers." *Pacific Stars and Stripes* Korea Edition, 2 May 1953, p. 7.
32. Marshall, pp. 165-166.
33. Ibid, p. 166.
34. Ibid, p. 167.
35. Ibid, p. 168.
36. Ibid, p. 174.
37. Ibid, p. 174.
38. Bekele Hora. Personal Interview. 10 Mar. 2012.
39. Ibid.
40. Tesfaye Woldeselassie. Personal Interview. 9 Mar. 2012.
41. Ibid.
42. Ibid.
43. Ibid.
44. Ibid.
45. Ibid.
46. Ibid.
47. Ibid.
48. Ibid.
49. United Press. "Ethiopian GI Gets New Leg." *The News Journal from Wilmington* 20 Feb. 1953. p. 12.
50. E.J. Khan, John Brooks. "U.N. Soldier." *The New Yorker*, 6 Jun. 1953. p. 32.
51. "Ethiopian Who Lost Leg in Korea Visits the U.N." *The New York Times*. 26 Ma 1953. p. 8.
52. UN Photo. "Ethiopian Soldier Amputee Visits United Nations." New York United Nations. 25 May 1953. Web.
53. Berkinesh Kebede. Personal Interview. 16 Mar. 2012.
54. Paul Claussen, Joan M. Lee, David W. Mabon Nina J. Noring, Carl N. Raethe William F. Sanford, Stanley Shaloff, William Z. Slany, Louis J. Smith. *Foreig Relations of the United States, 1952-1954, Volume XI* (Washington D.C.: U.S Government Printing Office, 1983), pp. 438-451.
55. Ibid.
56. Tesfaye Woldeselassie. Personal Interview. 9 Mar. 2012.
57. "Eight Americans Honored by Ethiopian Guard CG." *Pacific Stars and Stripes* Korea Edition, 17 Jun. 1953, p. 7.
58. Crosswell.
59. Wongele Costa. Personal Interview. 5 Mar. 2012.
60. Braun, Irwin. Personal Interview. 1 Dec. 2011.
61. Ibid.
62. Bekele Hora. Personal Interview. 10 Mar. 2012.
63. Wongele Costa Personal Interview. 5 Mar. 2012.
64. Tesfaye Woldeselassie. Personal Interview. 9 Mar. 2012.
65. Abebe Gebreyes. Personal Interview. 24 Dec 2013.
66. Melesse Tessema Personal Interview. 22 Feb. 2012.
67. Department of State Bulletin. Special Report of the United Nations Comman on the Armistice in Korea. Department of State. 24 Aug. 1953, p. 247.
68. "Korea Dead Honored by World Veterans." *The New York Times.* 19 Nov. 1953 p. 24.
69. Berkinesh Kebede. Personal Interview. 16 Mar. 2012.
70. "Never Caught': Kagnew Battalion Trains to Live up to its Name." *Pacific Stars and Stripes* – Korea Edition, 4 Apr. 1954, p. 8.

Chapter 4
1. "Ethiopian Decorated." *Pacific Stars and Stripes* – Korea Edition, 9 Jul. 1954, p 7.
2. "Ethiopian Battalion Honored in Korea." *Pacific Stars and Stripes*, 10 Jul. 1954 p. 6.
3. Wongele Costa. Personal Interview. 5 Mar. 2012.
4. Tesfaye Woldeselassie. Personal Interview. 9 Mar. 2012.
5. Ibid.
6. "Relieved Kagnew Soldiers." *The Ethiopian Herald*, 7 Aug. 1954.
7. Wongele Costa. Personal Interview. 5 Mar. 2012.
8. Tesfaye Woldeselassie. Personal Interview. 9 Mar. 2012.
9. Wongele Costa. Personal Interview. 5 Mar. 2012.
10. Silverstein, Sheldon A. "Ongaku." *Pacific Stars and Stripes*, 13 Feb. 1955, p. 11.
11. "Ethiopian Bn. Ends Korea Tour." *Pacific Stars and Stripes*, 18 Jul. 1955, p. 12.
12. Korea, Republic of: Landmine Monitor Summary. 2000. www.the-monitor.org Web. Accessed 11 Feb. 2017.
13. Raymond C. Smith, *Peacekeeping without the Secretary-General: The Korea Armistice Arrangements* (Peace Operations Training Institute), p. 11
14. 1974 Annual Historical Report USFK/EUSA, p. 16.
15. Smith, p. 12.

16. Staff Historian's Office, G-3. Eighth United States Army Chronology 1 July 1968 – 31 December 1968. Headquarters, Eighth U.S. Army APO 96301, p. 15.

17. 1974 Annual Historical Report USFK/EUSA, pp. 13-14.

18. National Archives and Records Administration. Group 59 – Central Foreign Policy Files, created 7/1/1973 – 12/31/1979. U.S. Department of State. Electronic Telegrams. "Ethiopian UNC Liaison Group to Withdraw." 6 Jul. 1975.

19. Ibid.

20. 1977 Annual Historical Report. Headquarters: United Nations Command, United States Forces Korea, Eighth United States Army, p. 33.

21. Ridgway, p. 221.

22. Truman Library. Substance of Statements Made at Wake Island Conference, October 15, 1950. Web.

23. Wayne Danzik, Participation of Coalition Forces in the Korean War (Newport RI: Naval War College, 17 Jun. 1994), p. 6.

24. Marshall, pp. 163-164.

25. "S.L.A. Marshall Strikes Back for American Troops." Sarasota Herald-Tribune. 16 Mar. 1962, p. 5.

26. Melesse Tessema. Personal Interview. 22 Feb. 2012.

27. McWilliams, pp. 173-174.

28. Brown, p. 27.

29. Ibid, pp. 27-29.

30. Paul M. Edwards, The Korean War Almanac (New York: Facts on File, 2006), p. 517.

31. Gordon Rottman. Korean War Order of Battle: United States, United Nations, and Communist Ground, Naval, and Air Forces, 1950-1953 (Westport: Praeger, 2002), p. 123.

32. "Ethiopia: Association to Commemorate 61st of Korean War." Allafrica.com. 25 Apr. 12. http://allafrica.com/stories/201204260161.html. Web. Accessed 17 Feb. 2018.

33. Haile Araya Amdemichael. "East African Crisis Response: Shaping Ethiopian Peace Force for Better Participation in Future Peace Operations." Naval Postgraduate School. Dec. 2006, p. 83.

34. Bekele Hora. Personal Interview. 10 Mar. 2012.

35. Vassilios Simatos. Personal Interview. 27 Feb. 2012.

36. Melesse Tessema. Personal Interview. 22 Feb. 2012.

37. Ibid.

38. Yilma Belachew. Personal Interview.

39. Abebe Gebreyes. Personal Interview. 24 Dec 2013.

40. "At Melting Pot: Swedes, Germans Train Selassie's War Troops." Washington Afro-American. 5 Jun. 1951, p. 8.

41. Fox, pp. 144-145.

42. US Army Photo. "Congratulations." Pacific Stars and Stripes, 11 Jan. 1952, p. 6.

43. Ofcansky & Berry, p. 292.

44. Spencer, p. 220.

45. Yilma Belachew. Personal Interview.

46. "Kagnew are Happy Soldiers: Tough Ethiopians Never Gave Ground in Ethiopia." Pacific Stars and Stripes – Korea Edition, 18 Feb. 1955, p. 8.

47. "Ethiopians Help Korea School Fund." Pacific Stars and Stripes – Korea Edition, 30 Jul. 1953, p. 7.

48. "Ethiopian Forces Give Church Money." Pacific Stars and Stripes – Korea Edition, 28 Jan. 1955, p. 6.

49. Abebe Gebreyes. Personal Interview. 24 Dec 2013.

Epilogue

1. Ofcansky & Berry pp. 256, 292.

2. Negarit. Volume 14, Number 12. 30 Jun. 1955.

3. Bemebratu Gebeyehu. Arayanet. Addis Ababa, 2012, p. 40.

4. Metasebya, (Addis Ababa: Finfinne, 1999 EC), pp. 146-147.

5. United Nations Archives. Summary of AG-008 United Nations Operations in the Congo (ONUC)(1960-1964).

6. "Bekongo Yemedalya Shelimat." Menen. Addis Ababa, Ethiopian Patriotic Association. Sept. 1960. Amharic Edition.

7. Ibid.

8. "U.S. Airmen Beatings Protested." Daily Independent Journal [San Rafael, CA]. 30 Aug. 1960, p. 1.

9. Cherenetu Besewer. Africawe Congo. Addis Ababa: Commerce, 1958 EC.

10. Staff Historian's Office, G-3. Eighth United States Army Chronology 1 January 1968 – 30 June 1968. Headquarters, Eighth U.S. Army APO 96301, p. 15.

11. Staff Historian's Office, G-3. Eighth United States Army Chronology 1 July 1968 – 31 December 1968. Headquarters, Eighth U.S. Army APO 96301. p. 11.

12. National Archives and Records Administration. Group 59 – Central Foreign Policy Files, created 7/1/1973 – 12/31/1979. U.S. Department of State. Electronic Telegrams. "A Minisketch of the Ethiopian Rebellion to Date." 24 Jun. 1974.

13. Ofcansky & Berry, p. 53.

14. National Archives and Records Administration. Group 59 – Central Foreign Policy Files, created 7/1/1973 – 12/31/1979. U.S. Department of State. Electronic Telegrams. "Yesterday's Executions and Today's Perceptions." 25 Nov. 1974.

15. Ofcansky & Berry, pp. 56, 65, 293.

16. Ibid, p. 299.

17. Tadesse Gebrekristos. Personal Interview. 6 Mar. 2012.

18. Desta Gemeda. Personal Interview. 16 Mar. 2012.

19. Gorman, p. 19. Web.

20. Robert F. Ensslin, Jr. Collection (AFC/2001/001/41587), Veterans History Project, American Folklife Center, Library of Congress, p. 8.

21. Anthony J. Sobieski, Fire for Effect! Artillery Forward Observers in Korea (Bloomington: AuthorHouse, 2005), p. 176.

22. Hightower and Hightower, p. 133.

23. Yilma Belachew. Personal Interview.

24. Melesse Tessema Personal Interview. 22 Feb. 2012.

25. Ibid.

26. The New York Times.

Colour section

1. Abebe Woldetensaye. Kehasena Tor Serawitu. 2000 EC, p. 40-41.

2. National Archives and Records Administration. Group 59 – Central Foreign Policy Files, created 7/1/1973 – 12/31/1979. U.S. Department of State. Electronic Telegrams. "Appointment of New Chief of Staff." 5 Jul. 1974.

3. Greenfield, Richard. Ethiopia: A New Political History (New York: Frederick A. Praeger, 1968), p. 407.

4. National Archives and Records Administration. Group 59 – Central Foreign Policy Files, created 7/1/1973 – 12/31/1979. U.S. Department of State. Electronic Telegrams. "Appointment of New Chief of Staff." 5 Jul. 1974.

5. National Archives and Records Administration. Group 59 – Central Foreign Policy Files, created 7/1/1973 – 12/31/1979. U.S. Department of State. Electronic Telegrams. "Political Developments." 26 Nov. 1974.

6. Negarit. Volume 17, Number 3.

7. Desta Gemeda. Personal Interview. 16 Mar. 2012..

8. Ibid.

9. Berkinesh Kebede. Personal Interview. 16 Mar. 2012.

10. Negarit. Volume 13, Number 8. 4 Jan. 1953.

11. Negarit. Volume 14, Number 12. 30 Jun. 1955.

12. Negarit. Volume 17, Number 6.

13. Yekedamawi Haile Selassie Tor Temehert Bet Birrawi Iyobel. Asmara: Kokeb Tsbah, 1952 EC. 151.

14. Damte Assemahegn. D., Tekilena Serawitu. Addis Ababa: Commerce, 1950 EC, pp. 325-326.

15. National Archives and Records Administration. Group 59 – Central Foreign Policy Files, created 7/1/1973 – 12/31/1979. U.S. Department of State. Electronic Telegrams. "Political Developments." 26 Nov. 1974.

16. Tesfaye Woldeselassie. Personal Interview. 9 Mar. 2012.

17. Negarit. Volume 17, Number 3.

18. Bulcha Olika. Personal Interview. 23 Feb 2012.

19. Melesse Tessema Personal Interview. 22 Feb. 2012.

20. Yilma Belachew. Personal Interview.

21. Vassilios Simatos. Personal Interview. 27 Feb. 2012.

22. Wongele Costa. Personal Interview. 5 Mar. 2012.

23. Abebe Gebreyes. Personal Interview. 24 Dec 2013.

24. Bekele Hora. Personal Interview. 10 Mar. 2012.

25. Tesfaye Woldeselassie. Personal Interview. 9 Mar. 2012.

26. Assefa Demissie. Personal Interview. 6 Mar. 2012.

27. James Owings. Personal Interview. 10-12 Nov. 2011.

28. Crosswell.

29. Columbus State University Archives. Col. Richard R. Hallock Papers (MC 284). Biographical Notes. https://archives.columbusstate.edu/findingaids/mc284.php. Web. Accessed 19 Feb 2017.

30. Level Einerth, "Orvar Nilsson." Dagens Nyheter. 11 Jan. 2009. Web. Accessed 22 Feb. 2018.

31. Andreas Tullberg, We Are in The Congo Now": Sweden and The Trinity of Peacekeeping During The Congo Crisis 1960-1964 (Lund: Lund University, 2012), p. 92.

32. Paul Harnesk, Vem är Vem? Svealand Utom Stor-Stockholm E Stockholm (Uppsala: Stadsbibliotekarien i Uppsala, 1964), p. 579–580.

33. Raigoza. Albuquerque Journal. http://obits.abqjournal.com/obits/show/146539. Web. Accessed 3 Mar. 2018.

34. McWilliams, p. 172.

Acknowledgments

The people who assisted me in various ways during my research could themselves fill a battalion.

Many thanks go to Andrew Hilton, author of *The Ethiopian Patriots*, for his inspiration and valuable guidance when I set off on this journey. I would also like to thank James Zobel at the MacArthur Memorial; everyone at the US National Archives; Fentahun Tiruneh at the Library of Congress; Carl Gustav Johanson of the Swedish Volunteer League; Korean War Veteran Bill "Lloyd" Hitt; Walter D. Ray of Southern Illinois University; the US Army Center of Military History and the various staff historians and authors including: Roy E. Appleman, William G. Bell, William T. Bowers, John S. Brown, Owen J. Curroll, William M. Hammond, John Miller Jr., George L. MacGarrigle, James F. Schnabel, Richard W. Stewart, and Margaret E. Tackley, for allowing me to cite their works in this book; Dr. Daniel Crosswell of Columbus State University who also allowed me to borrow freely from his manuscript on Colonel Rochard Hallock; Catherine Giordano at the Library & Archives for the Stars and Stripes, and Claudia Rivers at the University of Texas at El Paso Library Special Collections Department for reviewing and granting my reproduction request; the wonderful folks who run the US Embassy library in Addis Ababa for their help in cutting through all the red tape after my brief banishment from the National Library in Addis Ababa; the staff at the National Archives in Addis Ababa and the library at Addis Ababa University; John Mallgren for reviewing my proposal; everyone else, including friends who offered words of encouragement and the Yeshiwas family (Yeshiwas, Yodit, Dagmawi and Bethel) who graciously hosted my stay in the D.C. area.

I would like to express heartfelt gratitude for the following veterans and their families for sharing with me that which is most precious to them – their stories: Jane Hightower, daughter of Major General John Hightower; Sergeant Irwin Braun; General Paul F. Gorman; James Owings, son of Lieutenant Colonel Harold Myers; May and Nanna Nilsson, daughter and wife of Lieutenant Colonel Orva Nilsson; Myriam Hallock, wife of Colonel Richard Hallock; Mary Ensslin, wife of Major General Robert F. Ensslin Jr; Colonel Melesse Tessema and Captain Yilma Belachew for the thankless work they do at the Ethiopian Korean War Veterans Association and for allowing me access to the membership; Major General Abebe Gebreyes and his wife Nurse Haimanot Woldesellassie; Brigadier General Desta Gemeda and Nurse Berkinesh Kebede; Colonel Wongele Costa; Captain Bulcha Olika; Lieutenant Tadesse Gebrekristos; Sergeant Tesfaye Woldeselassie; Mr. Assefa Demissie; Mr. Bekele Hora; Mr. Vassilios Simatos; Captain Tegegn Mulatu, son of martyred Kagnew soldier Private Mulatu Woldetsadik, as well as other members and staff at the association. To all the veterans of Kagnew Battalion, thank you for welcoming me into your fraternity. I dedicate this book to you.

About the Author

Dagmawi Abebe was born in Addis Ababa, Ethiopia. His father was a naval officer and his mother was a nurse. He moved to the US as a teenager and later earned a bachelor's degree in Criminology. He currently works as a criminal investigator and has experience both in the private and public sectors. His interest in military history of the obscure nature ranges from the Barbary Wars to 20th Century Imperial Ethiopia. He is an antiquarian and avid traveller.